17 FEBRUARY - 18 MARCH 2017 NEW YORK

6 SEPTEMBER - 11 NOVEMBER 2017 SEOUL

24 JANUARY - 9 MARCH 2018 LONDON

TARA DONOVAN

COMPOSITIONS

PACE

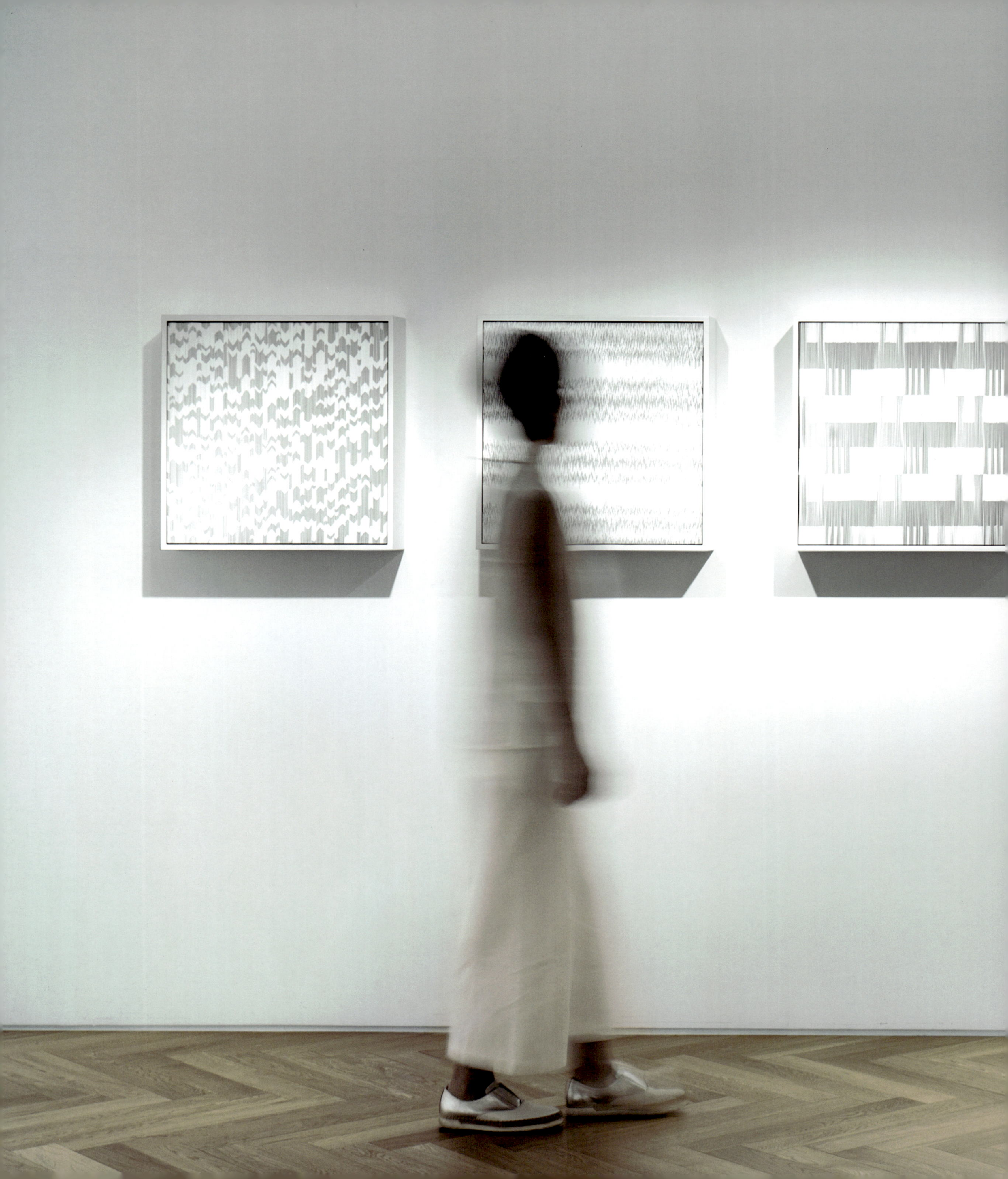

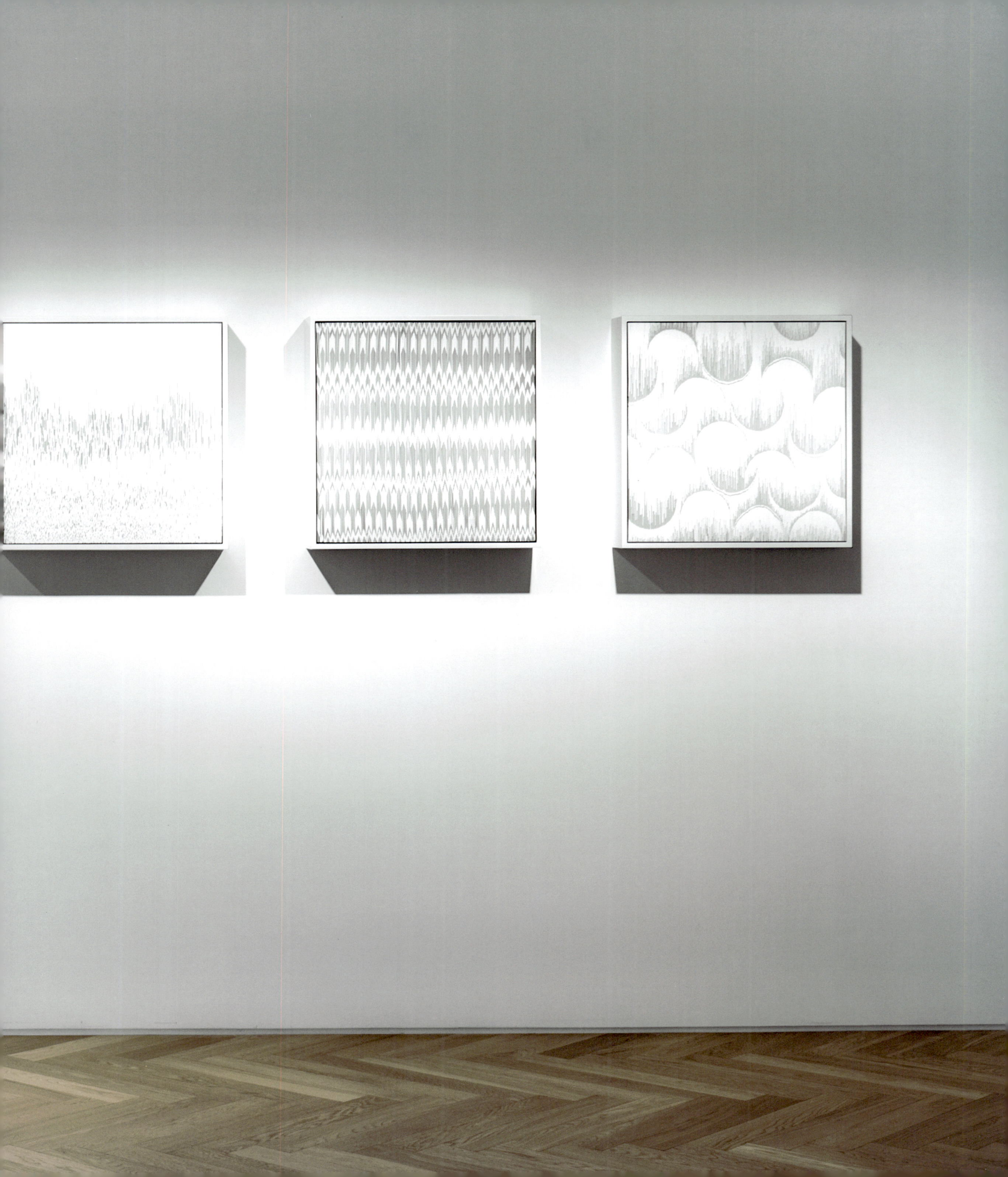

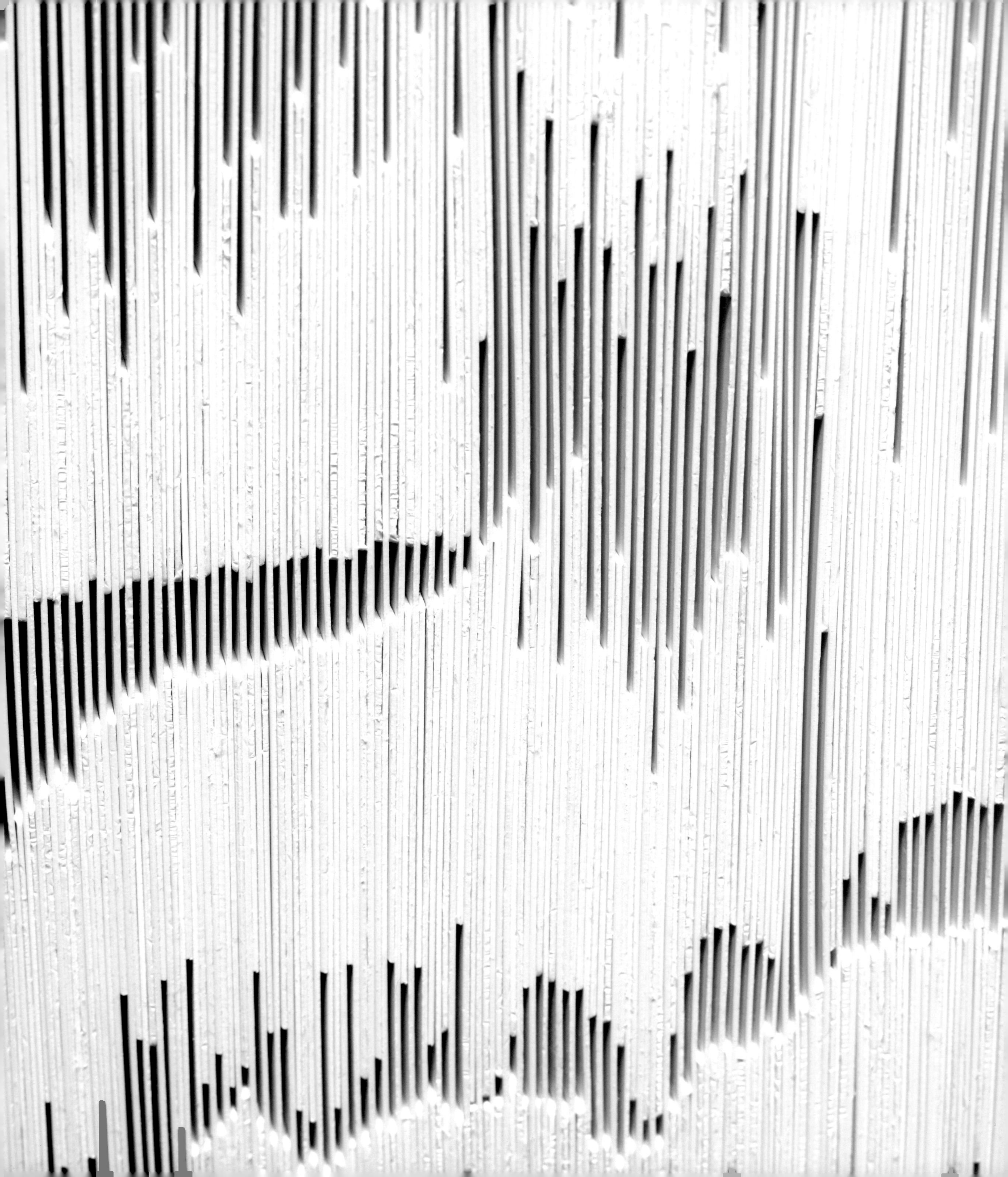

COMPOSITIONS (CARDS)

SUZANNE HUDSON

For her 2014 show at Pace Gallery's 25th Street location, Tara Donovan exhibited twelve spires, a towering fraternity of conical forms growing upward from the gallery floor. Engineered out of thousands of styrene index cards, layered parallel to the ground and ascending in horizontal strata, these monoliths suggest a propagative model befitting the steady advance of stalagmites. Material accretion marks time; coextensively, it occupies space. That such a uniform course does not yield identical solutions, but rather courts variability within immutable parameters, seems very much the point. Each spire is notably individuated, with undulating contours bowed in non-repeating passages that imply potentially infinite permutation within a standardized process of becoming. And even once deposited in the room as fully realized objects, they continue to adapt to their ambient environment of shifting light and moving bodies. Although each card is white—Donovan used the styrene in place of a 3 x 5 index card to ward off the discoloration typical of paper stock yellowing over time—the cumulative impression of their massing is shades of blues and sea greens, redolent of ice. Little surprise, perhaps, that soon afterward the work would be installed at the newly renovated Renwick Gallery in Washington, D.C., in a 2015 group show of immersive projects, simply titled *Wonder*.

For Donovan, *Untitled* (2014) occasioned something else. As the shimmering instantiation remained on view at the Renwick, Donovan began experimenting with the leftover cards. She ended up with a series, Compositions (Cards), which comprises three sizes of wall-mounted square frames with the namesake styrene cards tucked into arrangements that evoke, among other things, landscapes and textiles. (Indeed, these might be understood as resembling weaving without the weft.) This kind of tinkering-cum-aesthetic program recurs in Donovan's oeuvre. As with her appropriation of the cards—she got the idea to work with them while shuffling an Uno deck—the earlier and more capacious origin story regarding her practice involves a serendipitous studio mishap. As curators Jen Mergel and Nicholas Baume narrate in the exhibition catalogue published on the occasion of her first museum survey (at the Institute of Contemporary Art, Boston, in 2008), Donovan "knocked over a big box of toothpicks, picked it up, and then noticed that the spilled contents had latticed into a shape that echoed the perfect corner of their container."[1] Donovan later sourced some 500,000 toothpicks, which she succeeded in assembling into a large, freestanding cube, erecting it as one might construct a sand castle.

Since that time, *Untitled (Toothpicks)* (1996) has assumed symbolic priority. Donovan has used vernacular, mass-produced objects as her mainstays, arranging them in geometric, modular systems that recall minimal structures, replicating cellular organisms, vast, disorienting topographies, and much more. She has consistently required great quantities of whatever it is that she is using, be it plastic cups, buttons, rubber bands, or tape. These supplies are subjected to pragmatic procedures—rolling, aggregating, gluing, pouring, placing—that bring to mind Richard Serra's *Verb List* (1967–68), a manifesto of making through procedures that might initiate an activity of material self-organization (e.g., "to roll," "to crease," "to fold," "to store," "to bend," "to shorten," and "to twist"). Donovan's work is decidedly labor-intensive though, the agent of making resolutely present, even when the work is complete. In an important early example, *Haze* (2003), Donovan loaded clear drinking straws perpendicular to a wall plane, holding them in place with the corners of the room. For some reviewers, toil was the method as well as the nominal subject. David Frankel writes: "[*Haze*] is over twelve feet high and more than forty feet long. The gallery checklist names straws as the solitary medium—no glue, no pins, no stabilizing attachment of any kind. You wonder how she did it—or, at the least, how long it took."[2] And yet exertion is the means, not the end, even if its residue is palpable in the art.

Donovan's work evidences an old-fashioned way of making, one that admits its status as handmade at every juncture, despite the copious amounts of sourced, industrially fabricated things that she takes as her raw ingredients. Thus pieces foreground their willful crudity; they might fall apart, as did *Haze*, all the straws cascading in an unwitting jumble, or reveal their having been cut, if only at the edge, say, where Donovan has sliced prismatic film before situating it in an aperture in a wall. Given her courting of an otherwise gorgeous appearance, these are welcome, undermining aspects: a coupling between body and prop that exposes the skilled acts that ushered them into being. The cards are forthright on this count, too, with subtle distorting of grids or linear elements. Donovan draws an outline, or sometimes works freehand, matching the cards to the template. Once set into position, they are adhered to a bookbinding-like backing (layers of glue and cheesecloth affixed to a board), with the front flush with the edge of the frame; then Donovan turns them 90 degrees so that they read as vertical lines. While they are ultimately stable in a way that straws bookended by walls are not, many warp in the gluing and backing. Many do not outlive their genesis. In those that Donovan keeps, differences in density and orientation likewise demonstrate, paradoxically, care in fabrication that contradicts substitutable uniformity.

As the Compositions (Cards) foster abstract relationships within their respective casings, these subtle deviations remain even more explicit. First and foremost, they are built, manifestly made things. This ensures difference within repetition. Precisely because of what feels like a possible infinity of combinations—the analogue to an endless shuffling of deck chairs, or, as it were, a deck of cards—there exists, too, the inevitability that these works the size of easel pictures, are potentially interchangeable. The small but perceptible gaps and clumps, evidence of the aleatory and the handmade, arrest this. They are neither self-same nor mechanical. Lined up as friezes, they abet relational comparisons that secure rather than evacuate their specificity. Each pattern Donovan generates is unique: the waterfalls, plaids, camouflages, grids, arcs, diamonds, and the rest would not be the same again, even if made according to the same cartoon. The series as a whole seems to allow for iterability, even as it makes room for each instantiation of an autonomous form to exist on its own terms within the first principles guiding the actions.

This relates additionally to the contemporaneous series, Drawings (Pins), fields within which Donovan maps designs—shapes, geometries, and fades—through the use of silver pins that exploit the grayscale. Like the Compositions (Cards), they no longer make use of the entire room as a background; moreover, they similarly insinuate illusionism as something crafted of physical stuff rather than conjured through painterly tricks. In this, the cards likewise offer possibilities of intervals that survive this transition, preserving a sculptural logic in microcosm. In Compositions (Cards), the stacked cards do not always abut; where they leave a gap, light enters the picture plane, showing the surface to be far from seamless. The space between the cards determines how much light they shift. Some verge on iridescence. Like the pins, the cards remain obdurate entities, sensibly acknowledged as individual, matte, and colorless sheets. But like the pins' subtle glint that makes the argentine array possible, the cards become optical mirages of white, black, and gray. Where patterns overlap is the lightest. Elsewhere, they might verge on charcoal, lifting, as a viewer approaches, to opalescent silver; from the side, seen at an oblique angle, they are differently textured, differently poised to shift light or trap it in shadows that are also, fugitively, colored, moving even to blue where there is more material.

These optical effects result from stratification performed as a sculptural technique that in the end achieves a picture plane. Compositions (Cards) are simultaneously open, broken surfaces and portals. They thereby query the normative conventions of the mutually constitutive, binary traditions of sculpture and painting (without securing primary connection to either). Describing the origin of Compositions (Cards), Donovan says: "Revisiting the cards later gave me the opportunity to think about how the edges of the cards could be used to develop a linear composition with a two-dimensional surface, which is where the new series began taking shape. As I experimented further with the spacing of the cards, the linear surface began to act more and more as a screen laid over the top of a field with sculptural depth. I began thinking of the process as a very manual form of lenticular printing where offsetting layers create the illusion of depth and movement on a static surface."[3] The difference is that depth here is real: The offsetting layers are in fact negative spaces and positive volumes.

Beyond such visual volatility, the parallax that Compositions (Cards) engenders is also conceptual. Donovan herself has discussed the series in terms of the works being "sculptural paintings,"[4] as well as things that approximate the medium without hypostatization: "The idea that these *look* like paintings, but are most definitely not, is really interesting to me."[5] Donovan comes close to Donald Judd in his 1964 text "Specific Objects." Judd's most oft-cited quotation, which is also germane here, reads: "Half or more of the best new work in the last few years has been neither painting nor sculpture. Usually it has been related, closely or distantly, to one or the other."[6] While this treatise, issued in the midst of the polemics that would come to define minimal object and image production, might help to secure the neither-nor status of the Compositions (Cards), it also disagrees with Donovan's use of "sculptural" as a modifier for "painting." Donovan claims painting, however equivocally, as outcome if not genesis. This move is interesting, not least for the ways it pressures the medium from within as much as from without.

Games and the ludic dimension of art-making have served as apt metaphors for individual and historical advance, and the term "move" as just proffered above is necessarily inflected by these earlier discourses. The most relevant case is the exhibition *Endgame: Reference and Simulation in Recent Painting and Sculpture*, curated by Elisabeth Sussman and David Joselit at the Institute of Contemporary Art, Boston, in which the organizers argued that painting was no longer able to achieve the quality or weightiness that it once did (contrary to the title's fatalistic overtones, the point was not that picture-making was actually going to cease). Referencing Samuel

Beckett's play of the same name, the show, as David A. Ross explains in the catalogue's preface, drew on chess:

> Endgame is a term which describes the final set of moves which will lead to the mating of the King—the ritual killing which (out of respect) is never in fact carried out—but the indication of its inevitability signifies the termination of play. The endgame is most often played with a severely reduced number of pieces, creating need for a subtle yet effective strategy based on an economy of means. It is a time for desperate measures when, fighting against the odds and outnumbered, you freely invent as you struggle to survive. And then, it's over, and you quit the play perhaps to start again, recapitulating old patterns to evolve a new approach to an ancient game.[7]

The end could be a moment but also a strategy, a condition, or a performance of this condition, and hence the ground from which to produce, not to prohibit, new paintings. Donovan's Compositions (Cards) offer another, ultimately related prospect—of "sculptural paintings" coming out of sculpture and painting, and of infinite rearrangement in which different contests and positions still may be undertaken with the same deck. To Donovan's would-be verb list we might add "to shuffle."

1 Jen Mergel and Nicholas Baume, "Second Nature," in *Tara Donovan*, exh. cat. (New York: The Monacelli Press), 7.

2 David Frankel, "Tara Donovan at Ace Gallery," *Artforum* (Summer 2003), 186.

3 Allie Biswas, "Tara Donovan: 'I'm interested in exploring the moment when the conditional relationship of part to whole breaks down,'" *Studio International*, February 23, 2017, http://www.studiointernational.com/index.php/tara-donovan-interview-compositions-cards.

4 Kristen Tauer, "Tara Donovan Mounts Shows at Pace Gallery in Palo Alto and New York," *WWD*, January 31, 2017, http://wwd.com/eye/lifestyle/tara-donovan-pace-gallery-palo-alto-and-new-york-10748405/.

5 Pimploy Phongsirivech, "Tara Donovan's Decks," *Interview*, February 21, 2017, http://www.interviewmagazine.com/art/tara-donovan.

6 Donald Judd, "Specific Objects [1964]," *Arts Yearbook 8* (1965), 74; reprinted in Thomas Kellein, *Donald Judd: Early Work 1955–1968* (New York: D.A.P., 2002), 87.

7 David A. Ross, "Preface," in *Endgame: Reference and Simulation in Recent Painting and Sculpture*, exh. cat. (Cambridge and Boston, Mass.: The MIT Press; Institute of Contemporary Art, 1986), 7.

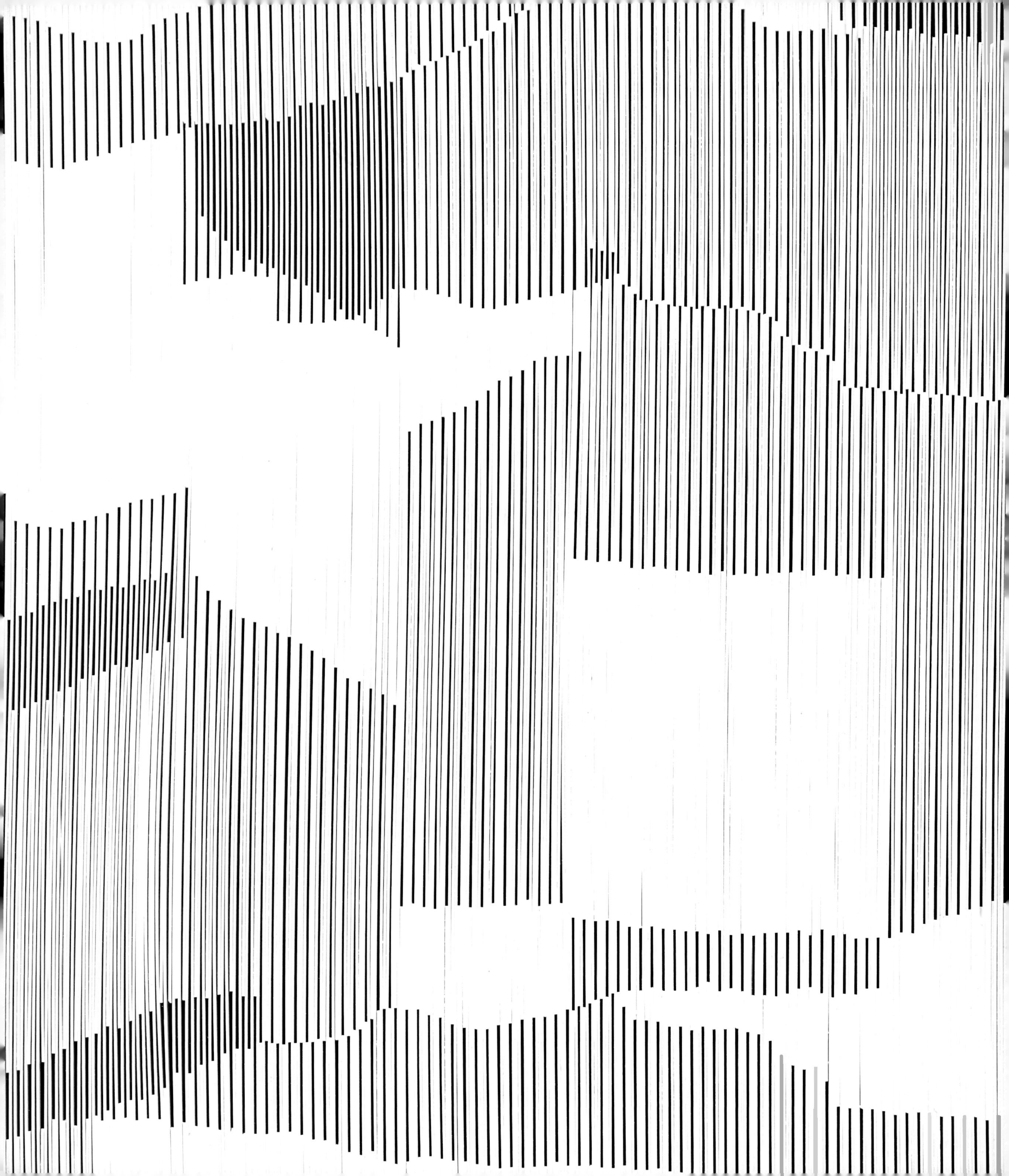

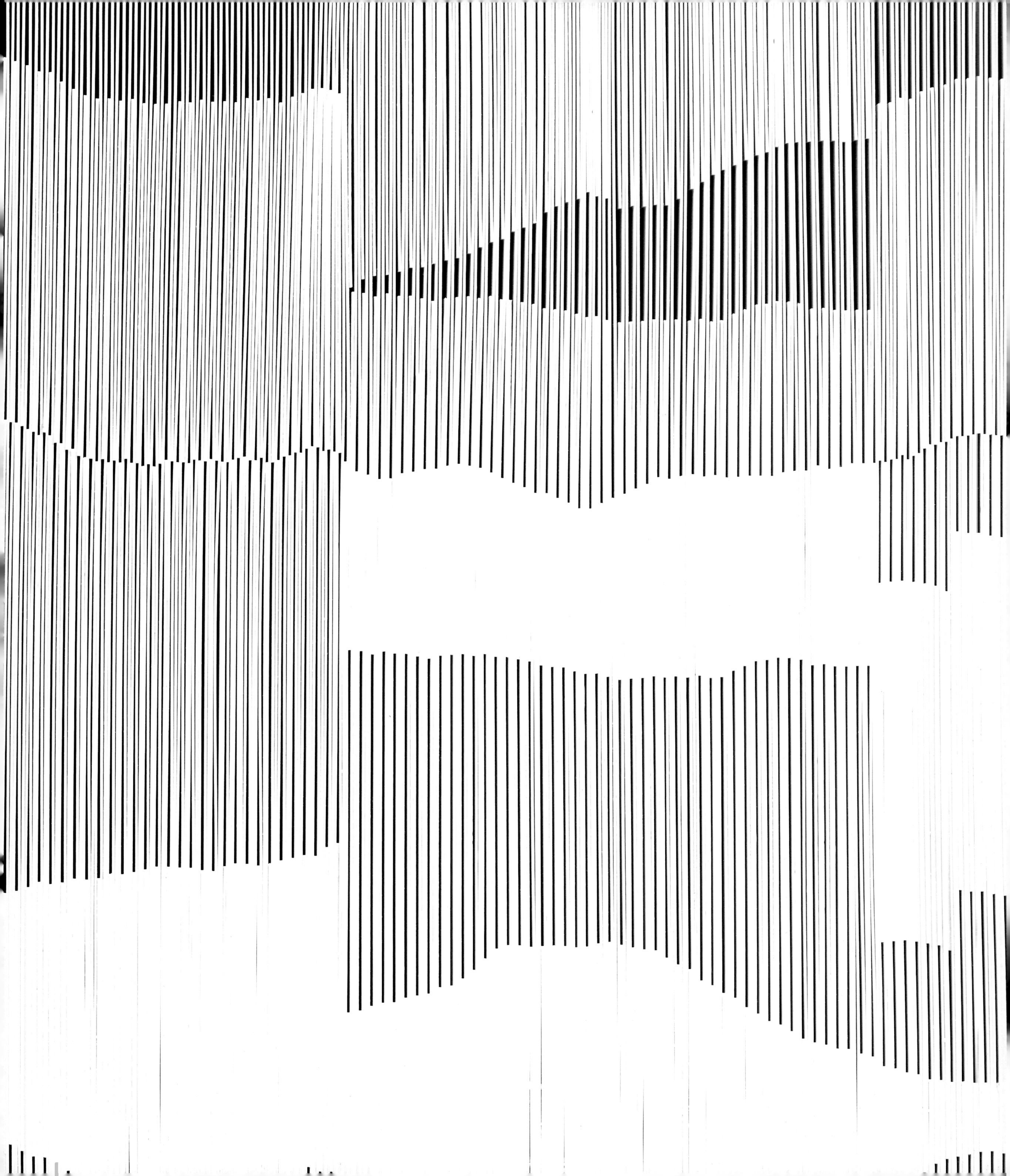

COMPOSITION (CARDS) 2017 39 ¼ x 39 ¼ x 4" | 99.7 x 99.7 x 10.2 cm

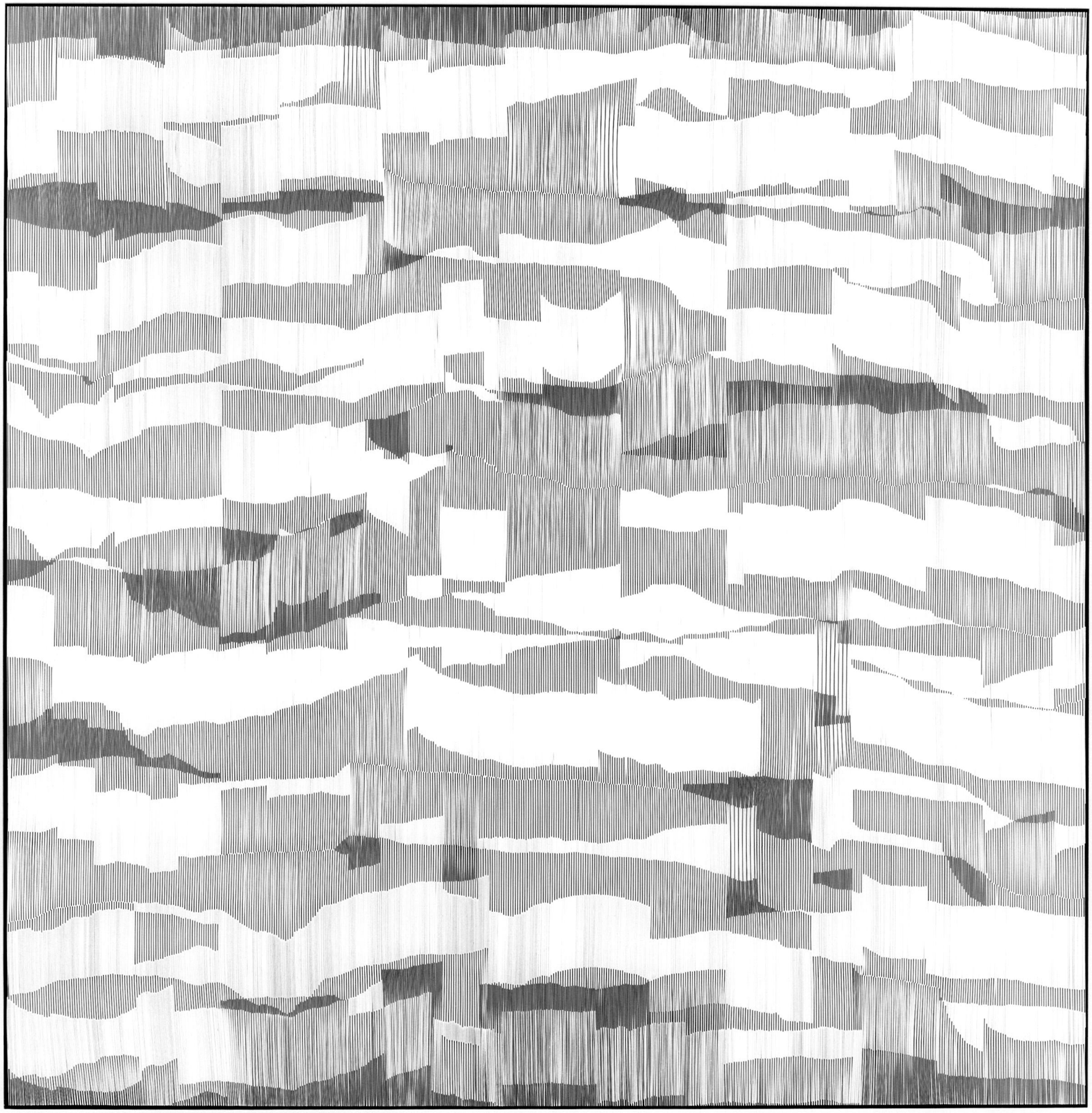

COMPOSITION (CARDS) 2017 39 ¼ x 39 ¼ x 4" | 99.7 x 99.7 x 10.2 cm

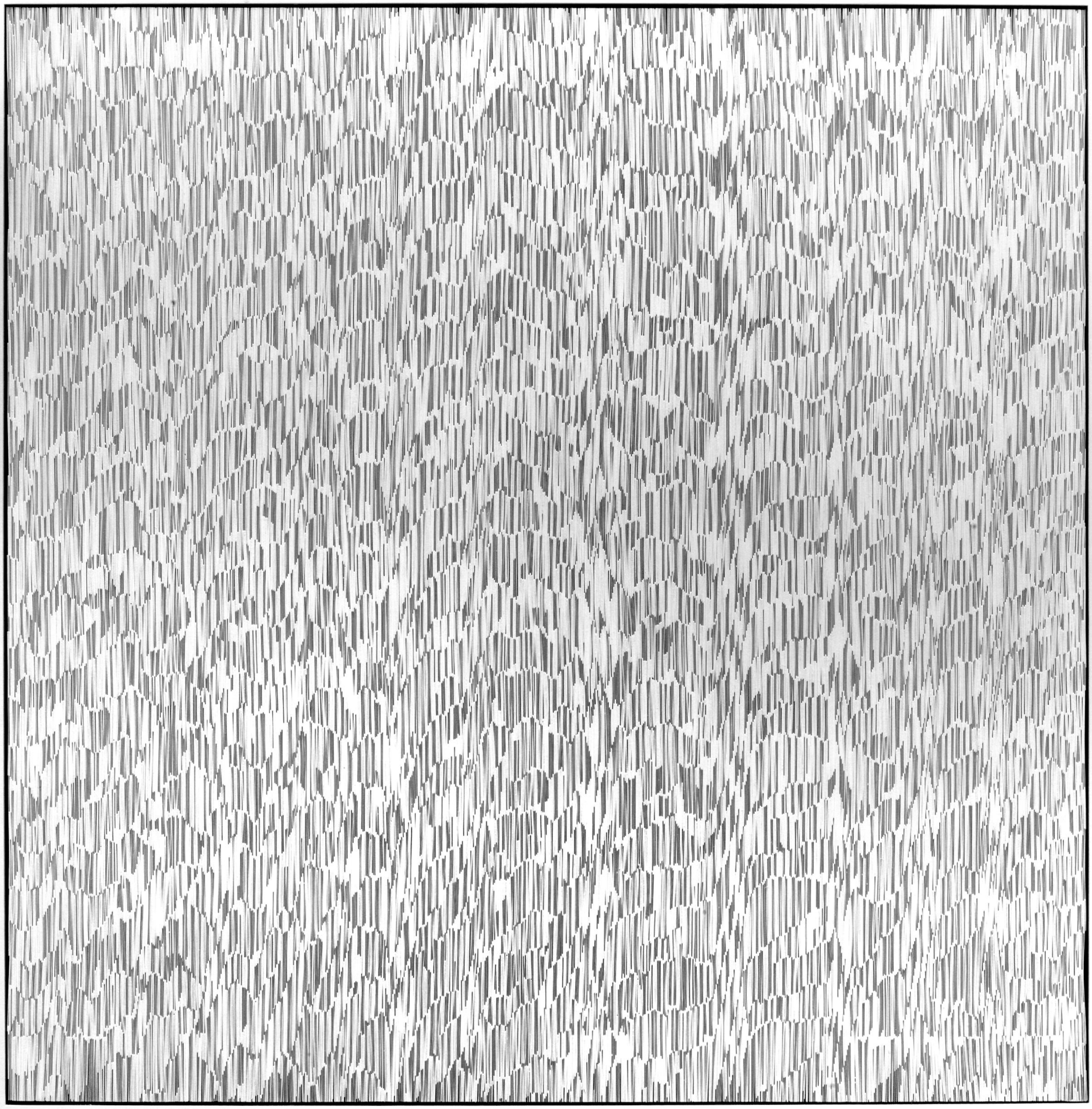

COMPOSITION (CARDS) 2017 39 ¼ x 39 ¼ x 4" | 99.7 x 99.7 x 10.2 cm

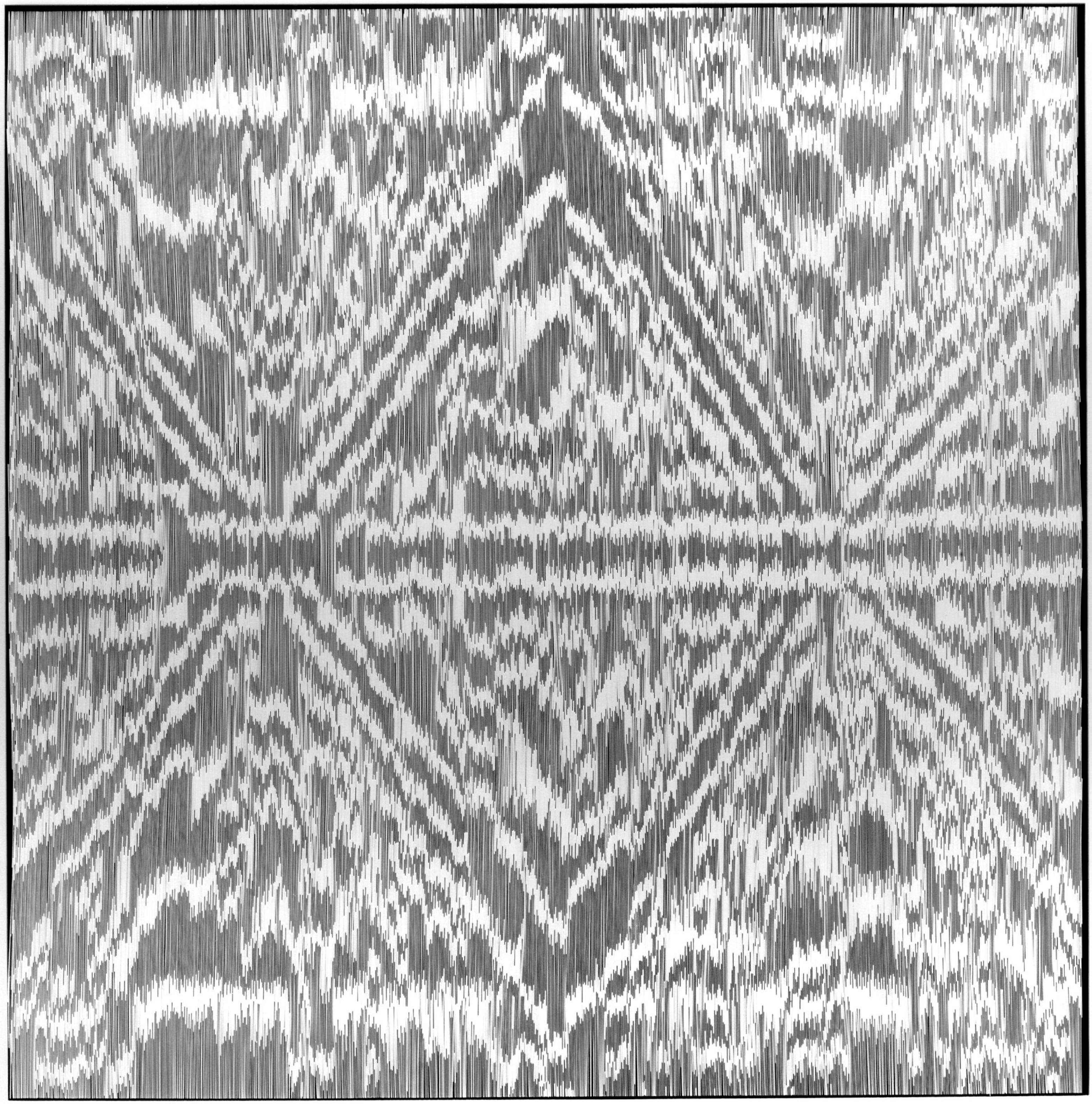

COMPOSITION (CARDS) 2017 39 ¼ x 39 ¼ x 4" | 99.7 x 99.7 x 10.2 cm

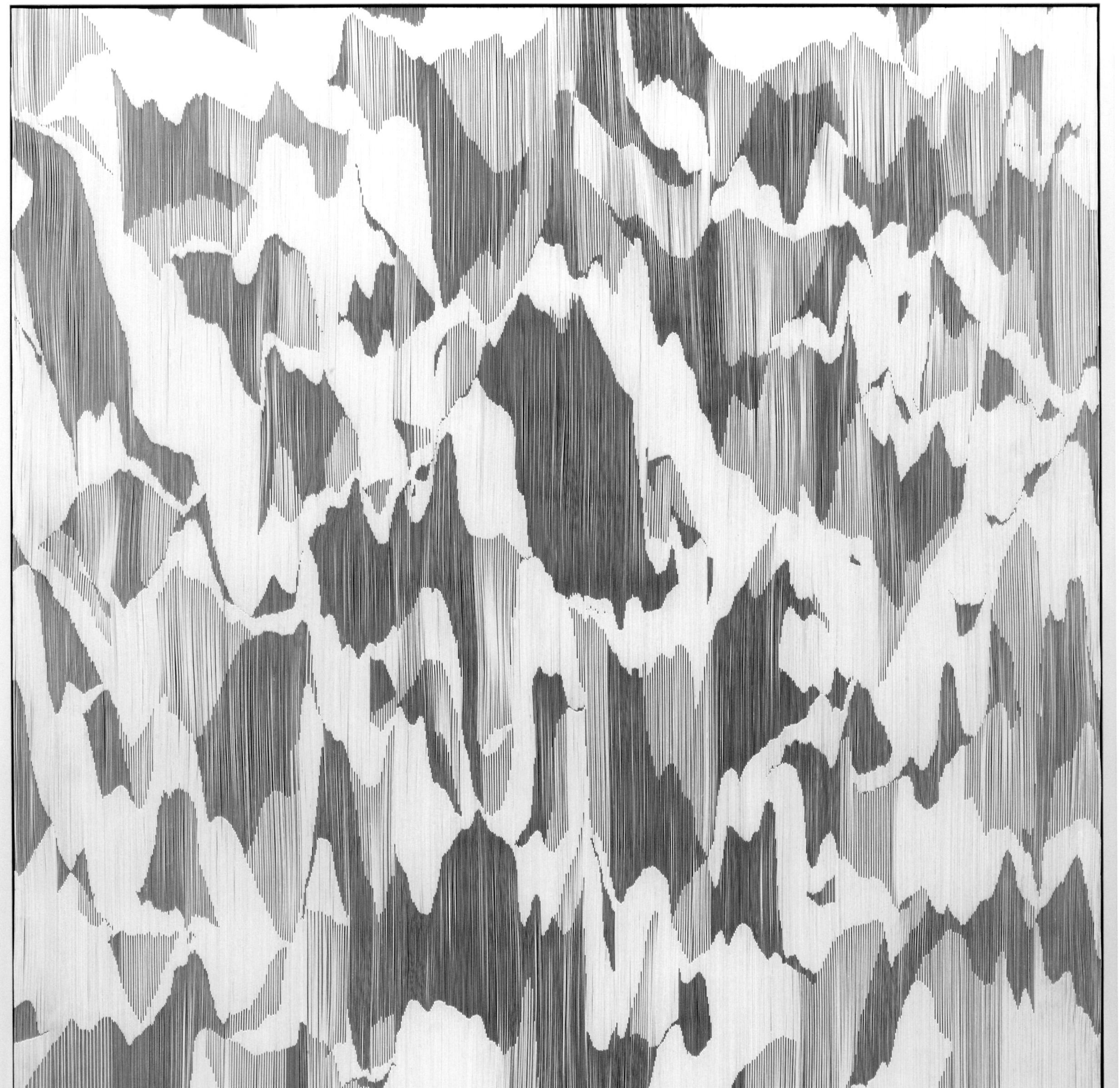

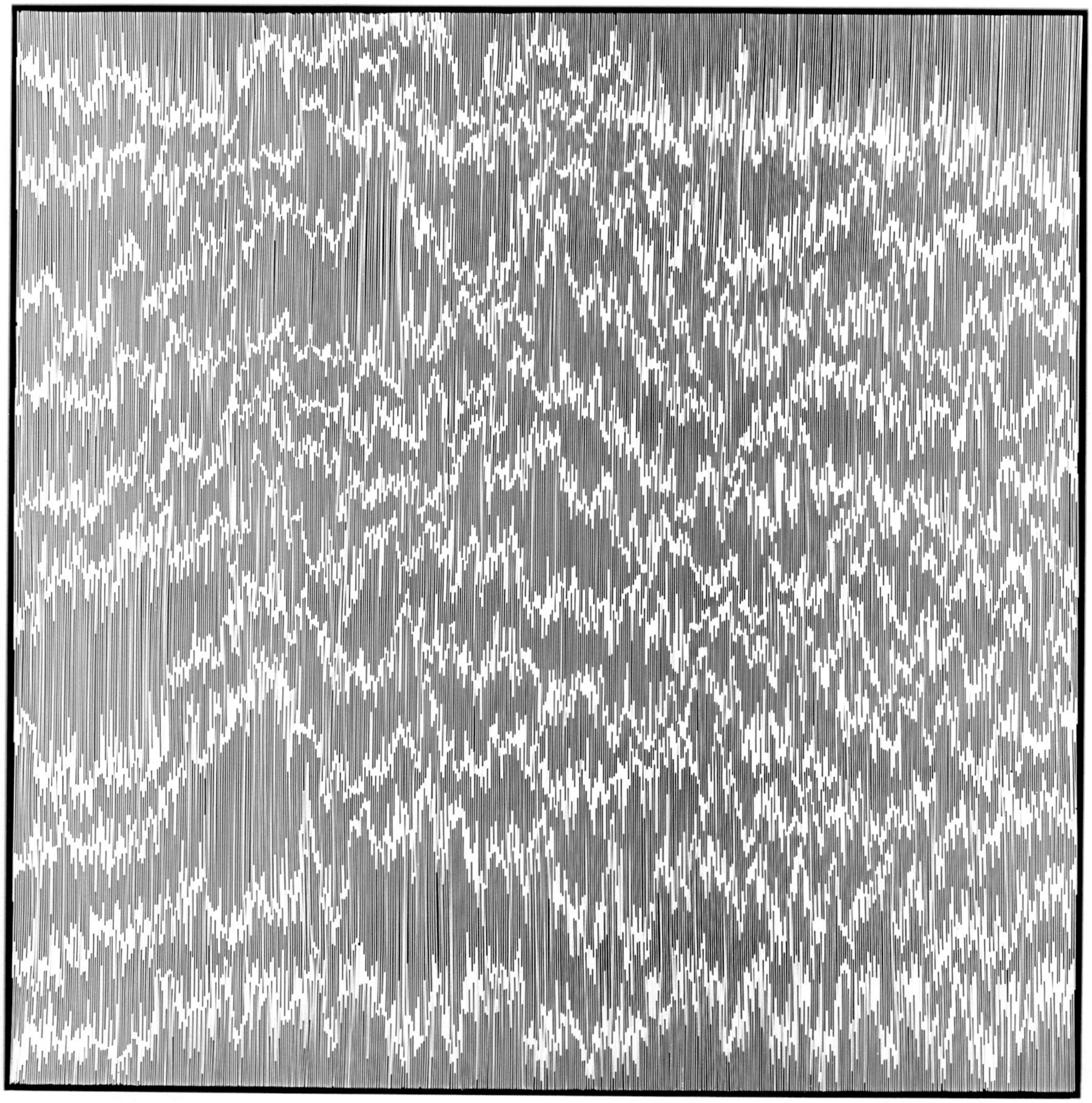

COMPOSITION (CARDS) 2017   22 ¼ x 22 ¼ x 4" | 56.5 x 56.5 x 10.2 cm

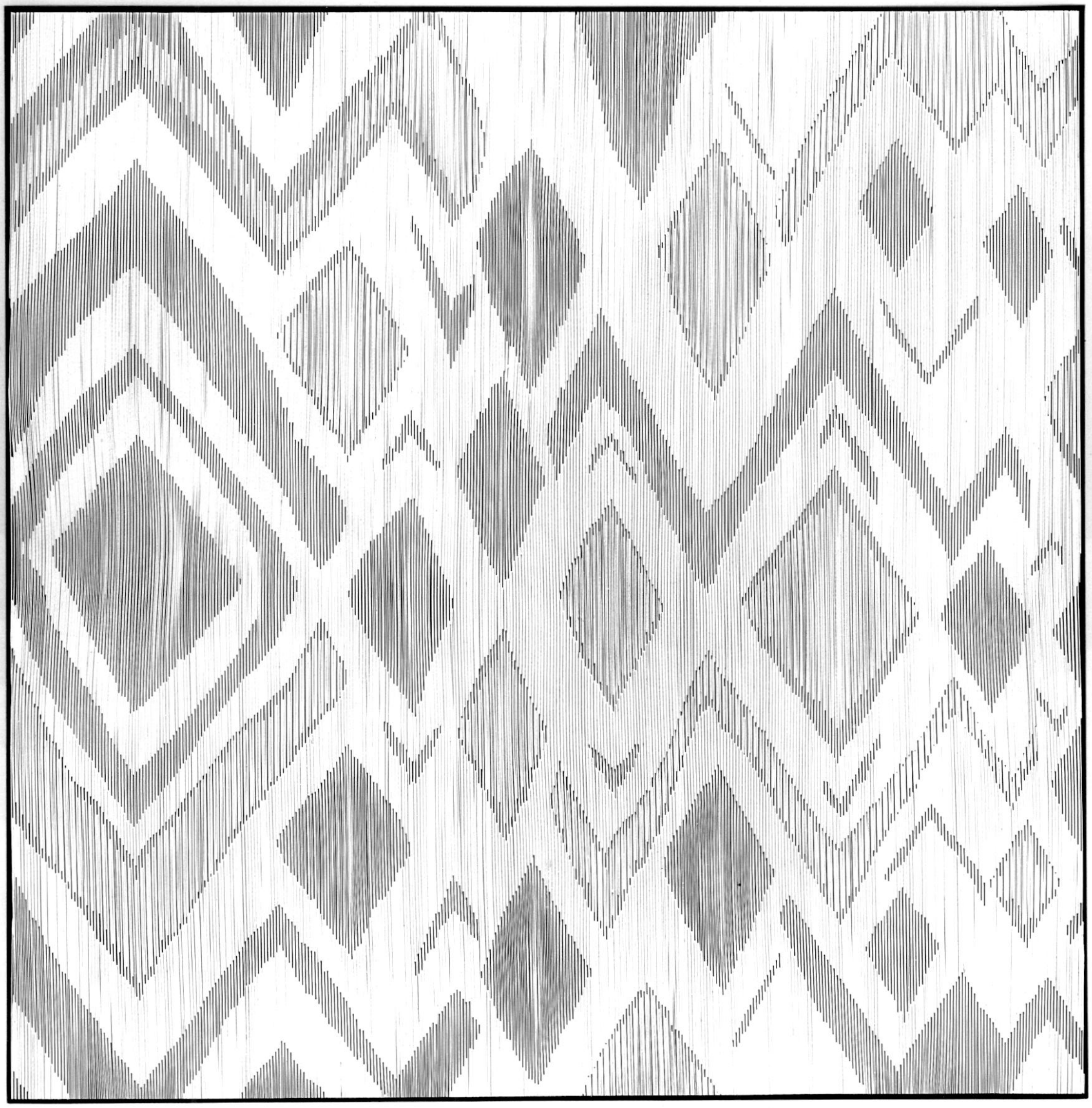

COMPOSITION (CARDS) 2017 22 ¼ x 22 ¼ x 4" | 56.5 x 56.5 x 10.2 cm

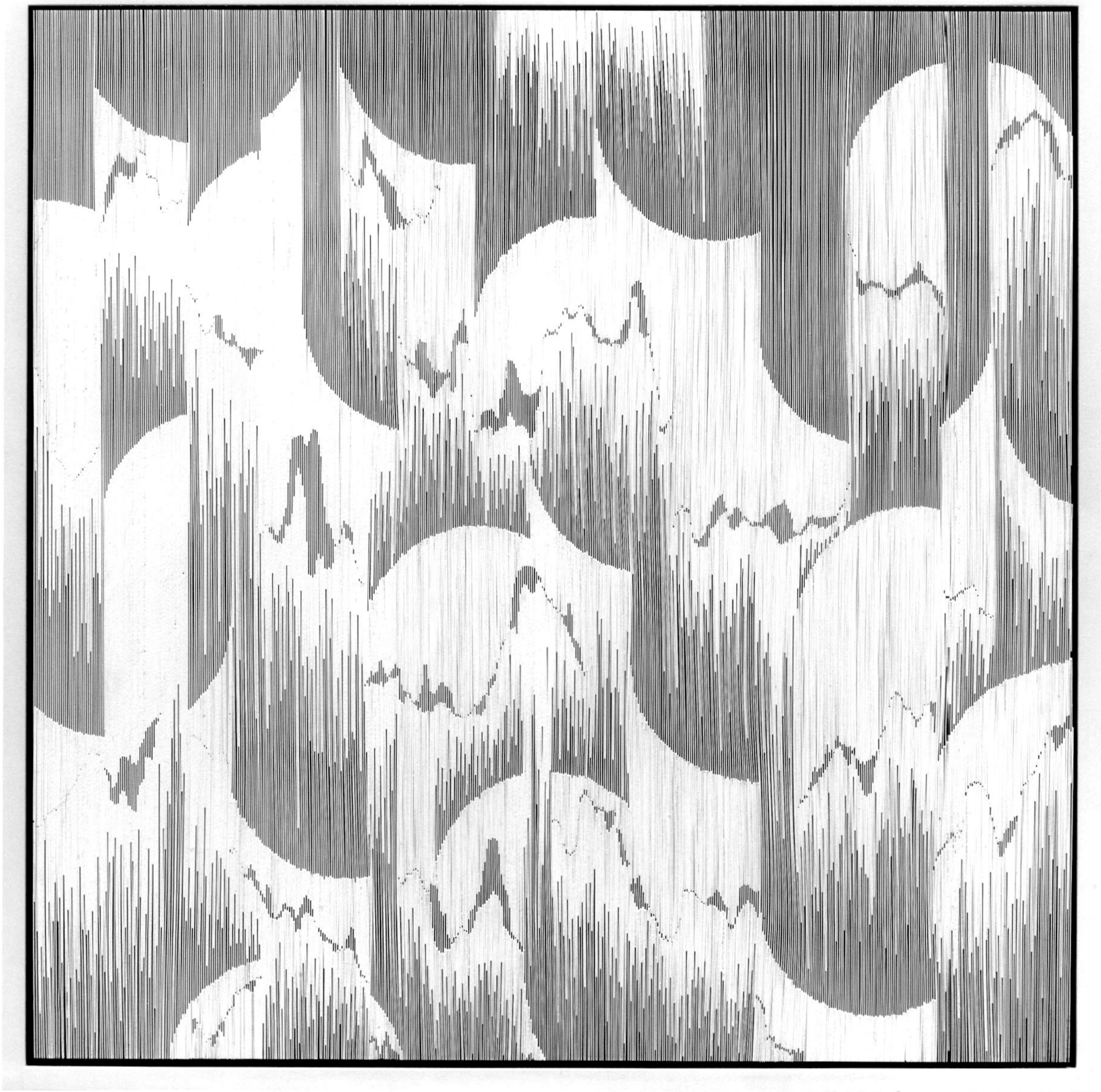

COMPOSITION (CARDS) 2017 22 ¼ x 22 ¼ x 4" | 56.5 x 56.5 x 10.2 cm

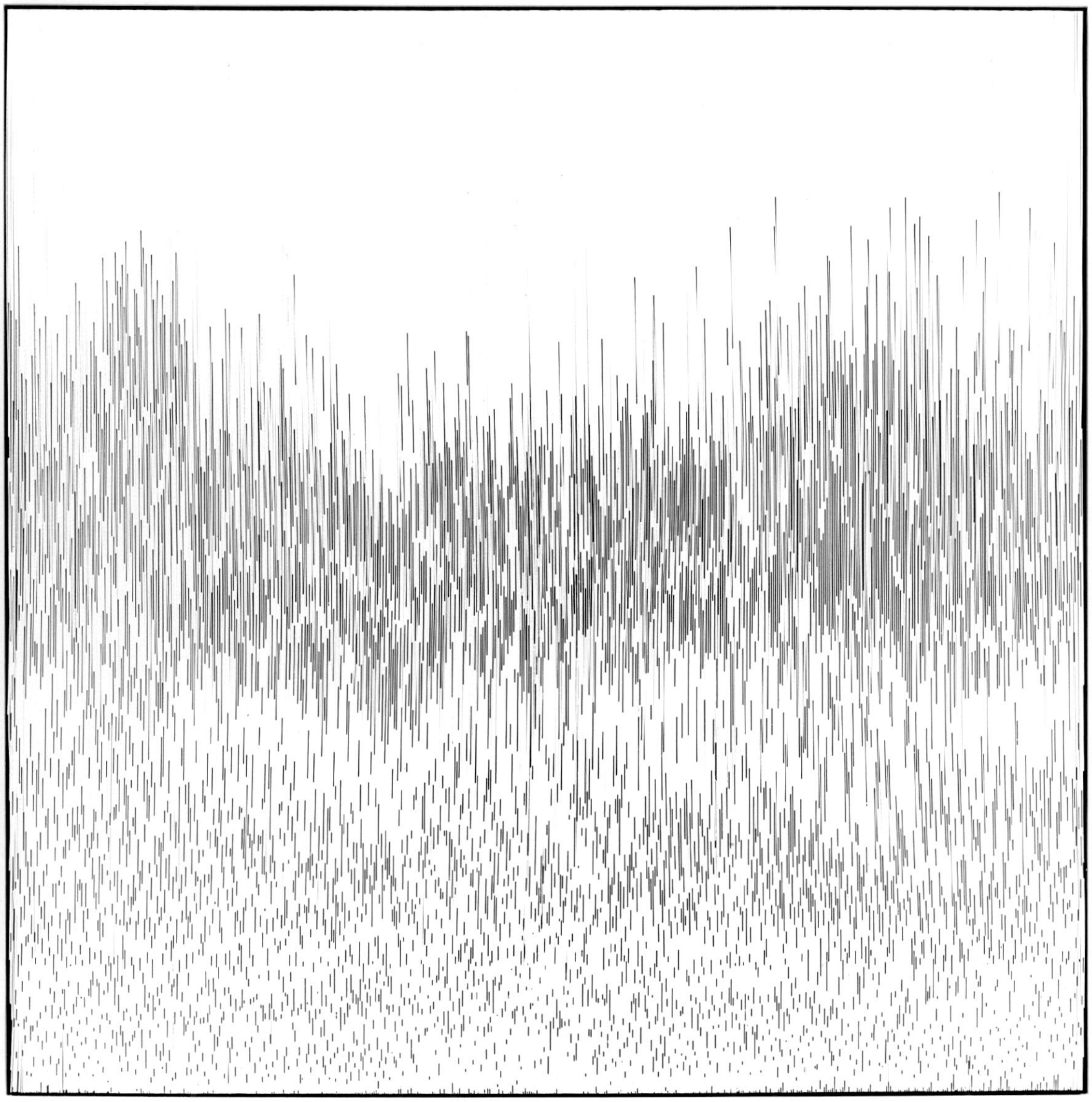

COMPOSITION (CARDS) 2017 22 ¼ x 22 ¼ x 4" | 56.5 x 56.5 x 10.2 cm

COMPOSITION (CARDS) 2017   39 ¼ x 39 ¼ x 4" | 99.7 x 99.7 x 10.2 cm

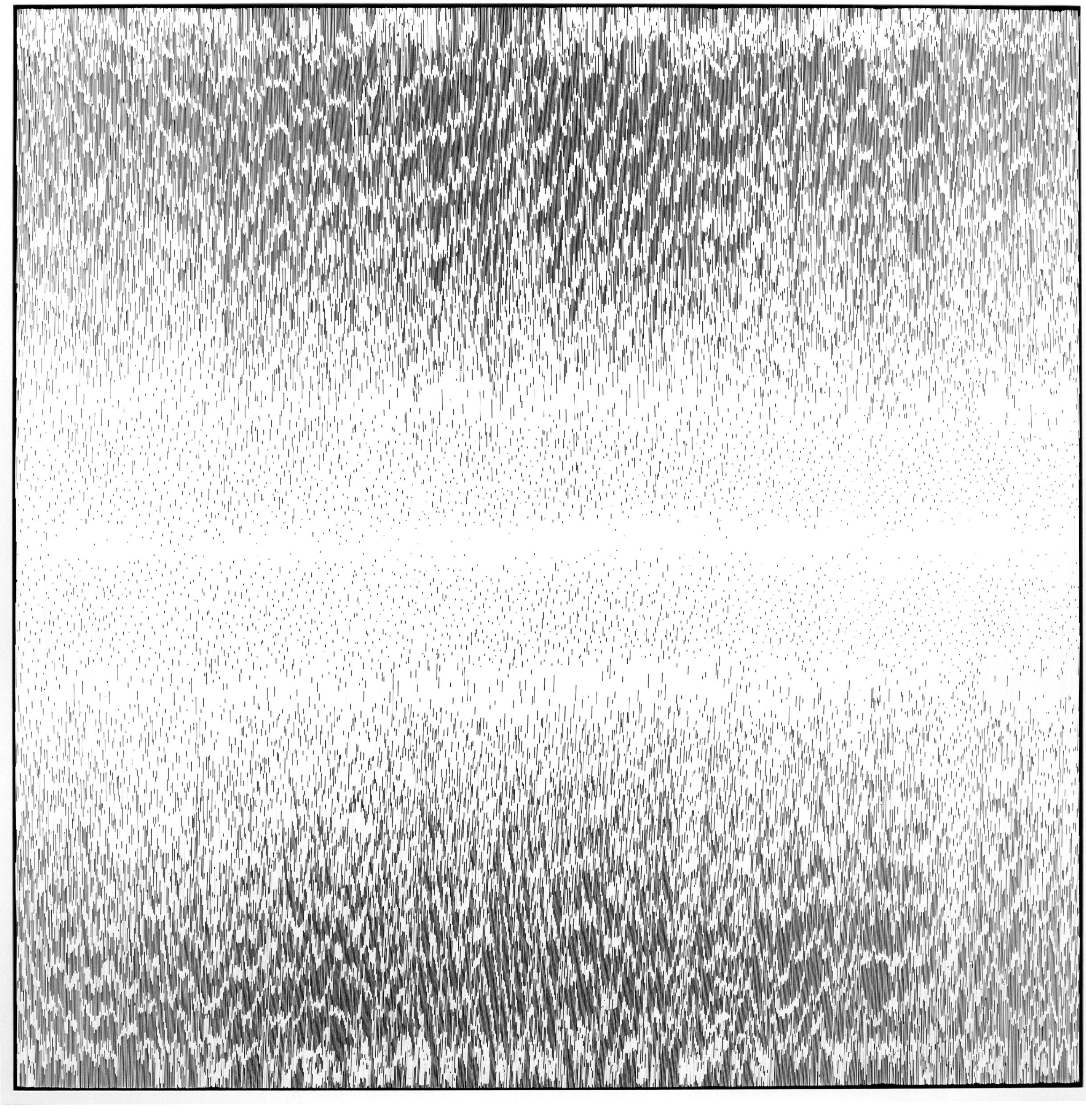

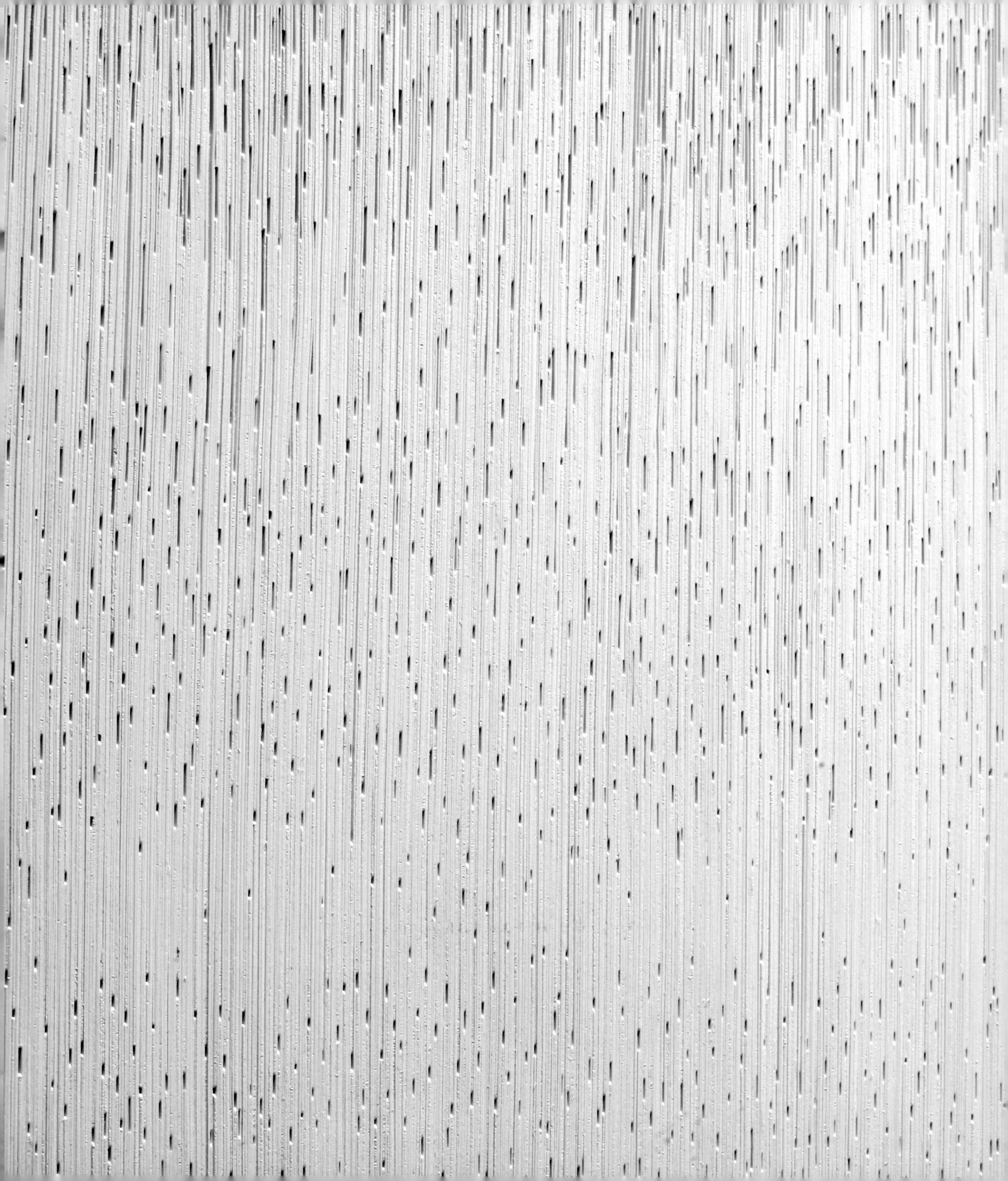

COMPOSITION (CARDS) 2017   39 ¼ x 39 ¼ x 4" | 99.7 x 99.7 x 10.2 cm

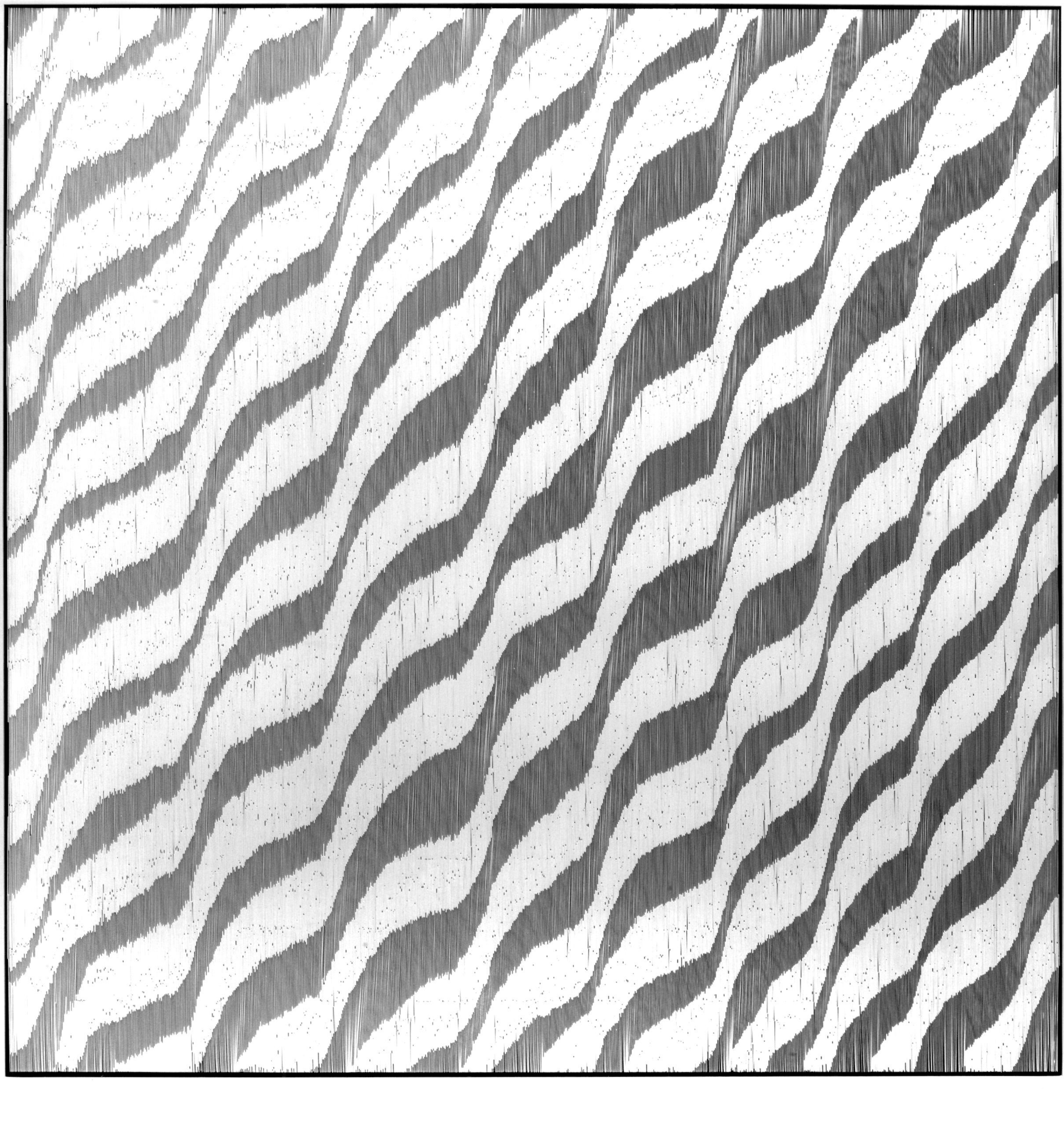

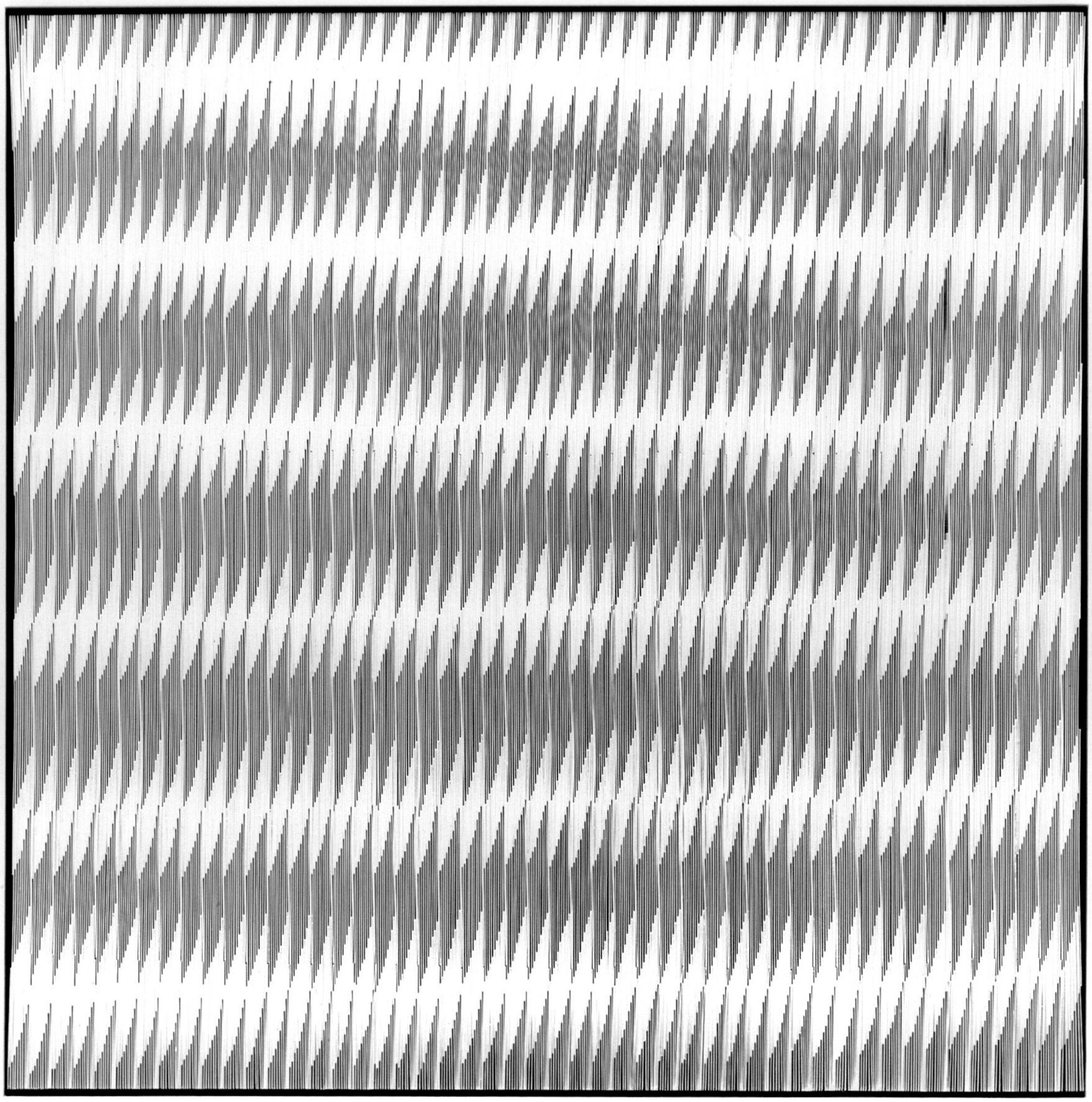

COMPOSITION (CARDS) 2017 22 ¼ x 22 ¼ x 4" | 56.5 x 56.5 x 10.2 cm

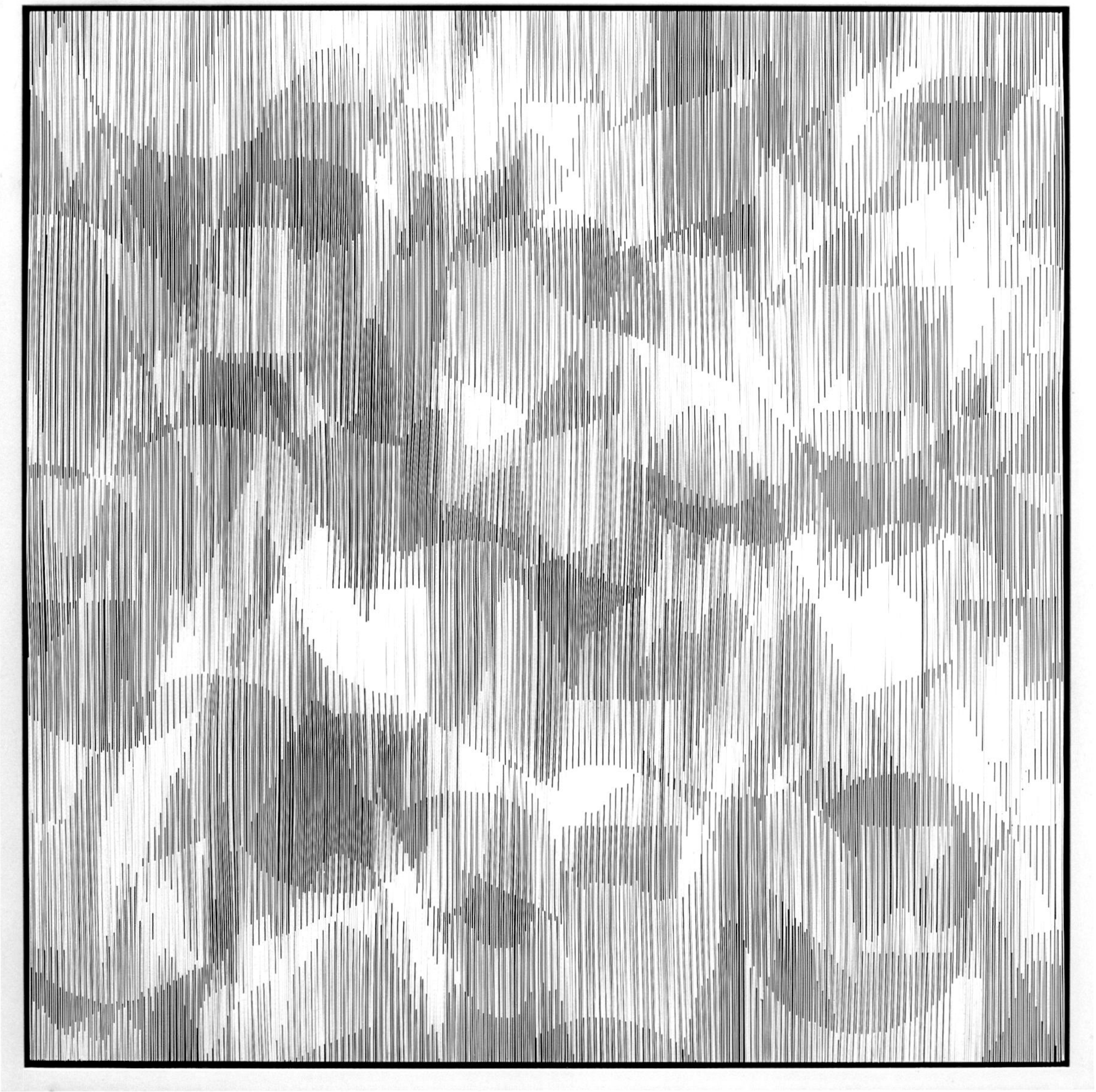

COMPOSITION (CARDS) 2017 22 ¼ x 22 ¼ x 4" | 56.5 x 56.5 x 10.2 cm

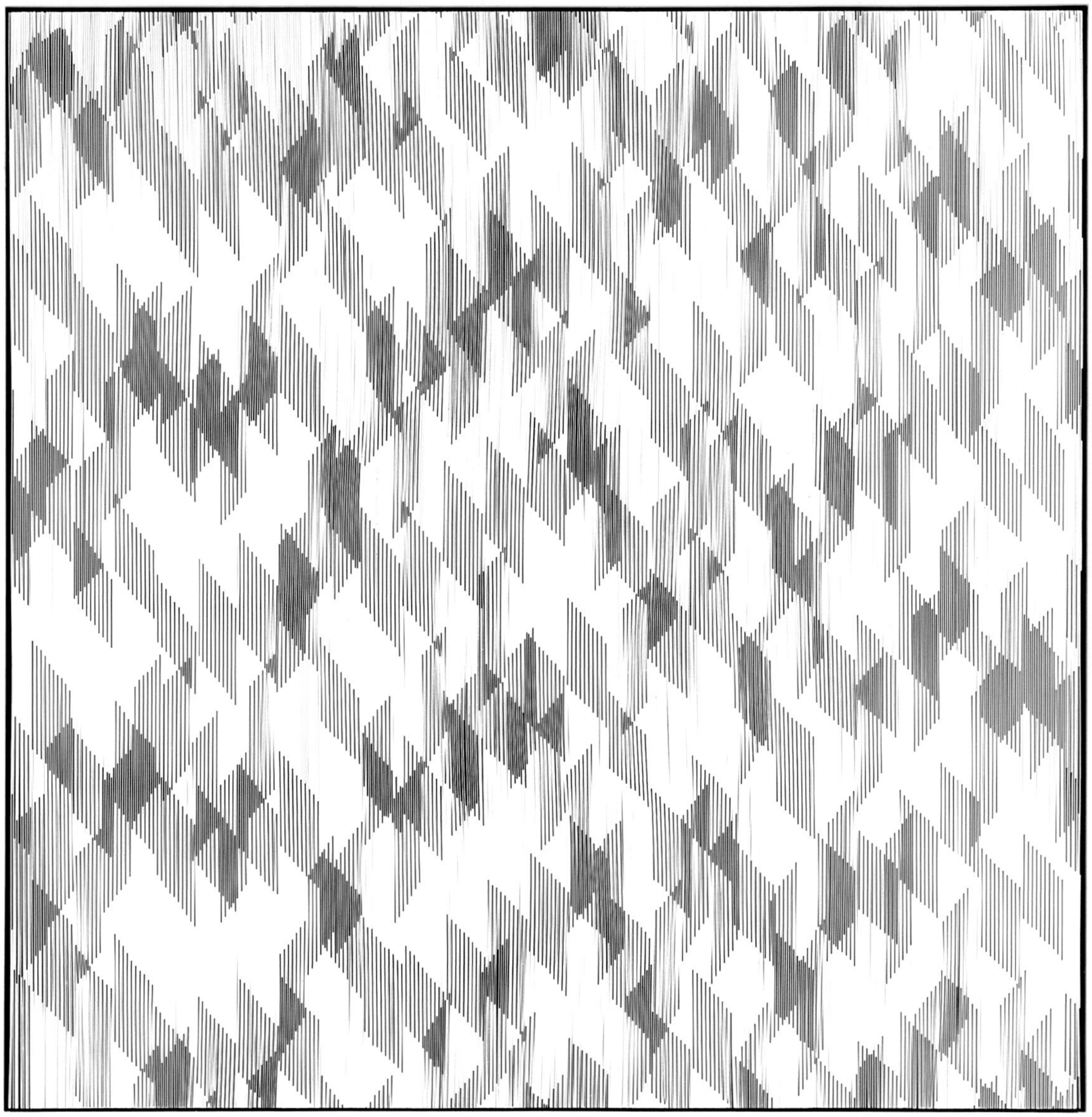

COMPOSITION (CARDS) 2017   22 ¼ x 22 ¼ x 4" | 56.5 x 56.5 x 10.2 cm

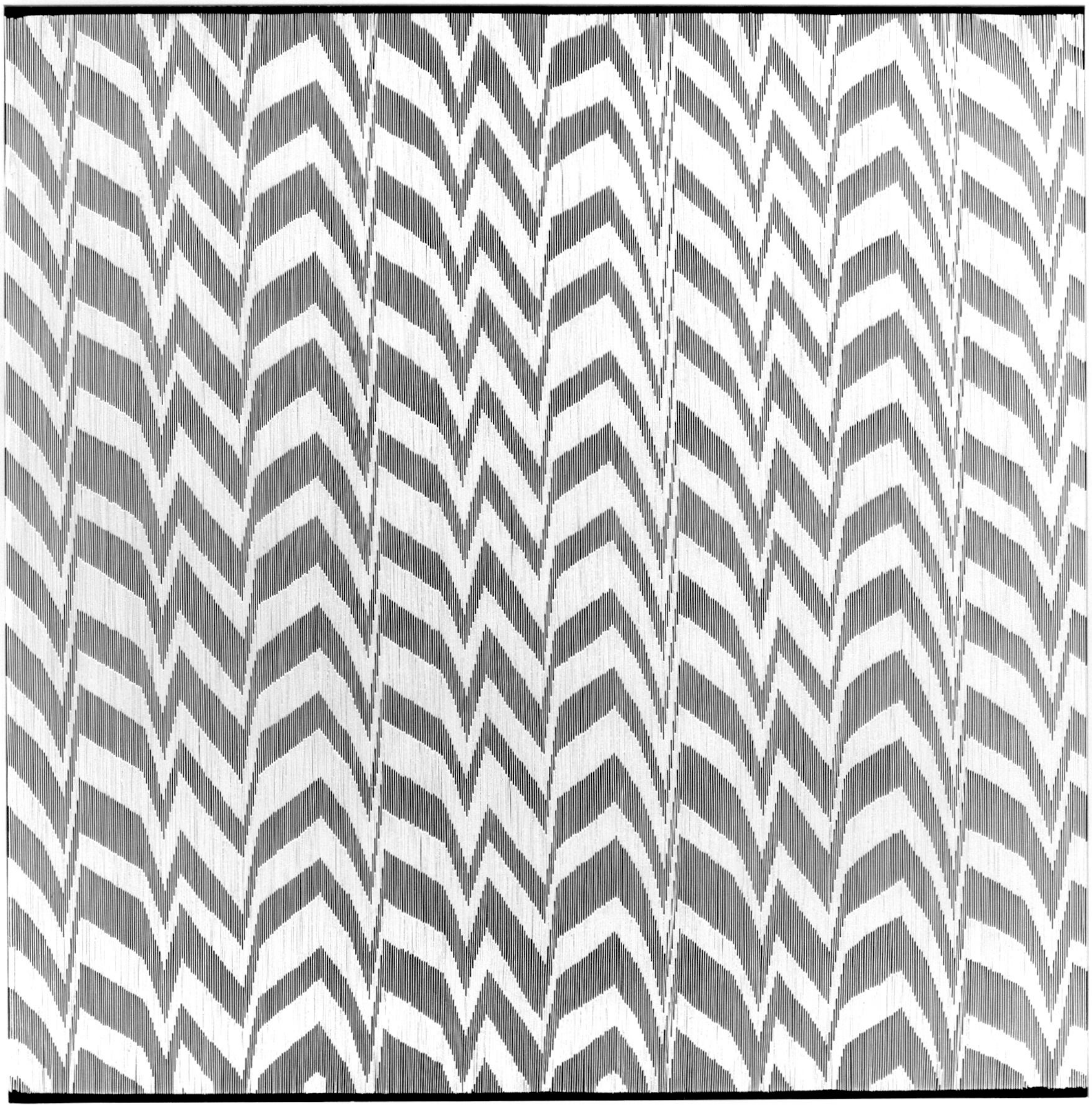

COMPOSITION (CARDS) 2017 22 ¼ x 22 ¼ x 4" | 56.5 x 56.5 x 10.2 cm

COMPOSITION (CARDS) 2017 39 ¼ x 39 ¼ x 4" | 99.7 x 99.7 x 10.2 cm

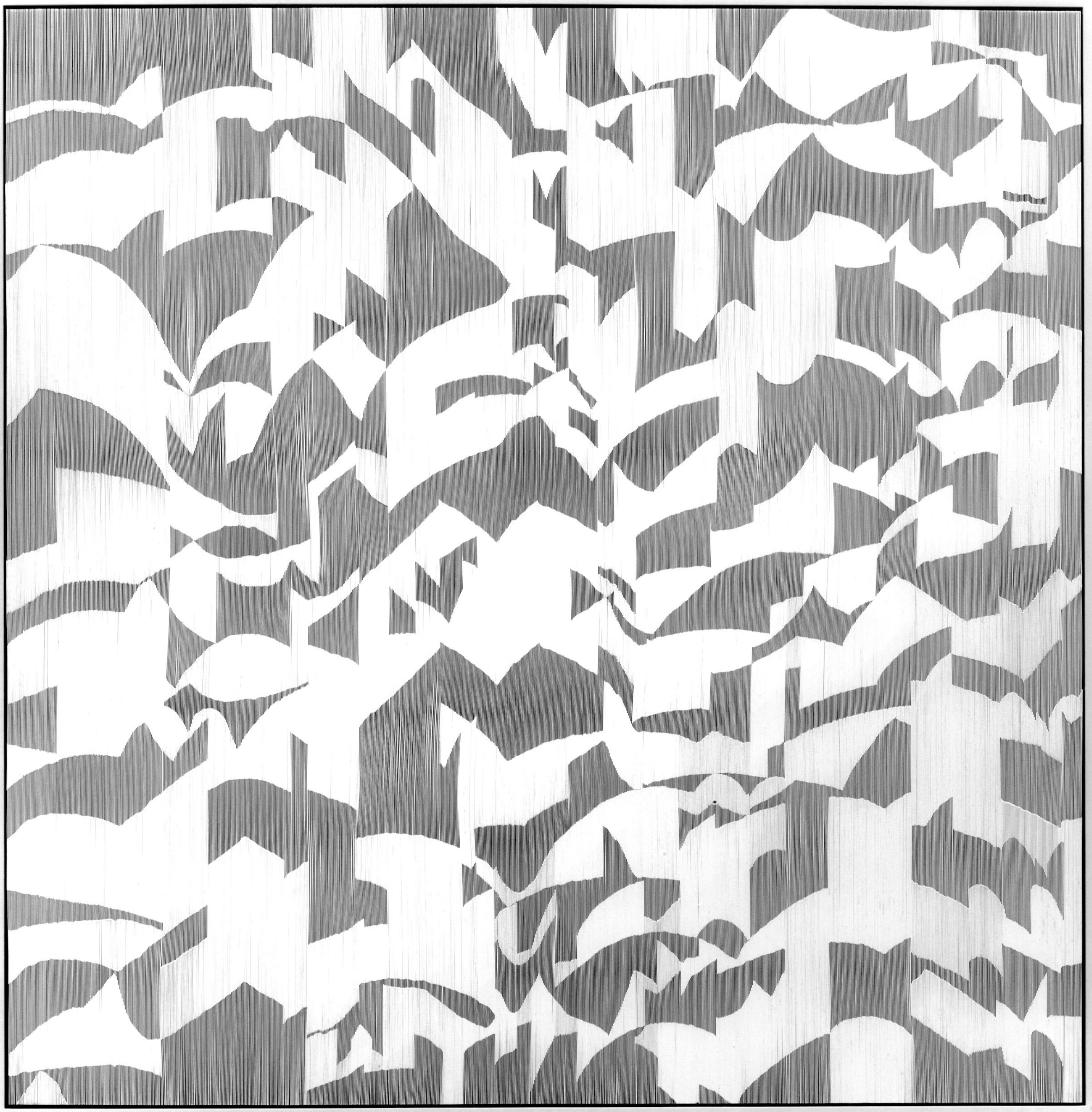

COMPOSITION (CARDS) 2017 39 ¼ x 39 ¼ x 4" | 99.7 x 99.7 x 10.2 cm

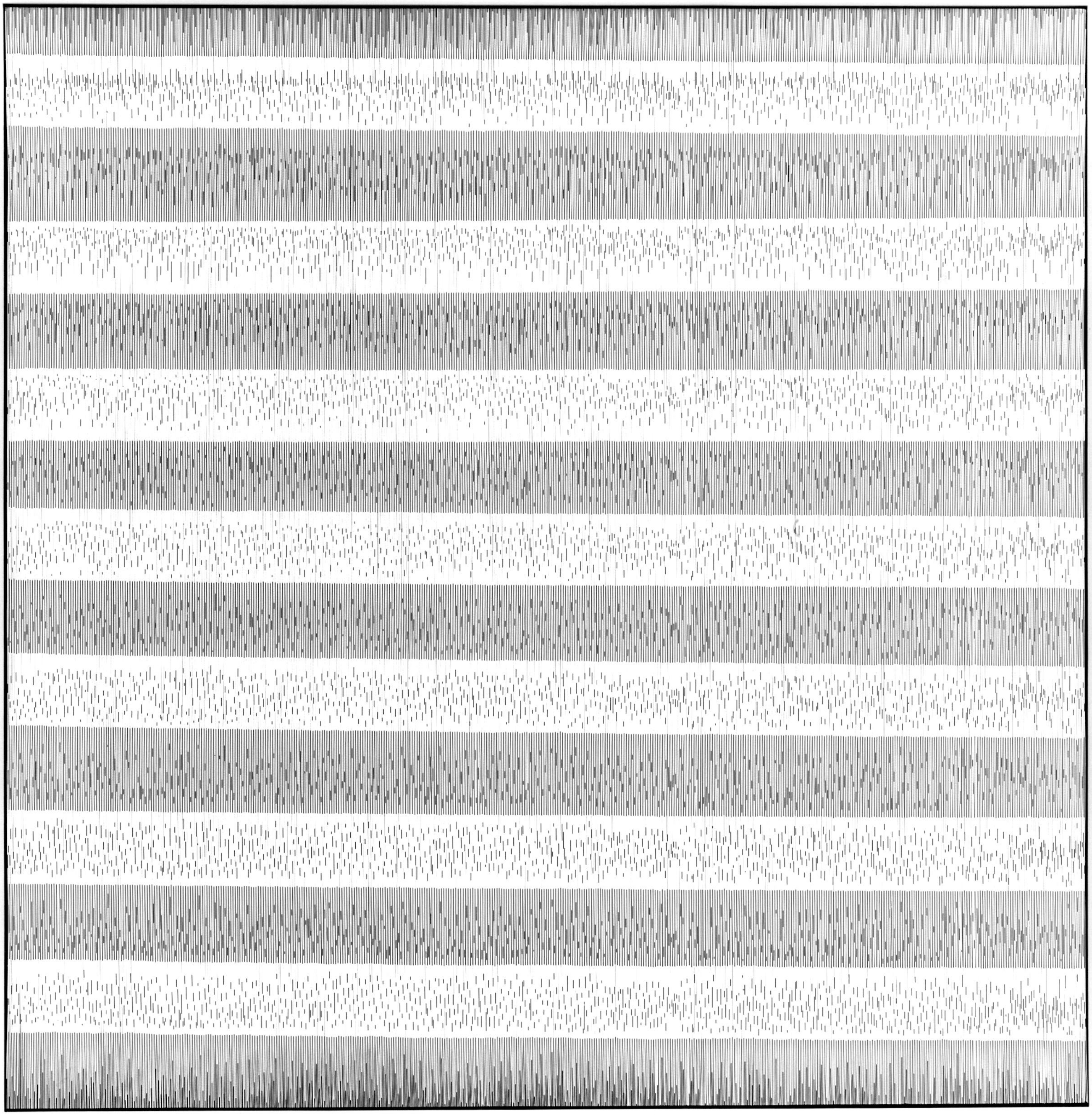

COMPOSITION (CARDS) 2017   39 ¼ x 39 ¼ x 4" | 99.7 x 99.7 x 10.2 cm

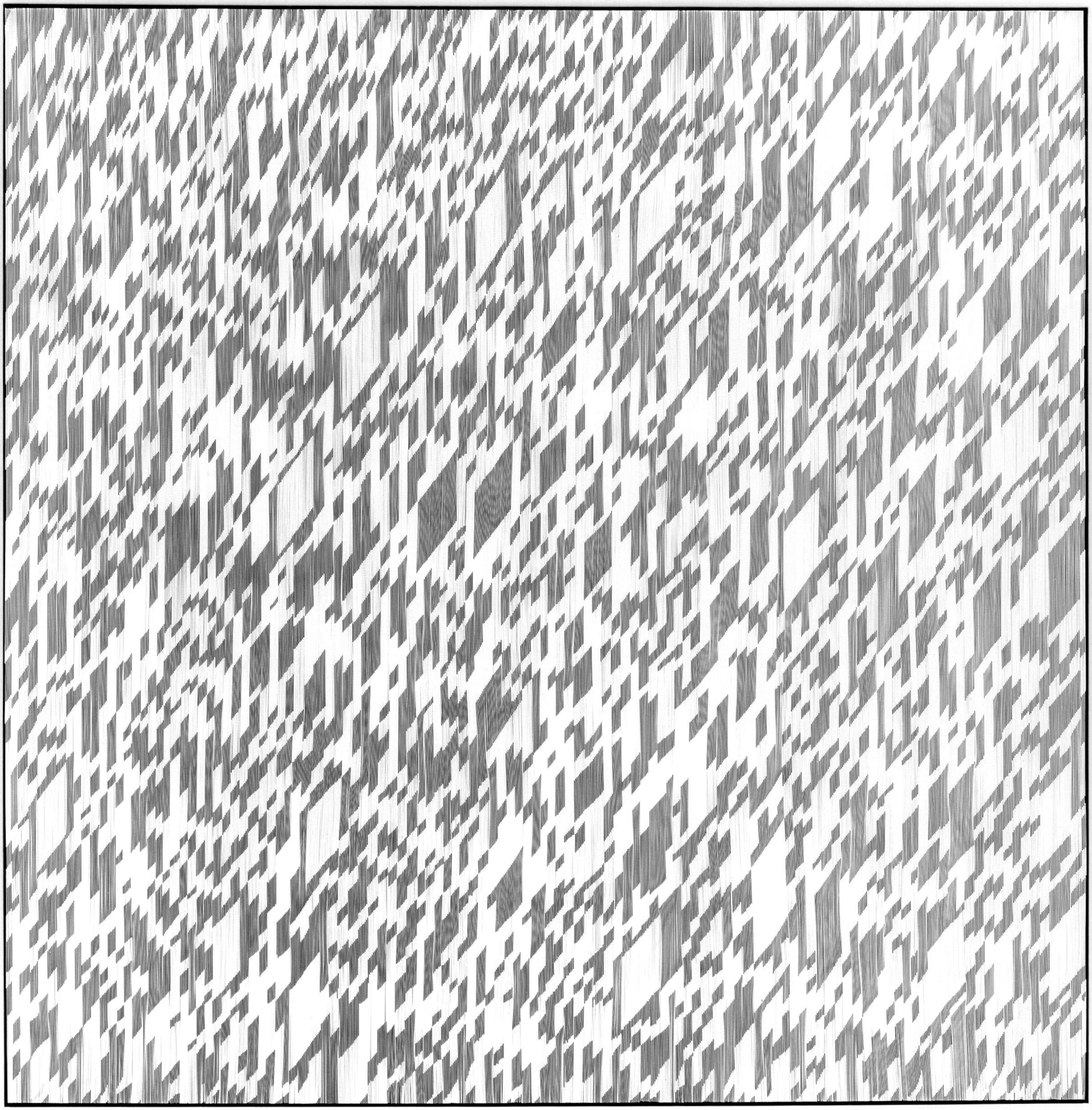

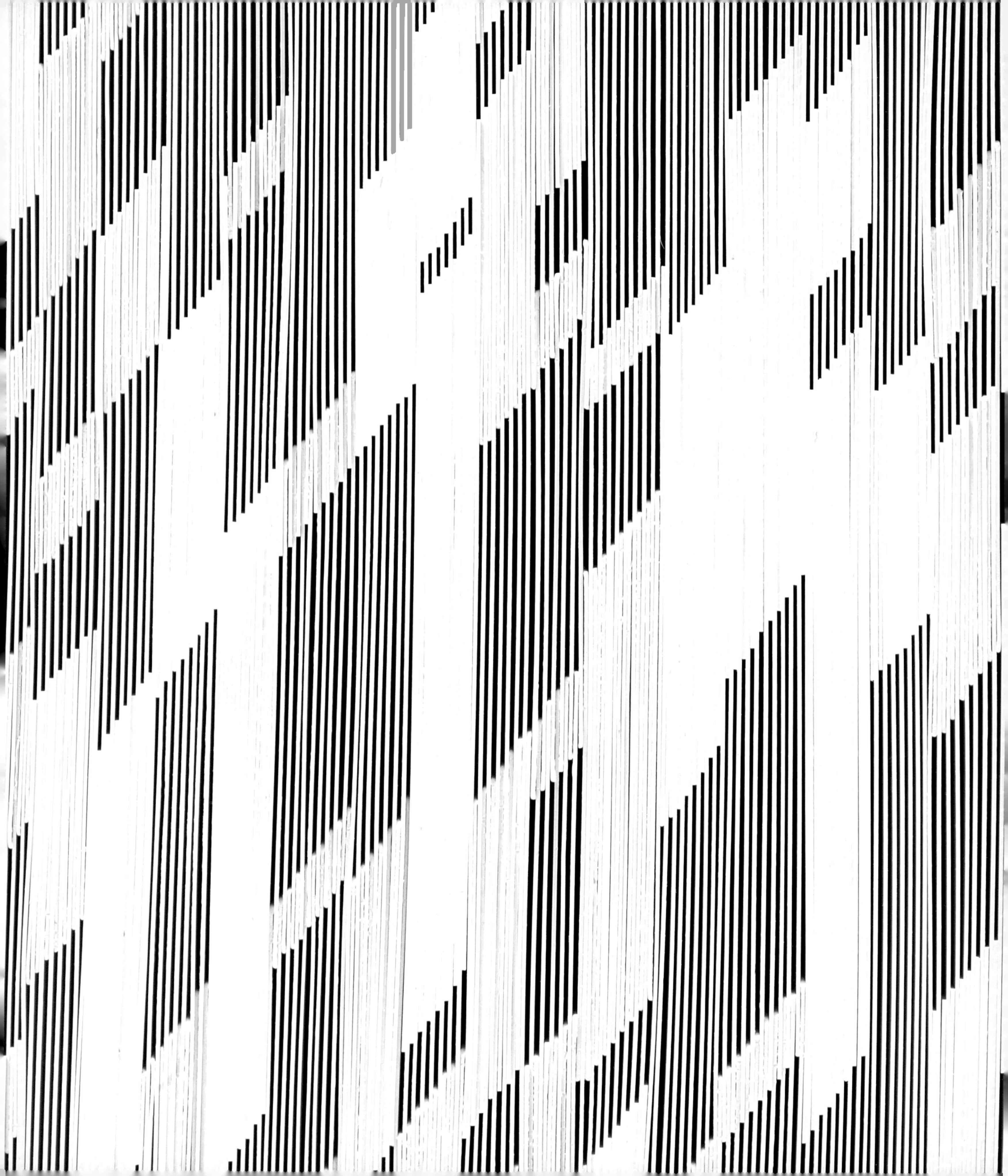

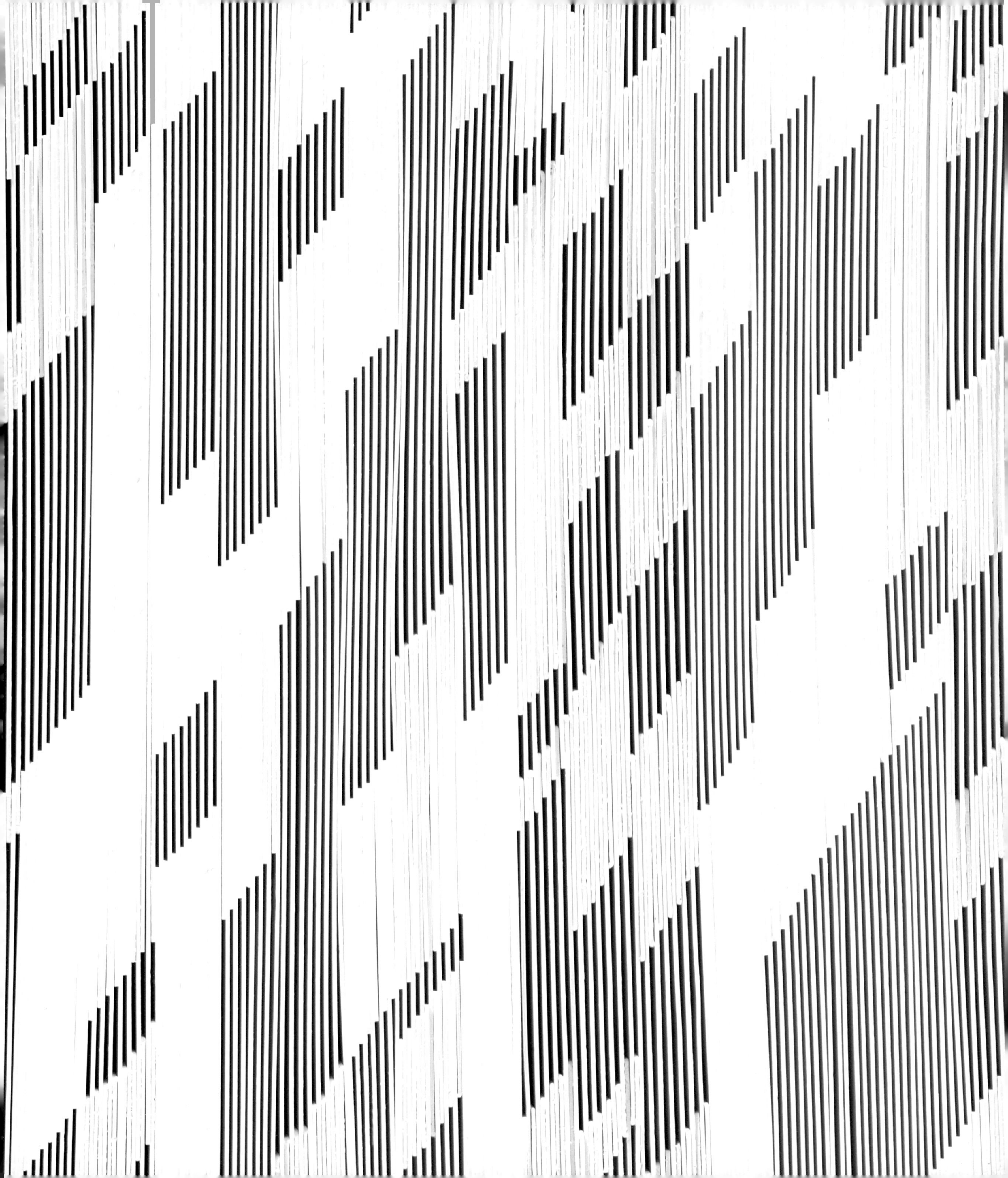

COMPOSITION (CARDS) 2016 39 ¼ x 39 ¼ x 4" | 99.7 x 99.7 x 10.2 cm

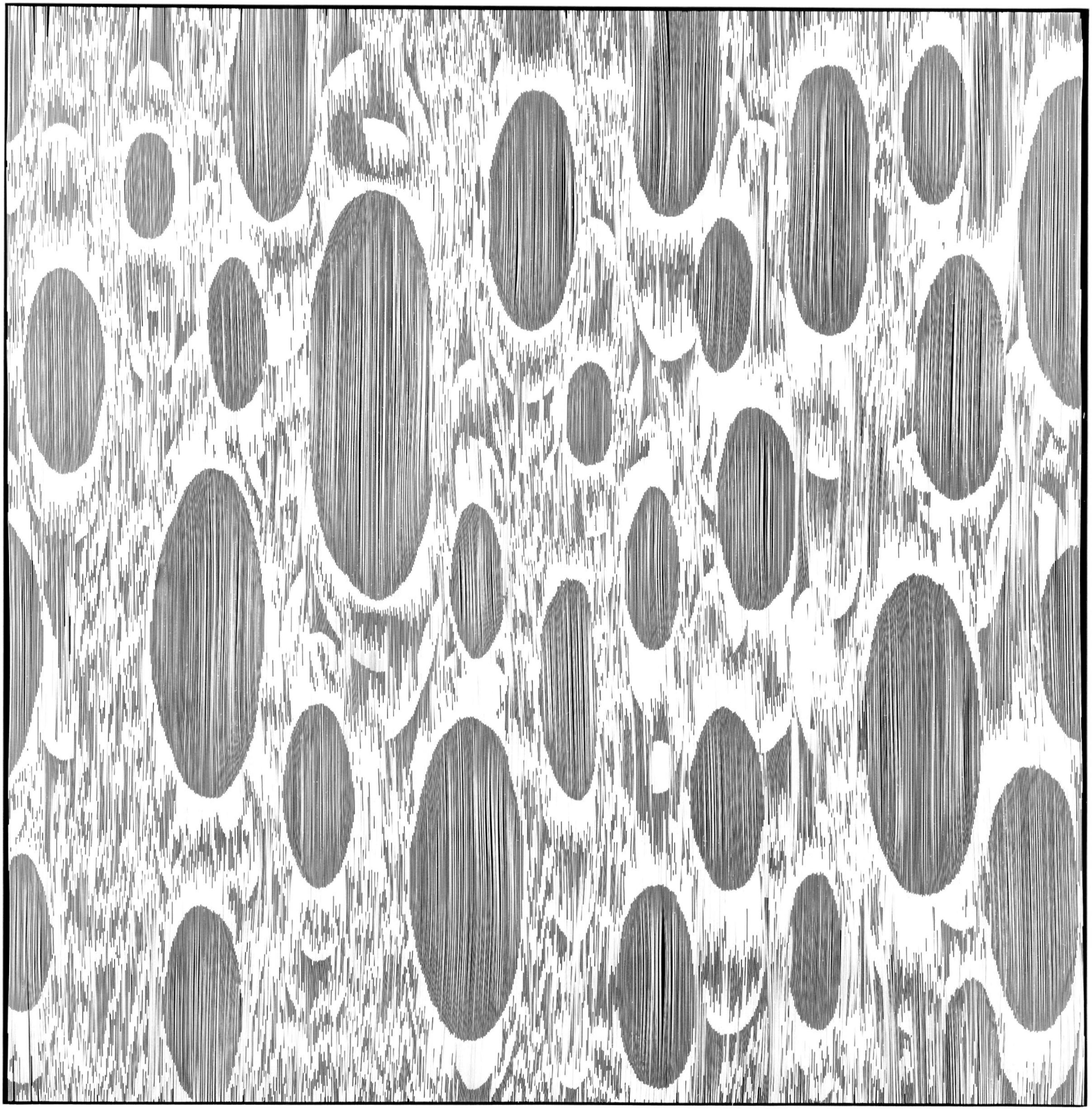

COMPOSITION (CARDS) 2017 39 ¼ x 39 ¼ x 4" | 99.7 x 99.7 x 10.2 cm

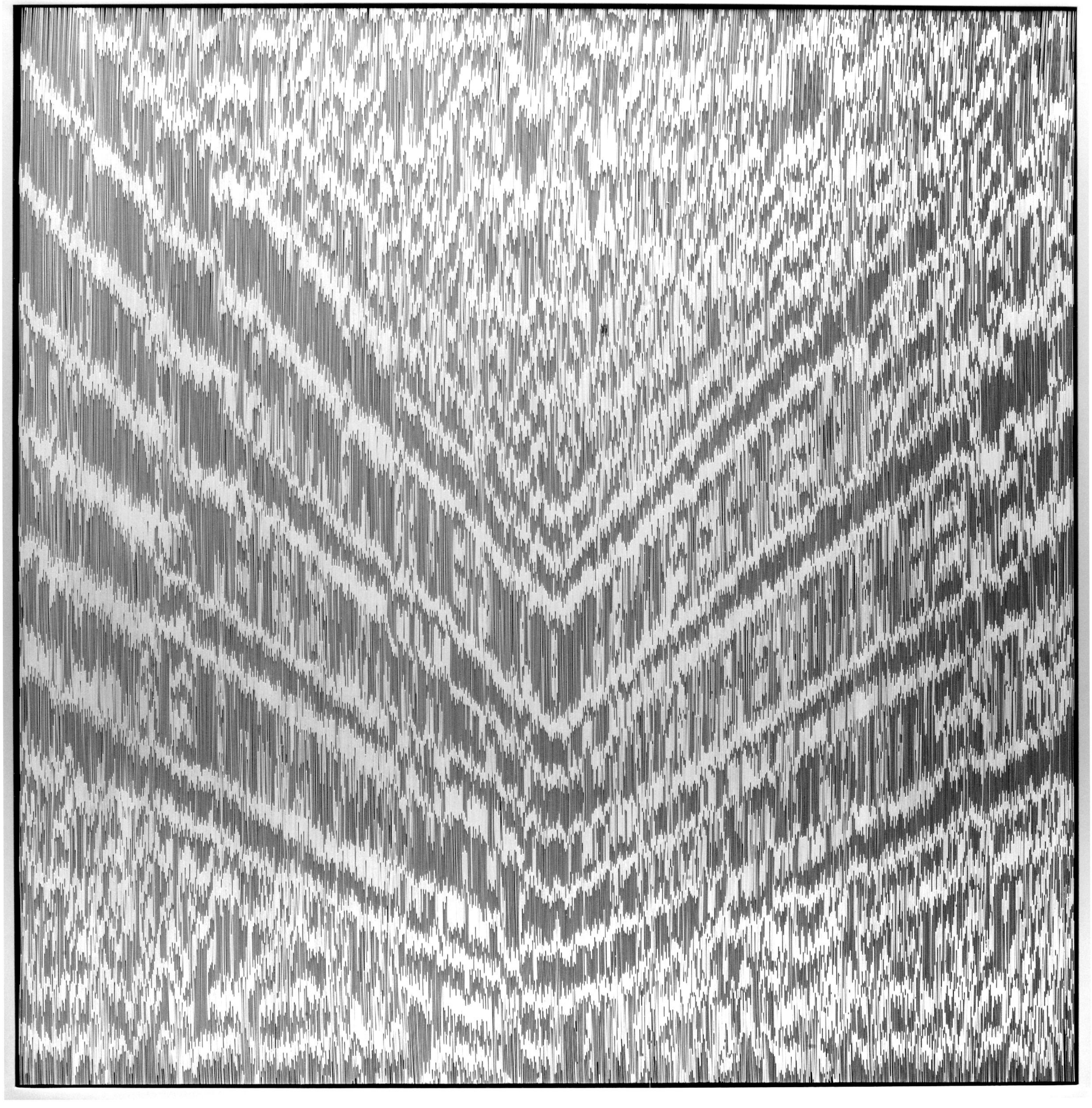

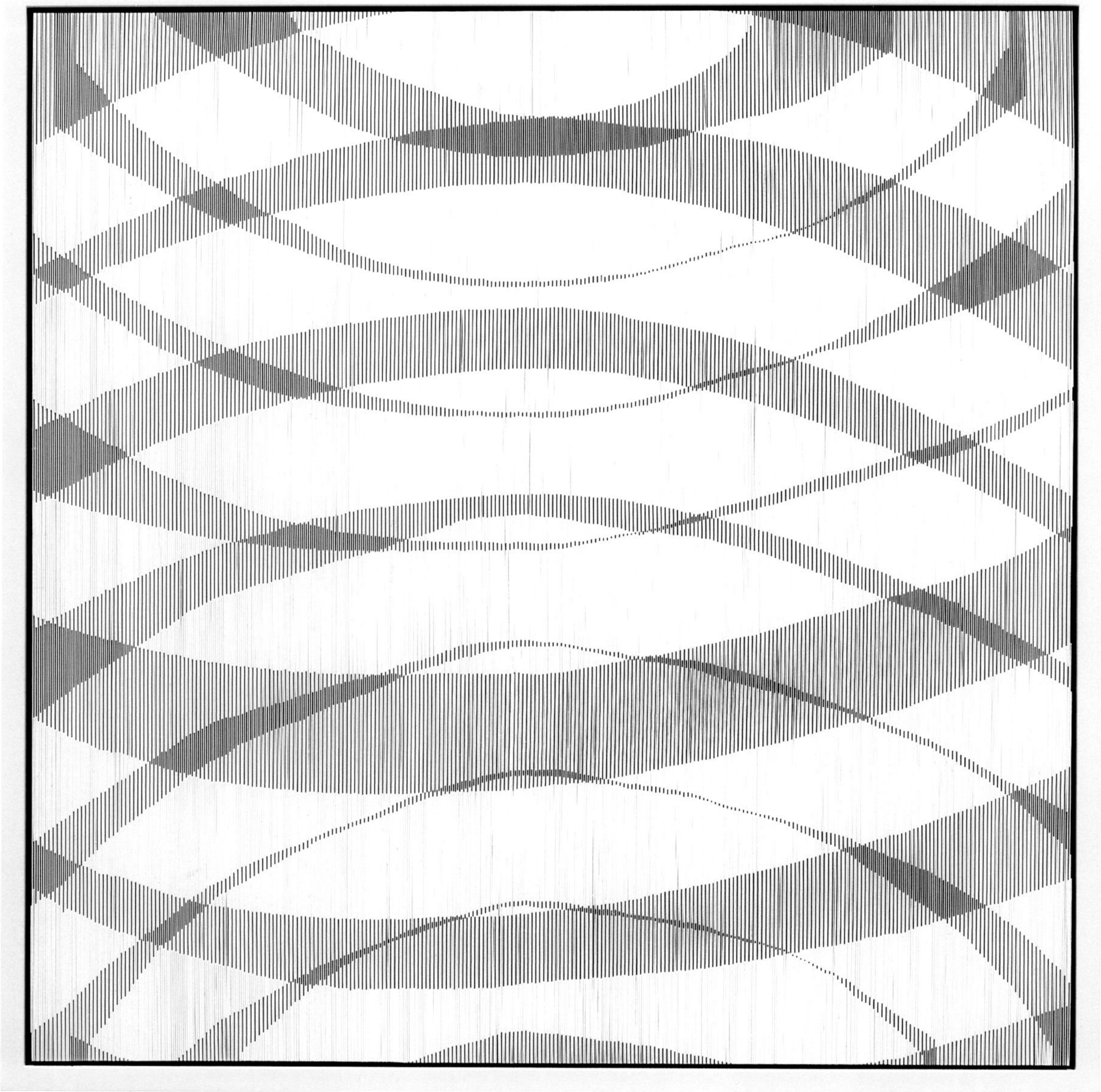

COMPOSITION (CARDS) 2017 22 ¼ x 22 ¼ x 4" | 56.5 x 56.5 x 10.2 cm

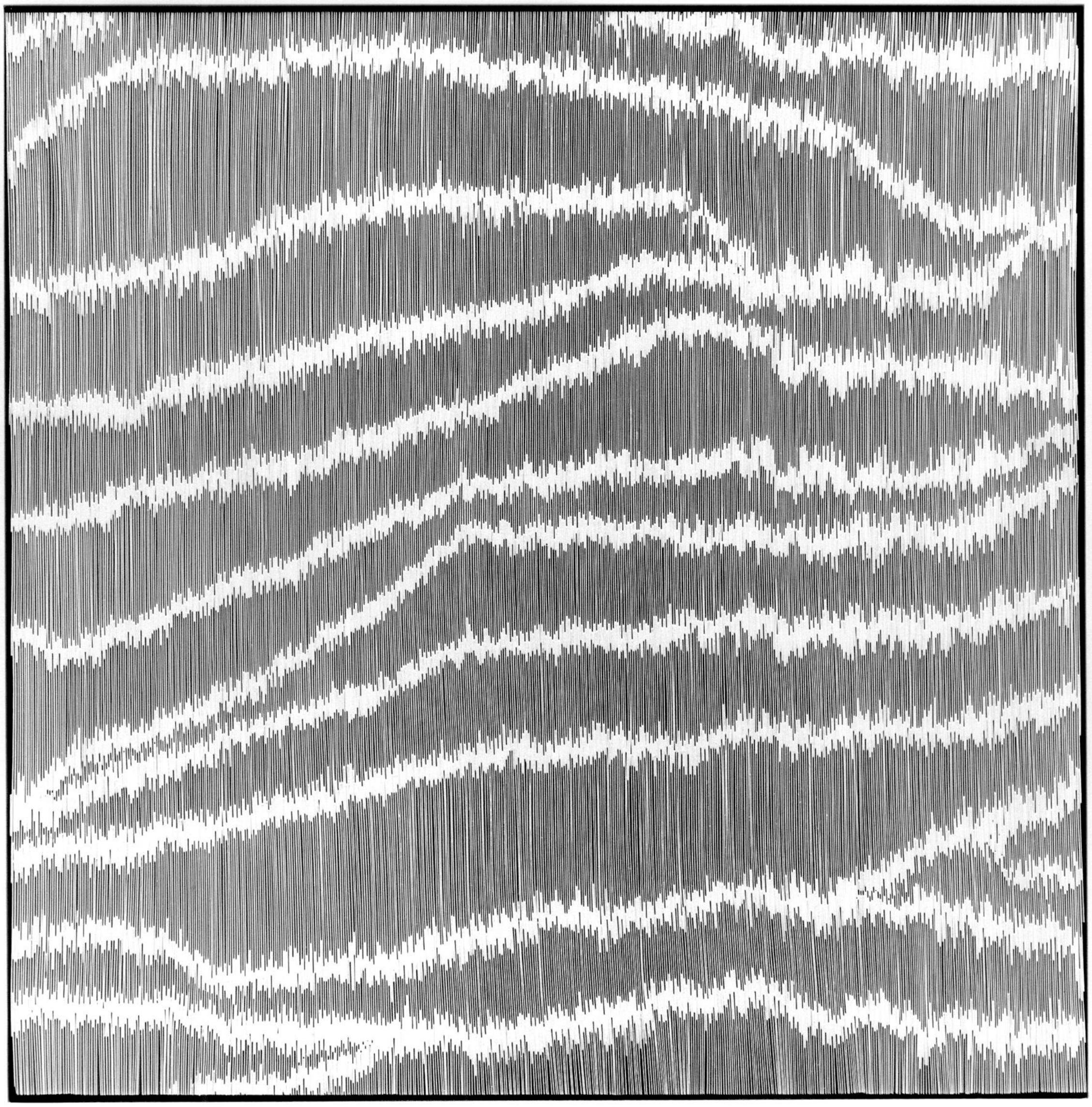

COMPOSITION (CARDS) 2017 22 ¼ x 22 ¼ x 4" | 56.5 x 56.5 x 10.2 cm

COMPOSITION (CARDS) 2017   39 ¼ x 39 ¼ x 4" | 99.7 x 99.7 x 10.2 cm

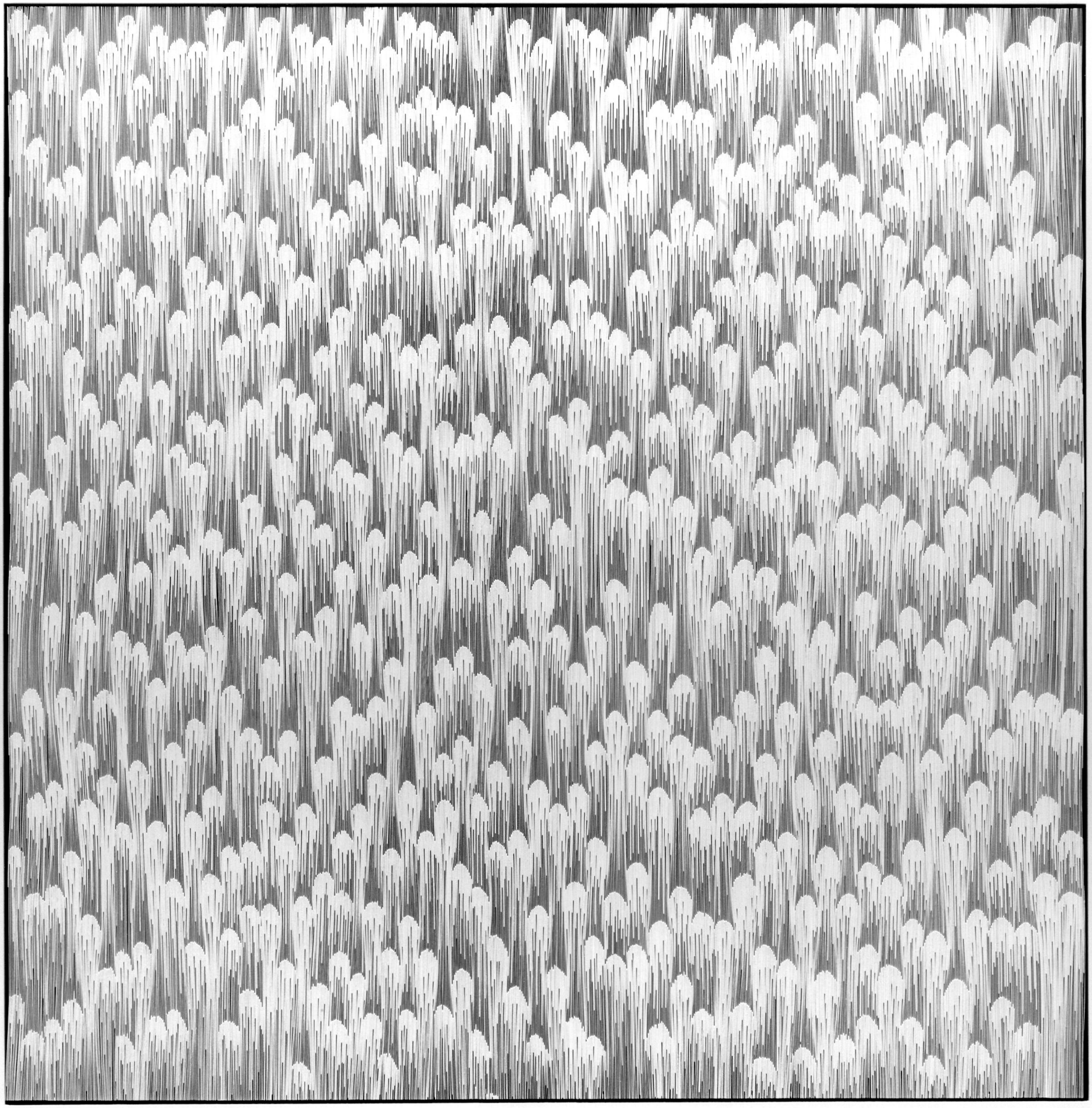

COMPOSITION (CARDS) 2017 39 ¼ x 39 ¼ x 4" | 99.7 x 99.7 x 10.2 cm

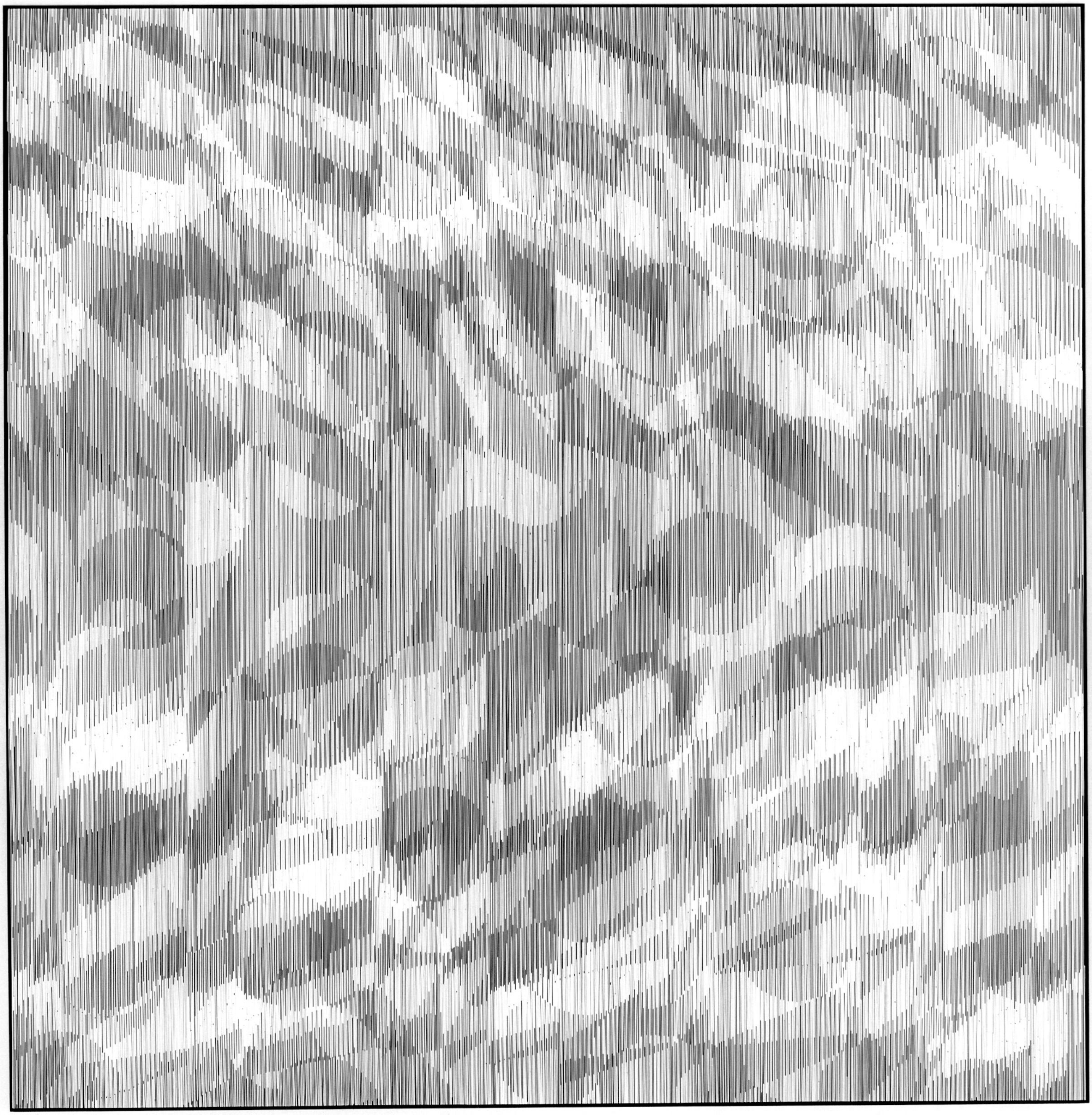

COMPOSITION (CARDS) 2017   39 ¼ x 39 ¼ x 4" | 99.7 x 99.7 x 10.2 cm

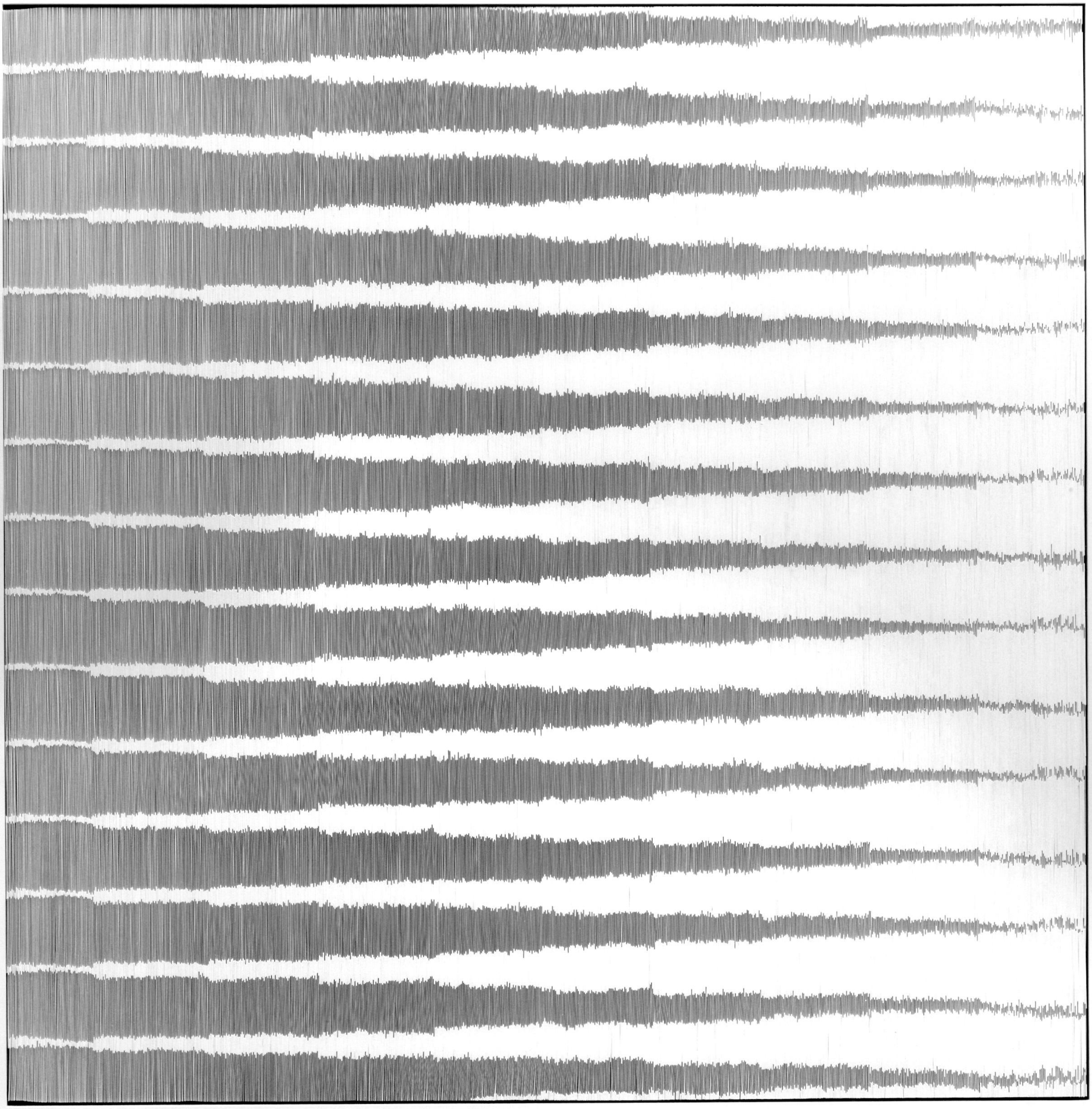

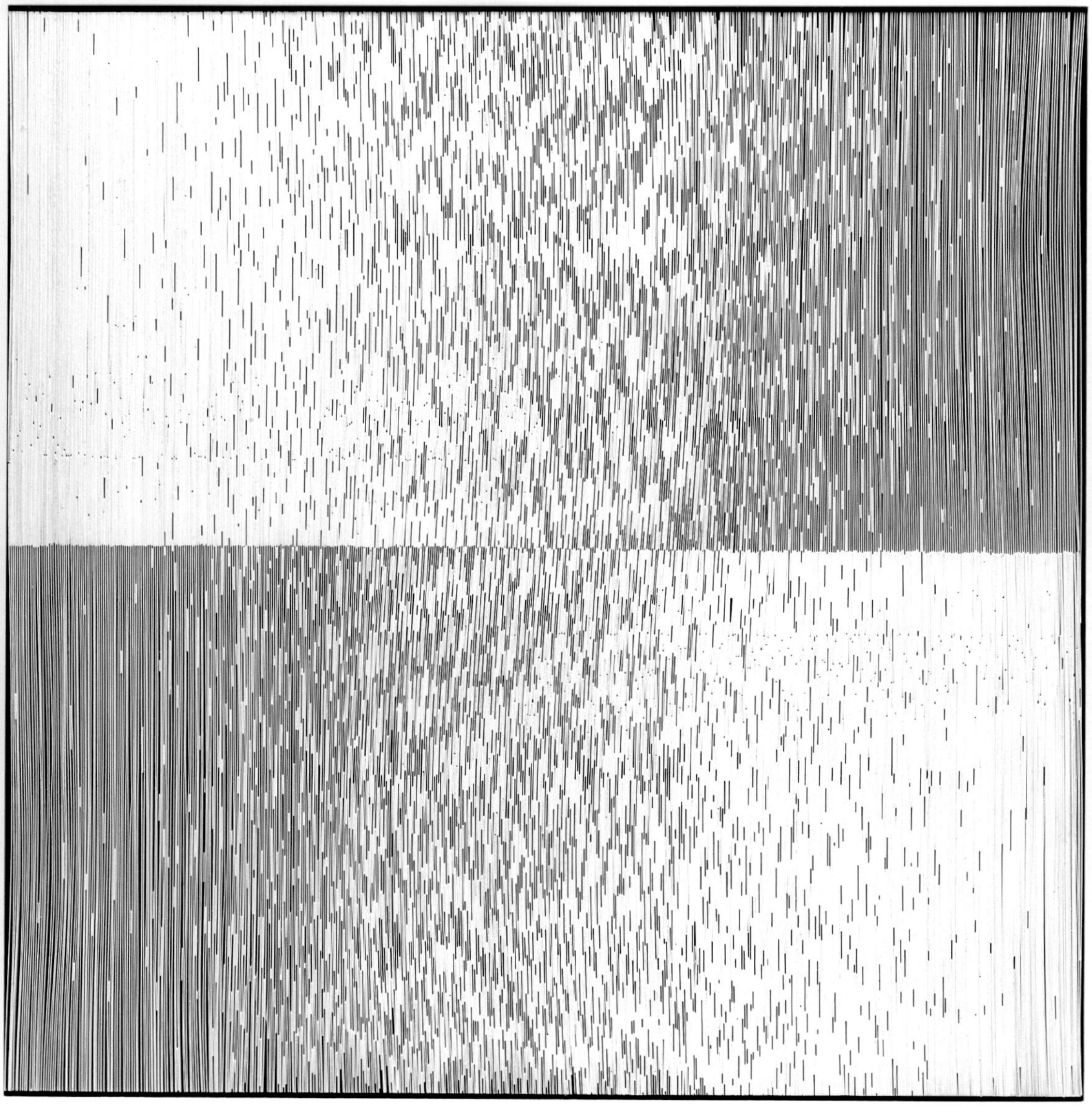

COMPOSITION (CARDS) 2017 22 ¼ x 22 ¼ x 4" | 56.5 x 56.5 x 10.2 cm

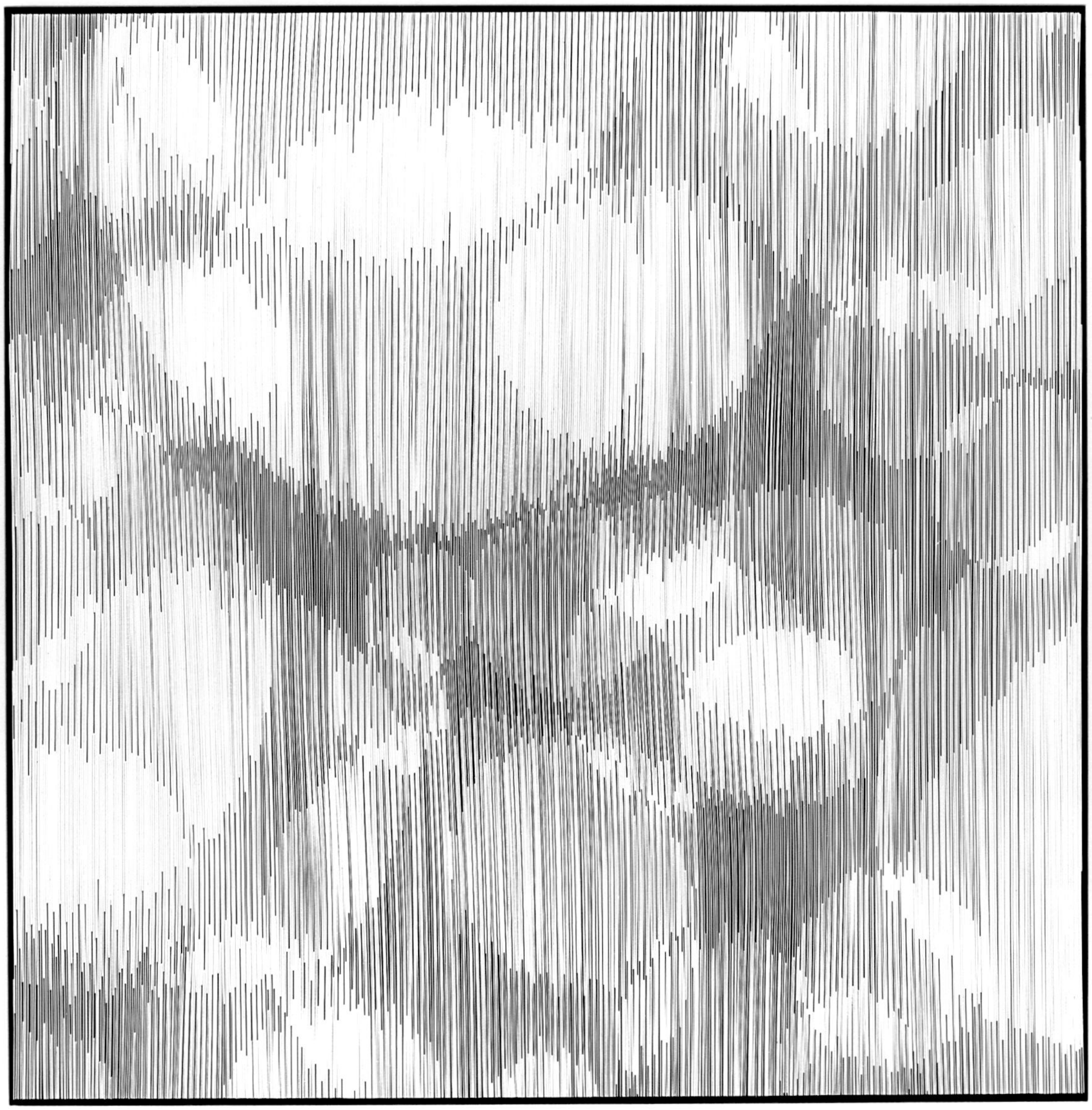

COMPOSITION (CARDS) 2017   22 ¼ x 22 ¼ x 4" | 56.5 x 56.5 x 10.2 cm

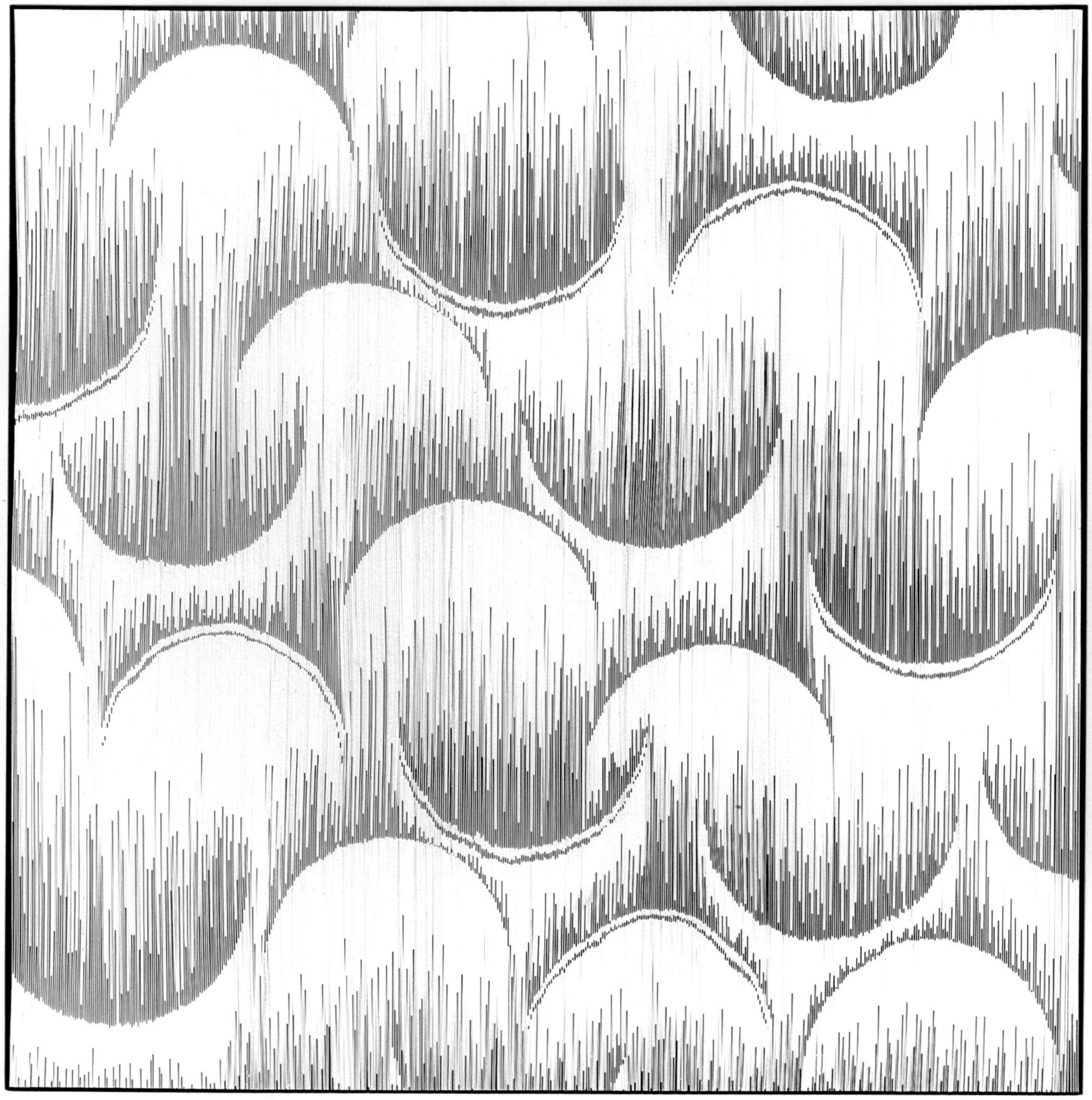

COMPOSITION (CARDS) 2017 22 ¼ x 22 ¼ x 4" | 56.5 x 56.5 x 10.2 cm

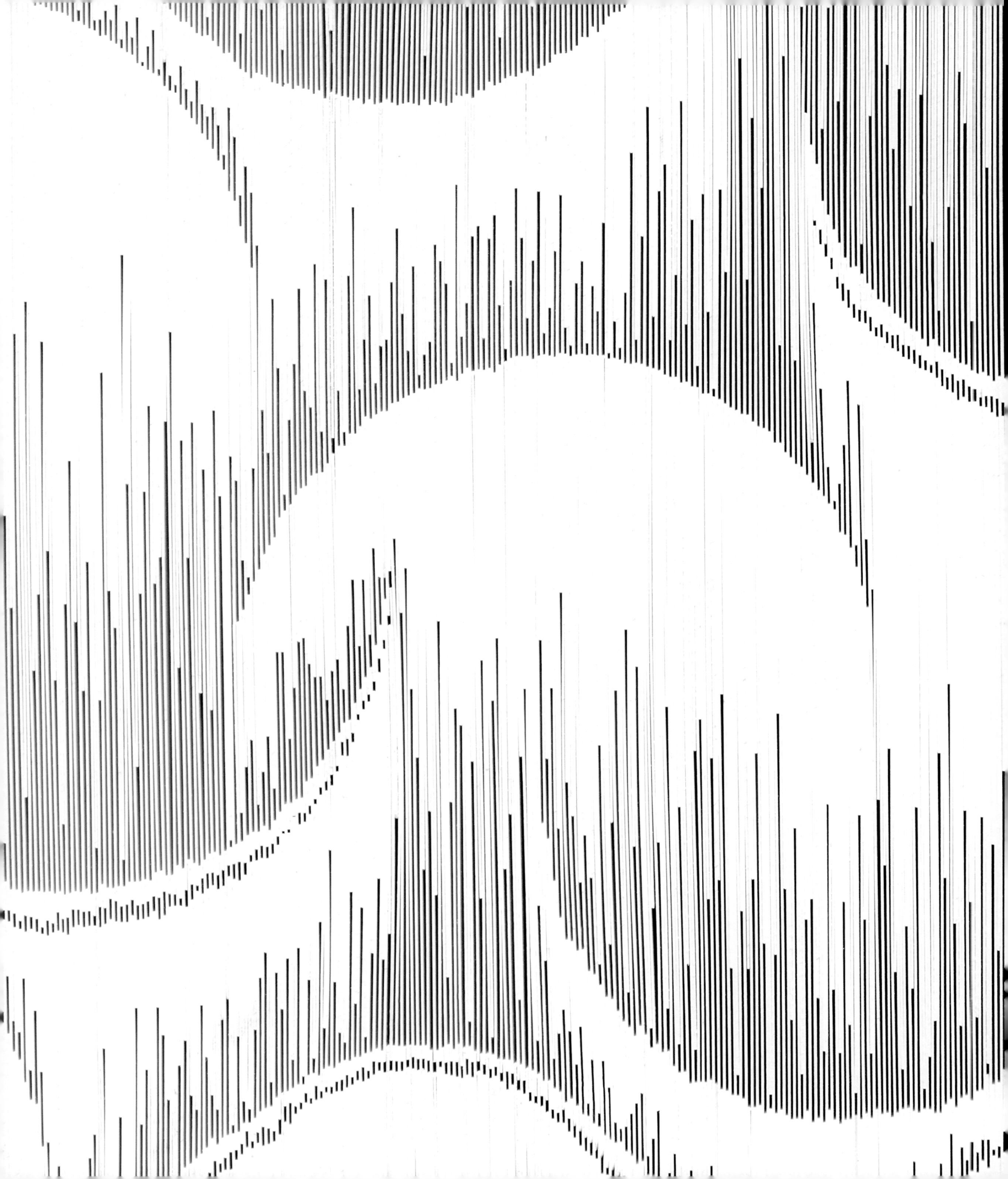

COMPOSITION (CARDS) 2017 39 ¼ x 39 ¼ x 4" | 99.7 x 99.7 x 10.2 cm

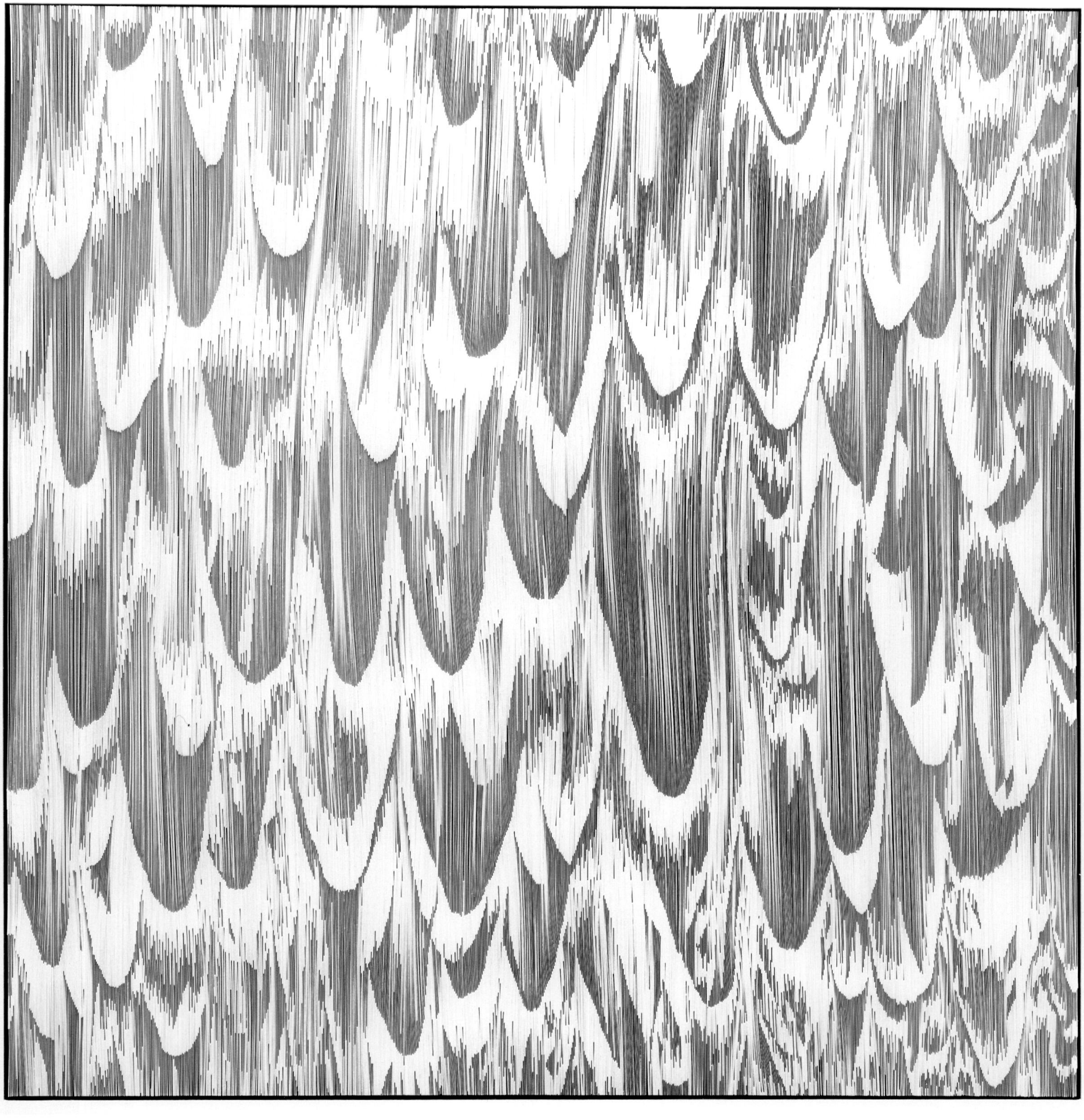

COMPOSITION (CARDS) 2017 39 ¼ x 39 ¼ x 4" | 99.7 x 99.7 x 10.2 cm

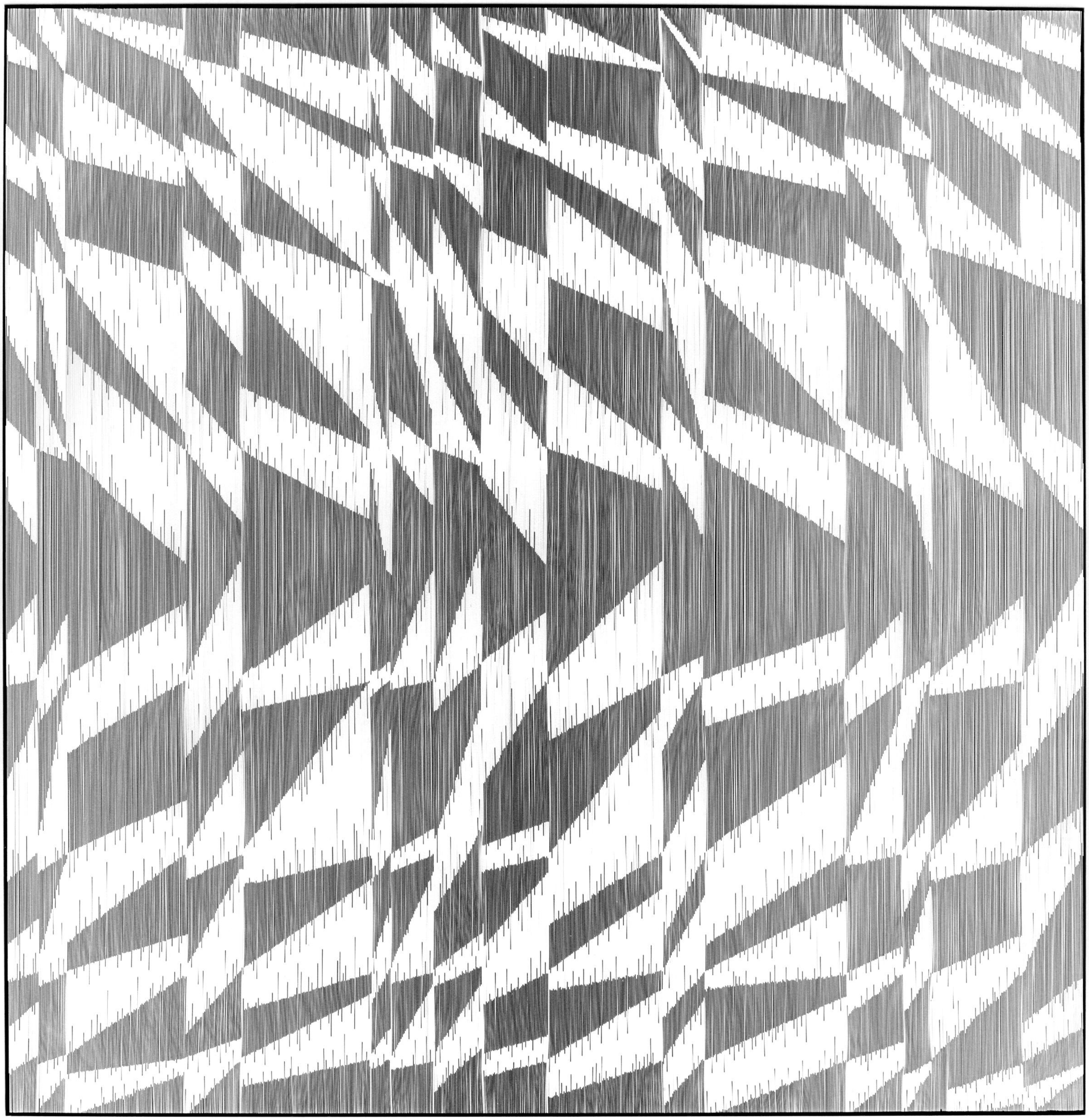

COMPOSITION (CARDS) 2016 39 ¼ x 39 ¼ x 4" | 99.7 x 99.7 x 10.2 cm

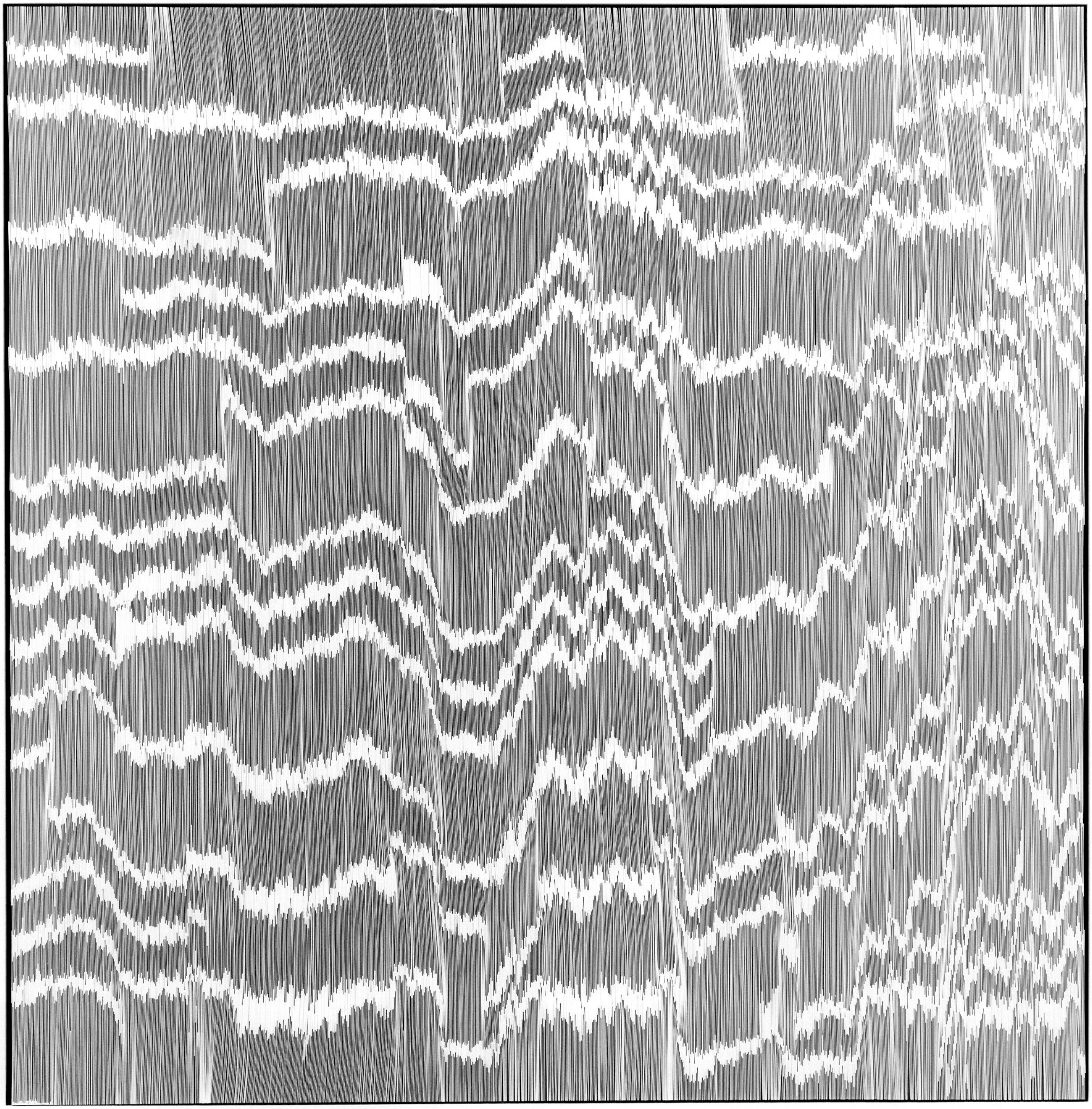

COMPOSITION (CARDS) 2017 39 ¼ x 39 ¼ x 4" | 99.7 x 99.7 x 10.2 cm

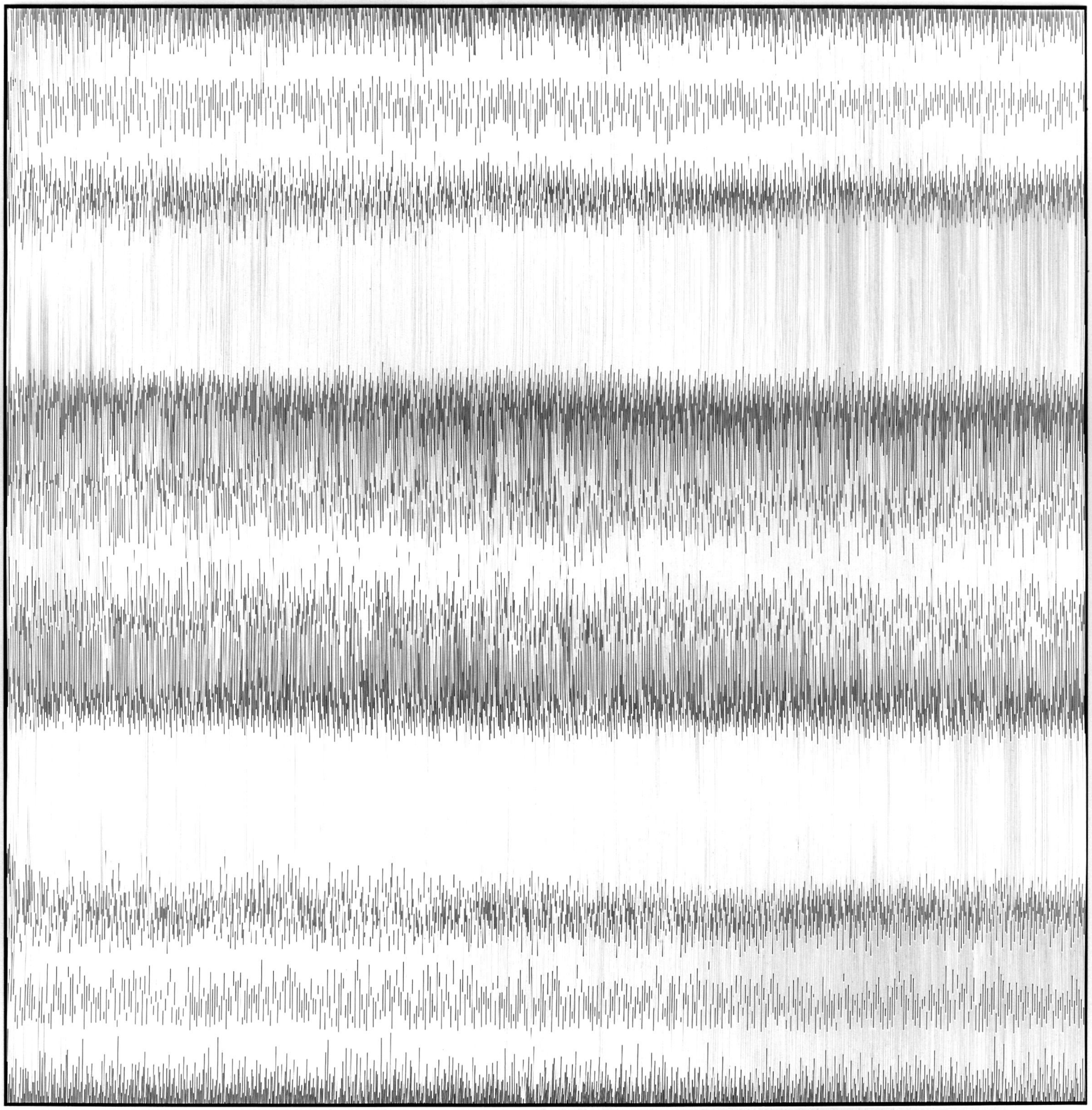

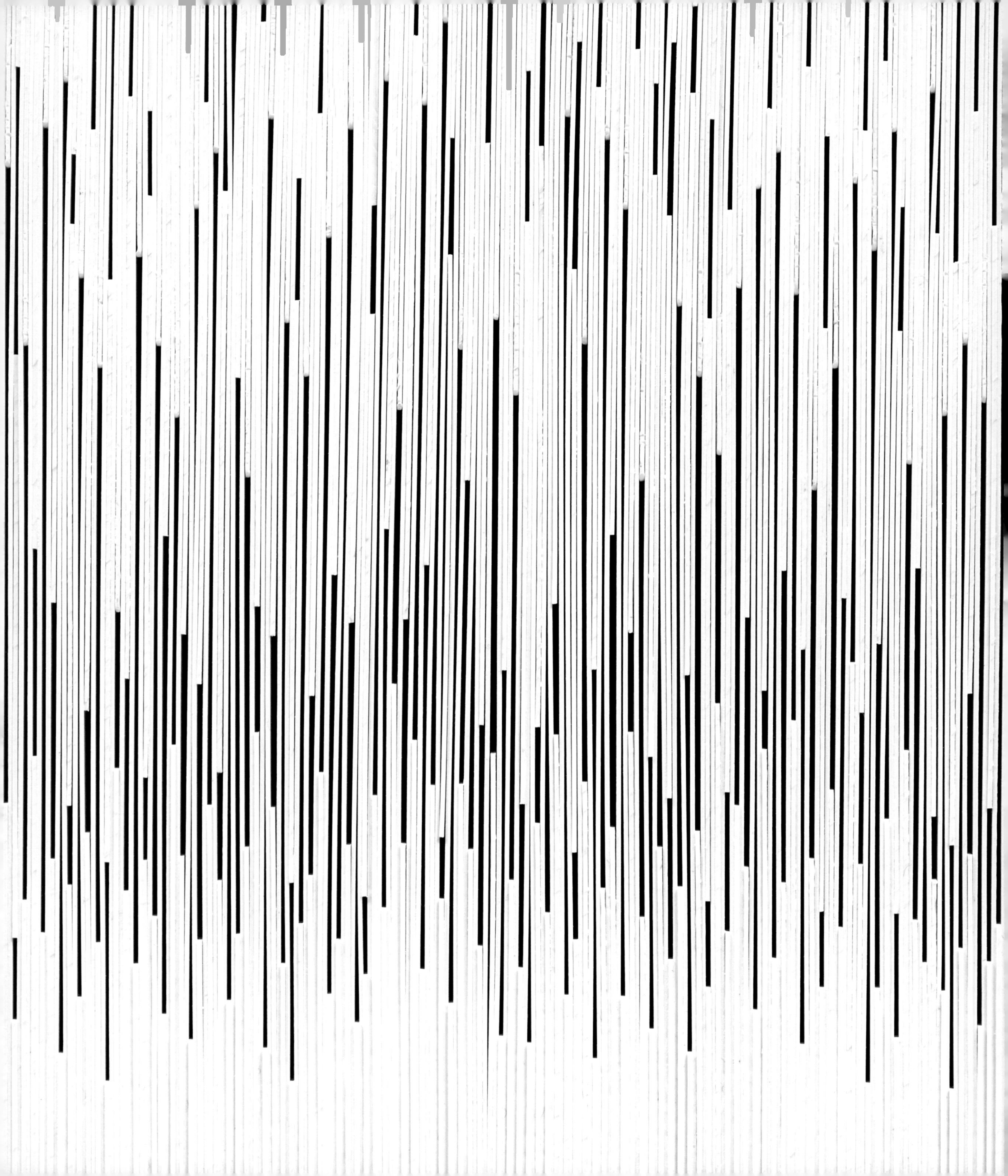

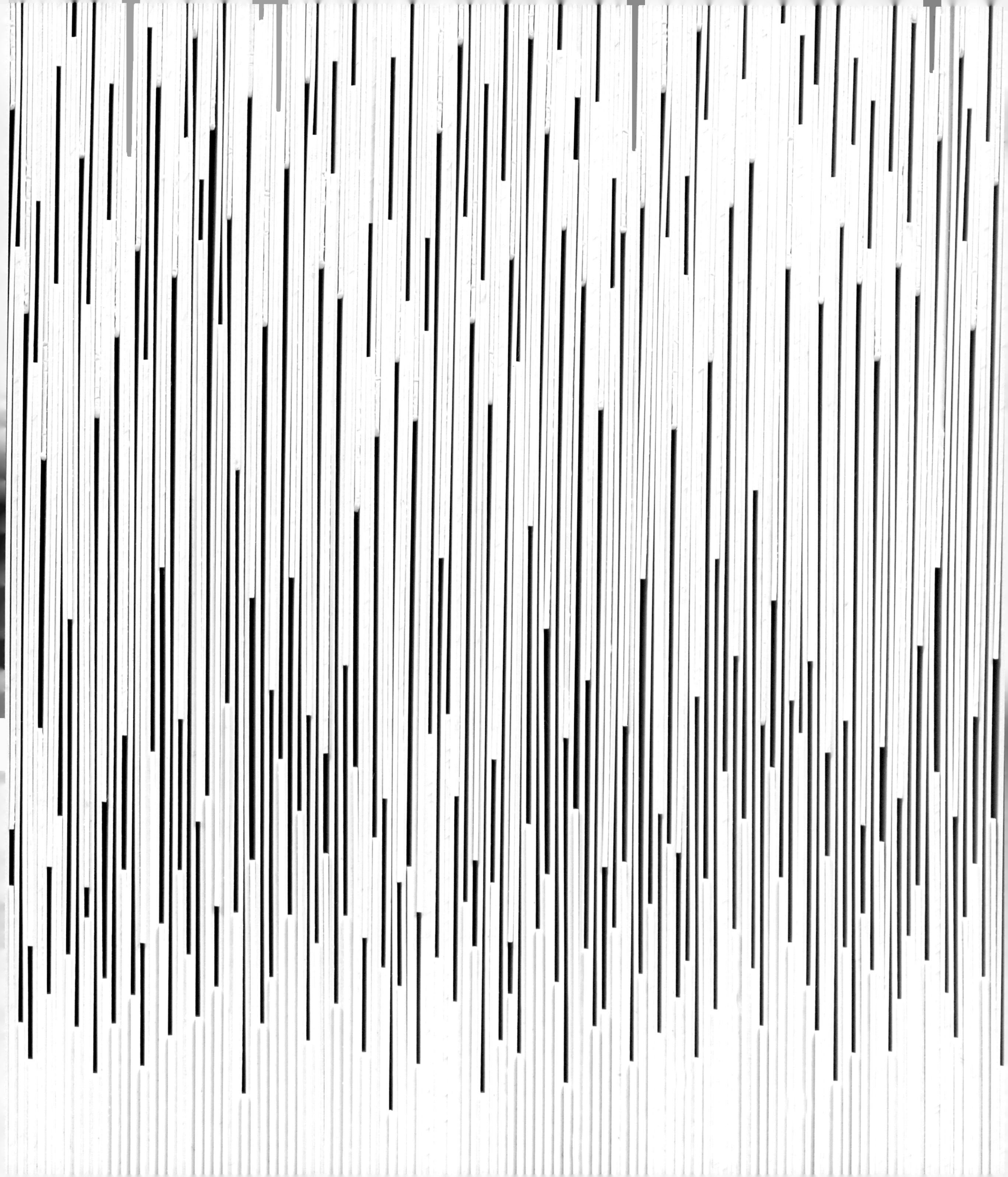

COMPOSITION (CARDS) 2017 39 ¼ x 39 ¼ x 4" | 99.7 x 99.7 x 10.2 cm

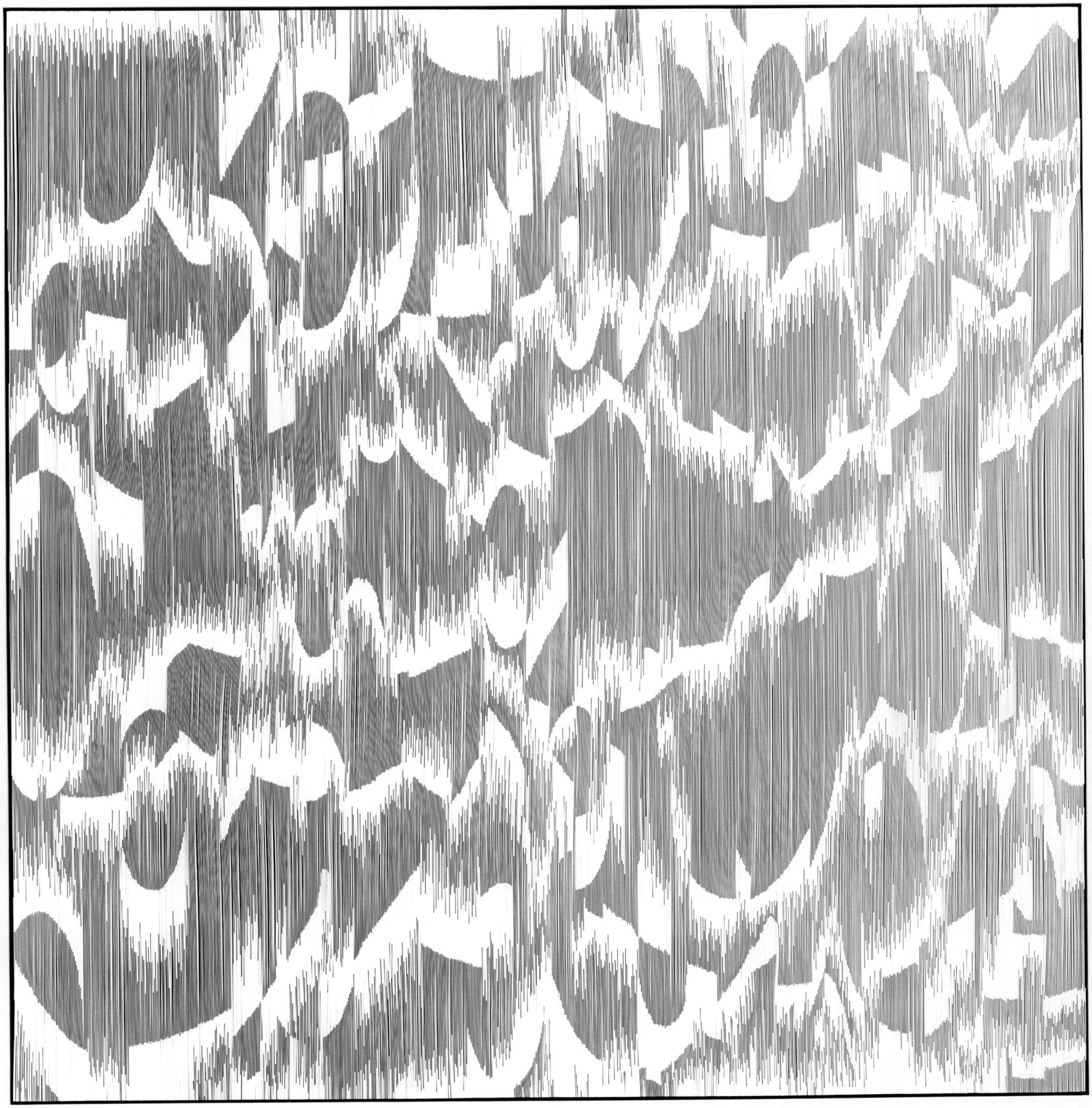

COMPOSITION (CARDS) 2017 39 ¼ x 39 ¼ x 4" | 99.7 x 99.7 x 10.2 cm

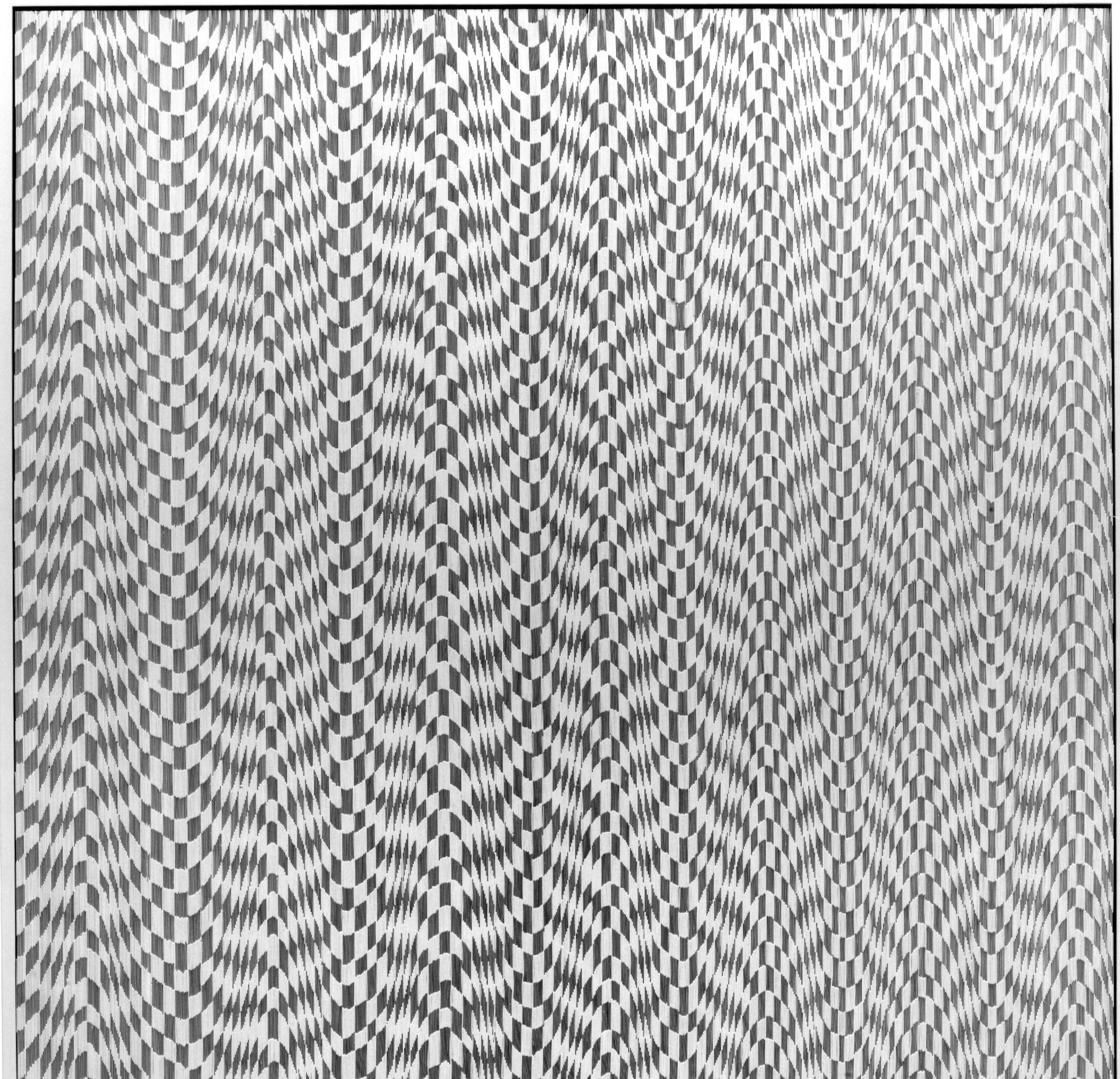

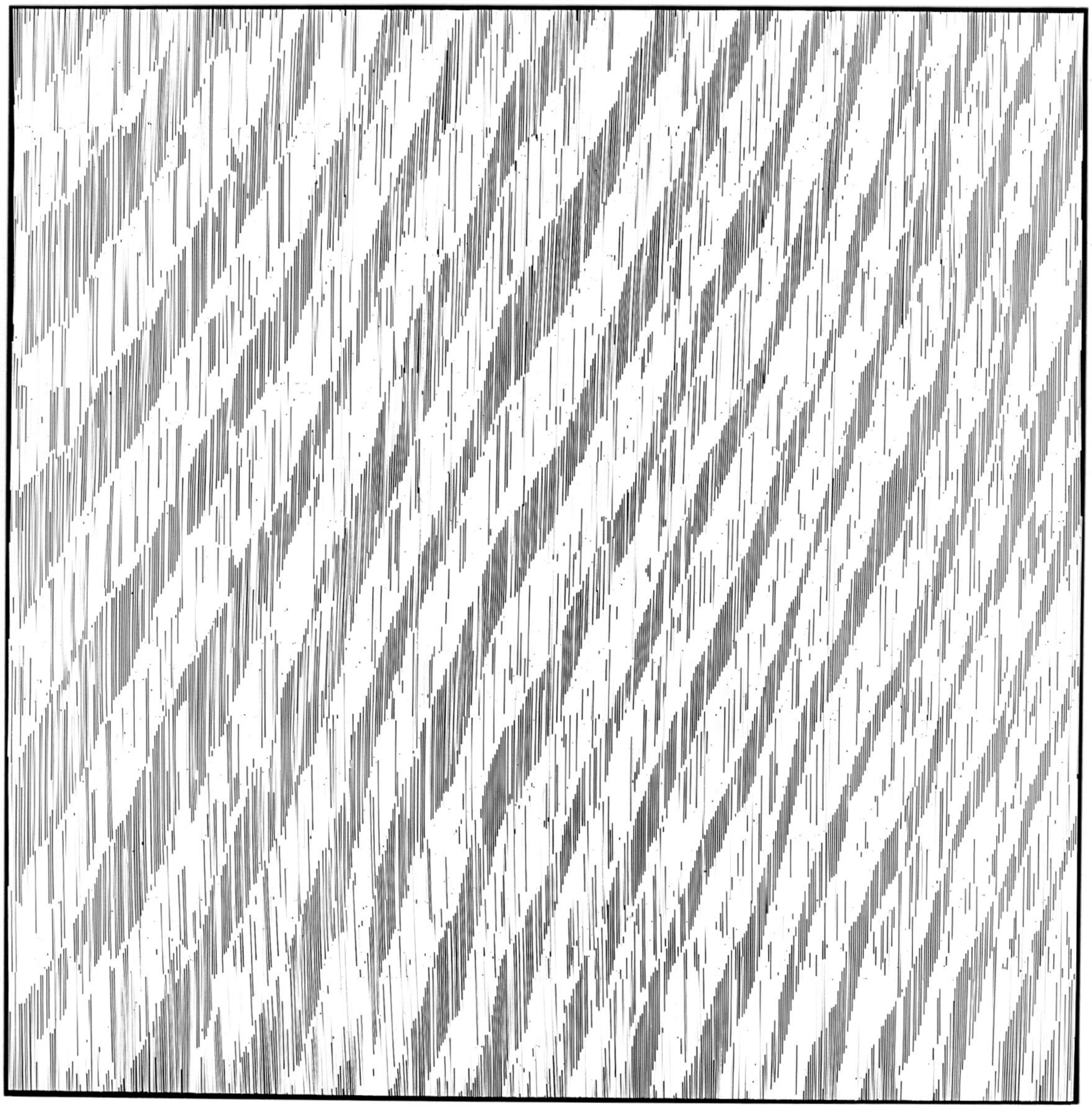

COMPOSITION (CARDS) 2017   22 ¼ x 22 ¼ x 4" | 56.5 x 56.5 x 10.2 cm

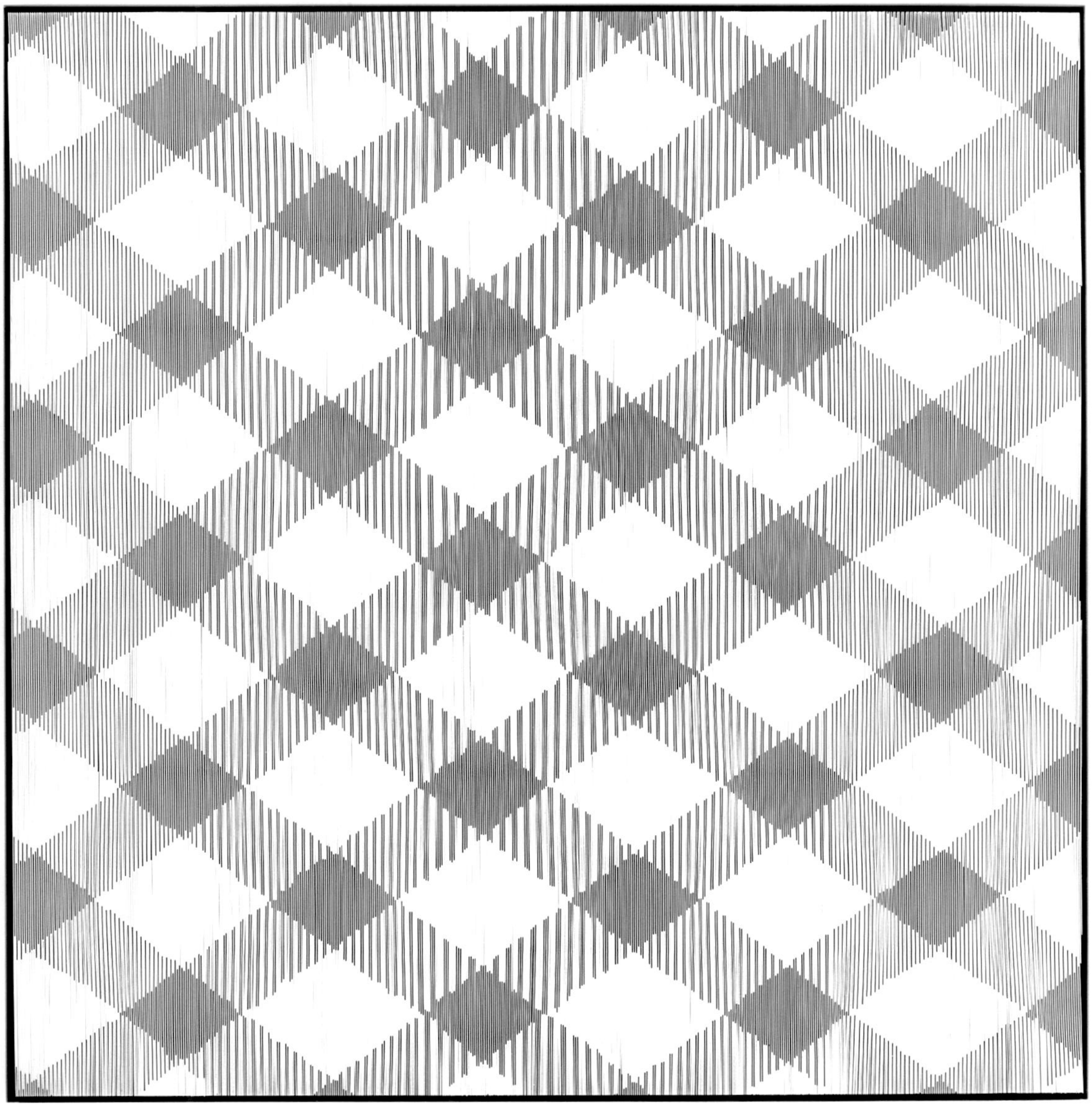

COMPOSITION (CARDS) 2017 22 ¼ x 22 ¼ x 4" | 56.5 x 56.5 x 10.2 cm

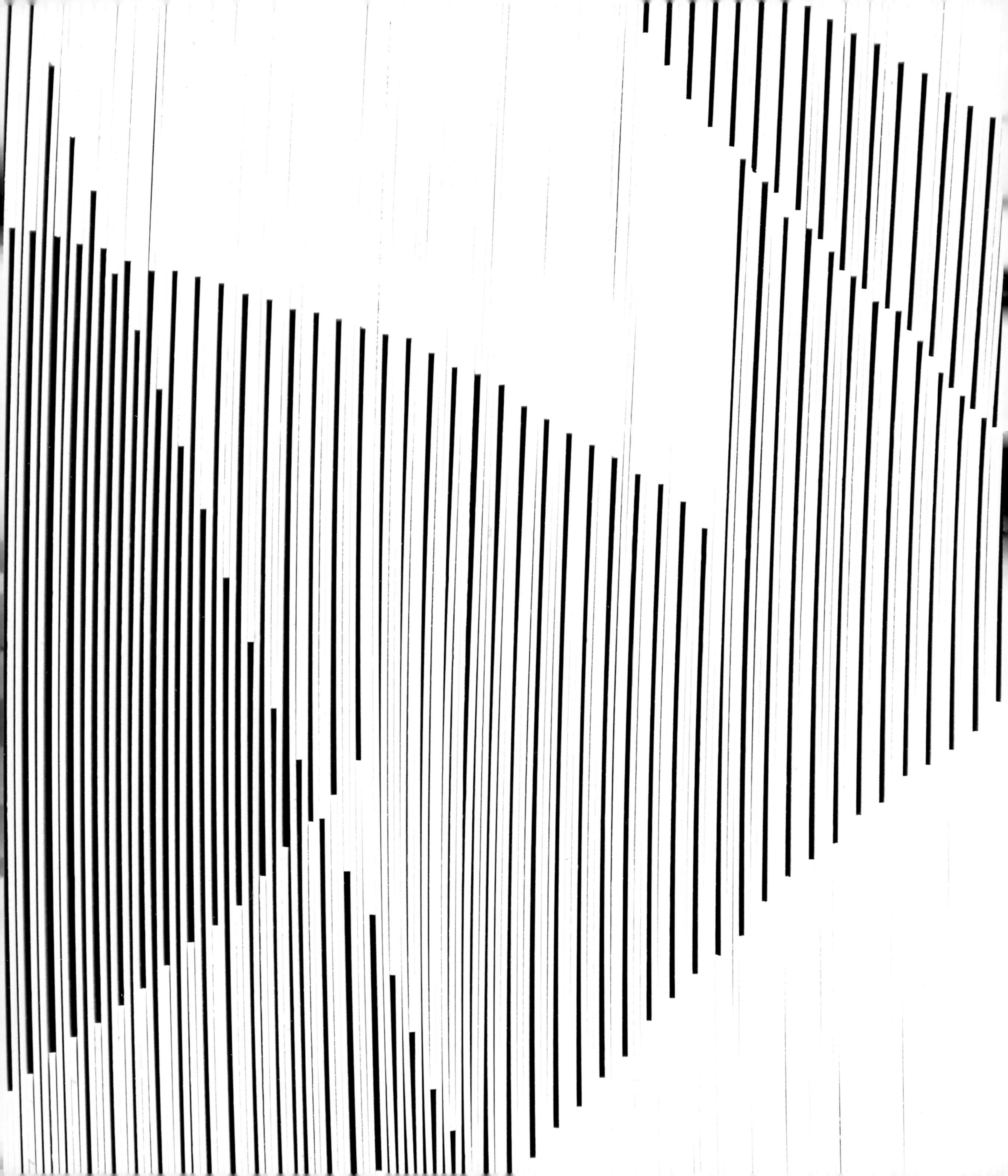

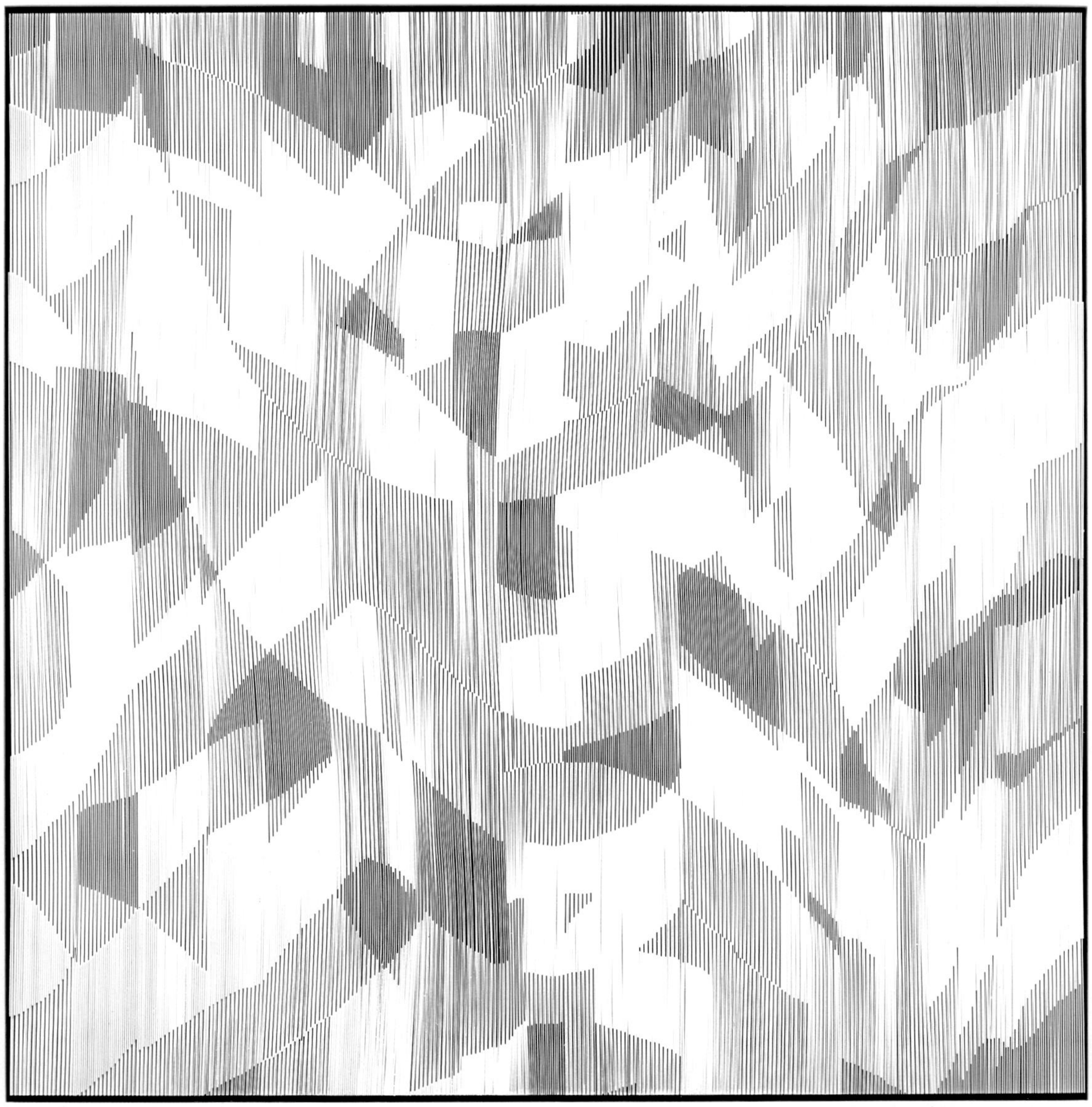

COMPOSITION (CARDS) 2017 22 ¼ x 22 ¼ x 4" | 56.5 x 56.5 x 10.2 cm

COMPOSITION (CARDS) 2017   39 ¼ x 39 ¼ x 4" | 99.7 x 99.7 x 10.2 cm

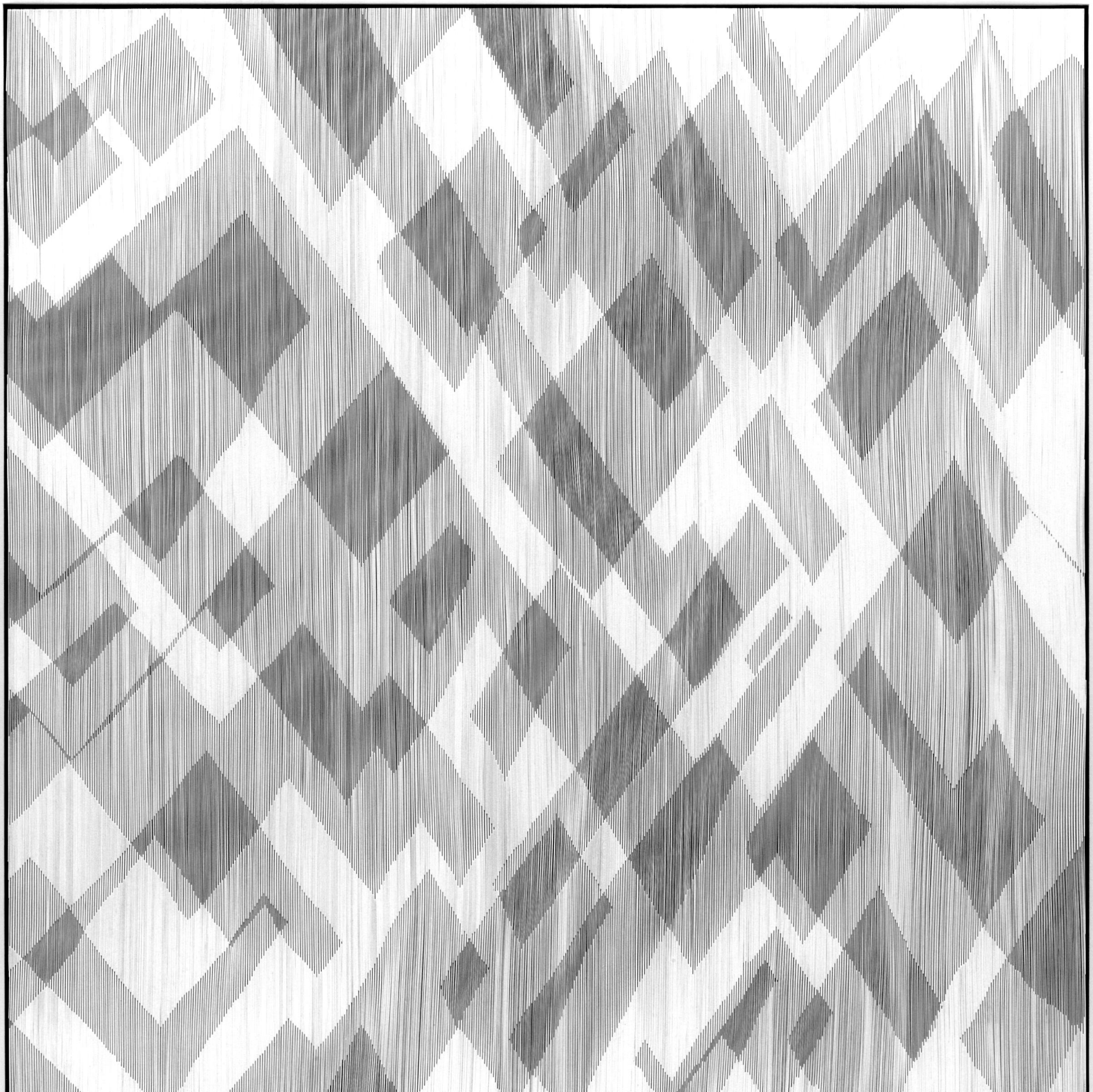

COMPOSITION (CARDS) 2017 39 ¼ x 39 ¼ x 4" | 99.7 x 99.7 x 10.2 cm

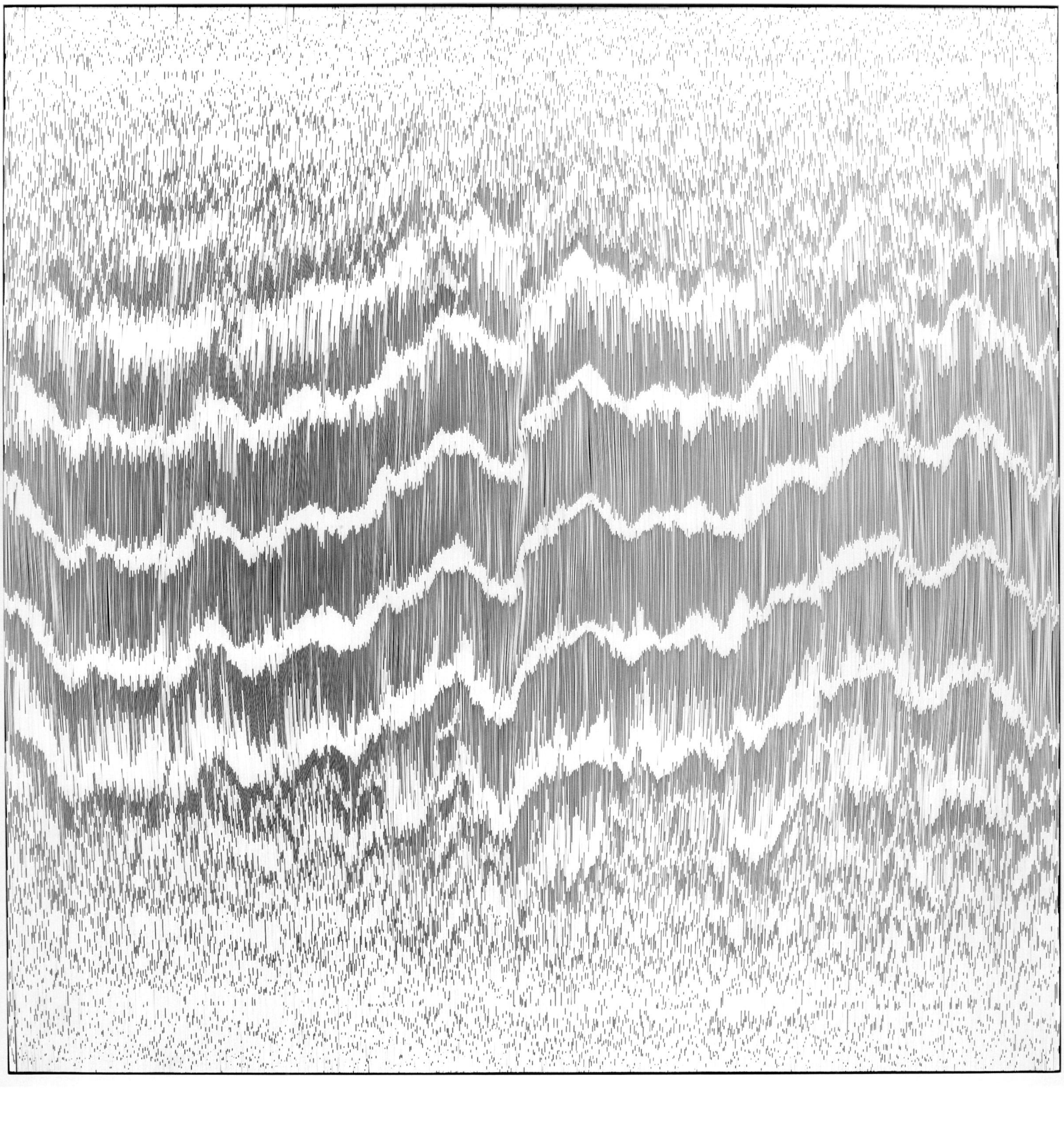

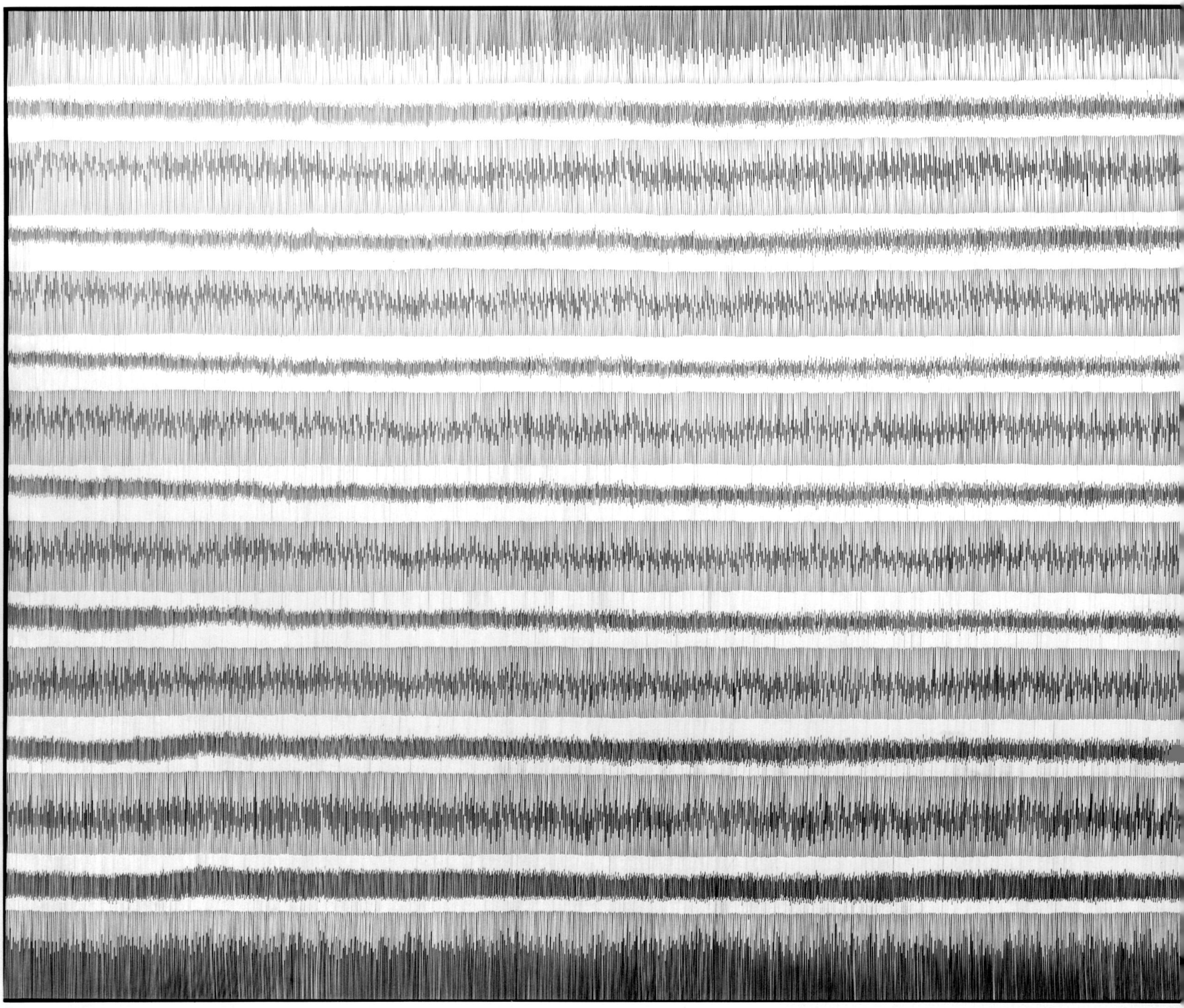

COMPOSITION (CARDS) 2017 45 ¼" x 9' 5 ¼" x 4" | 114.9 x 287.7 x 10.2 cm

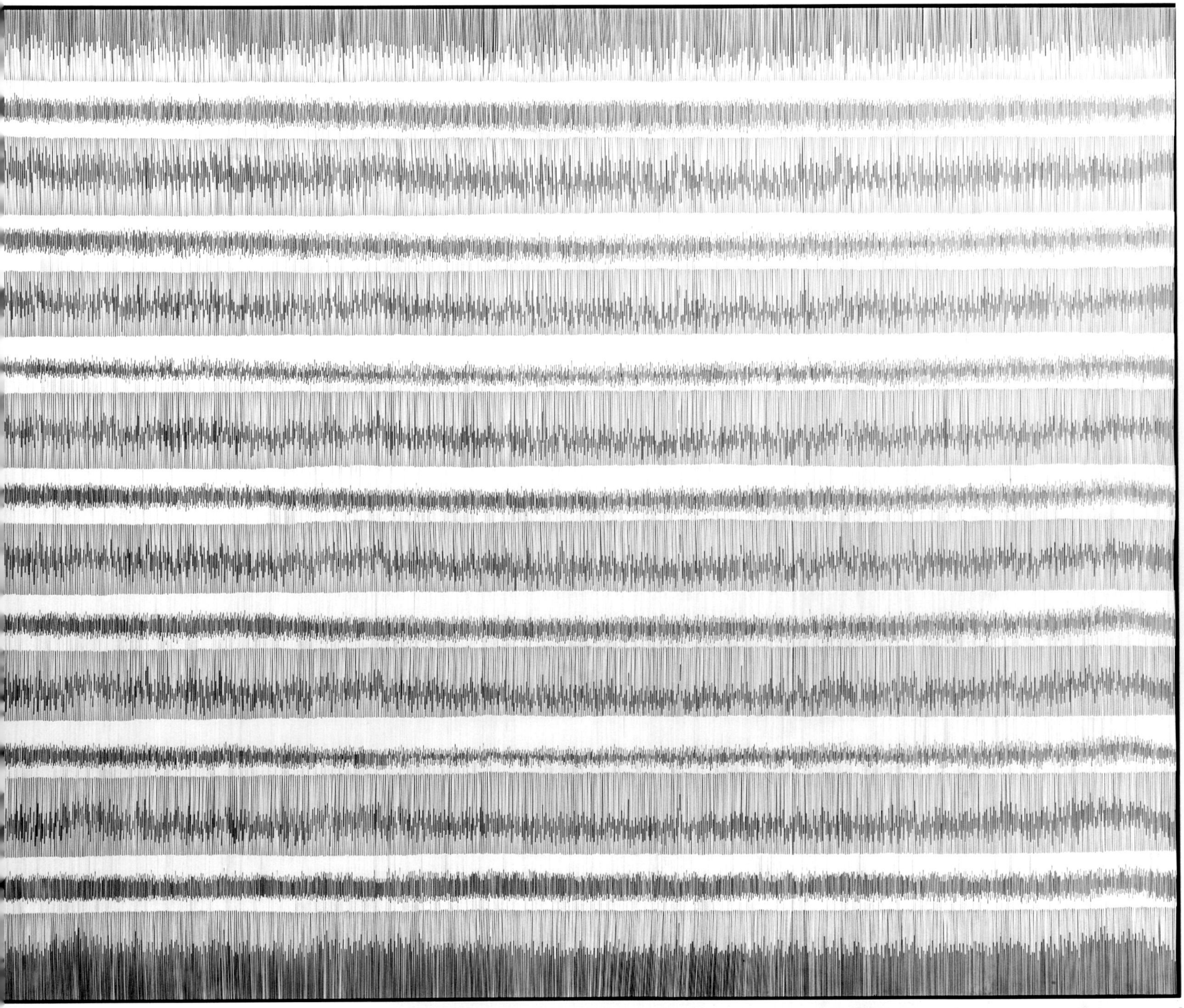

COMPOSITION (CARDS) 2017 39 ¼ x 39 ¼ x 4" | 99.7 x 99.7 x 10.2 cm

COMPOSITION (CARDS) 2017   36 ¼ x 36 ¼ x 4" | 92.1 x 92.1 x 10.2 cm

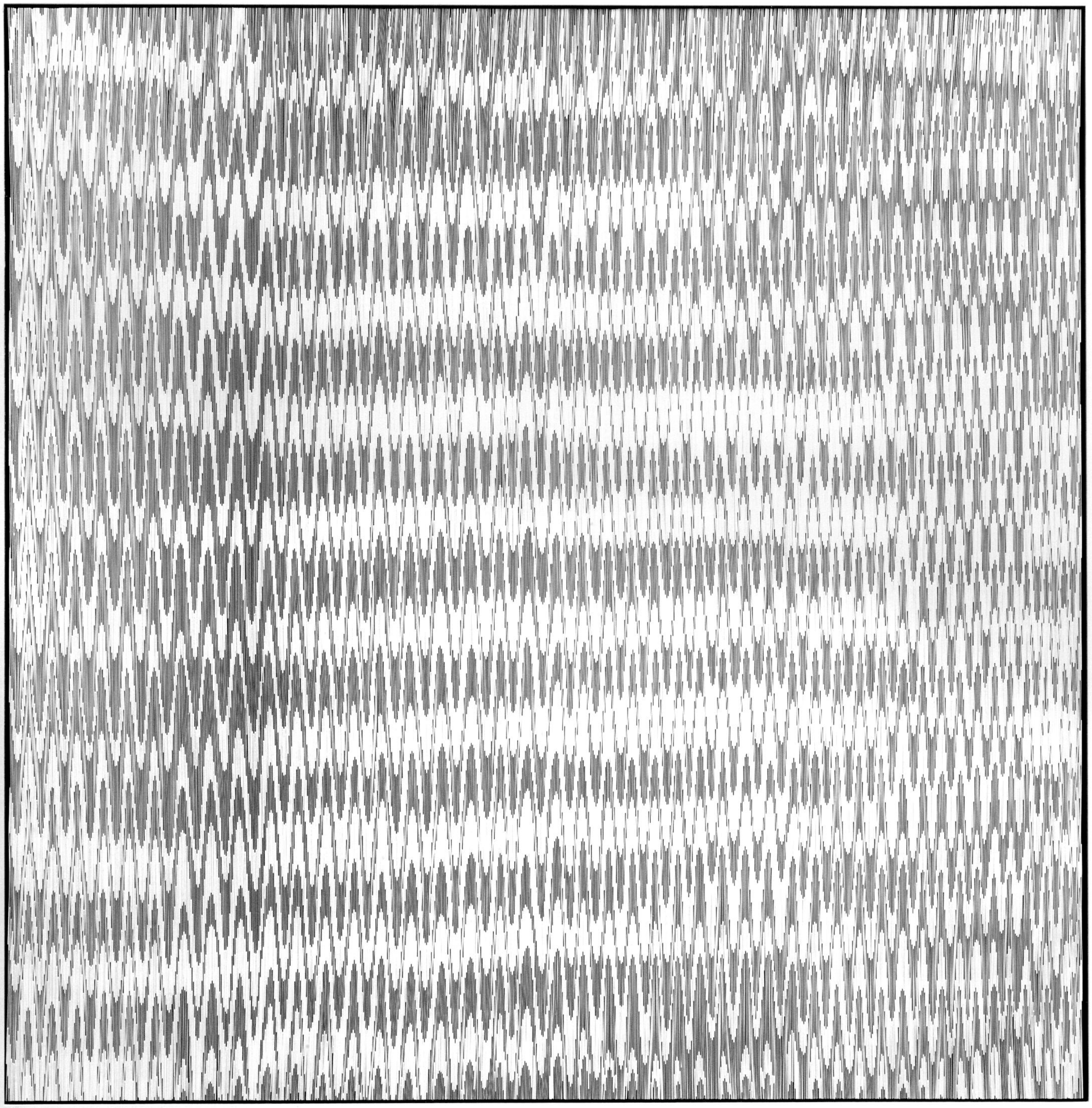

COMPOSITION (CARDS) 2017 39 ¼ x 39 ¼ x 4" | 99.7 x 99.7 x 10.2 cm

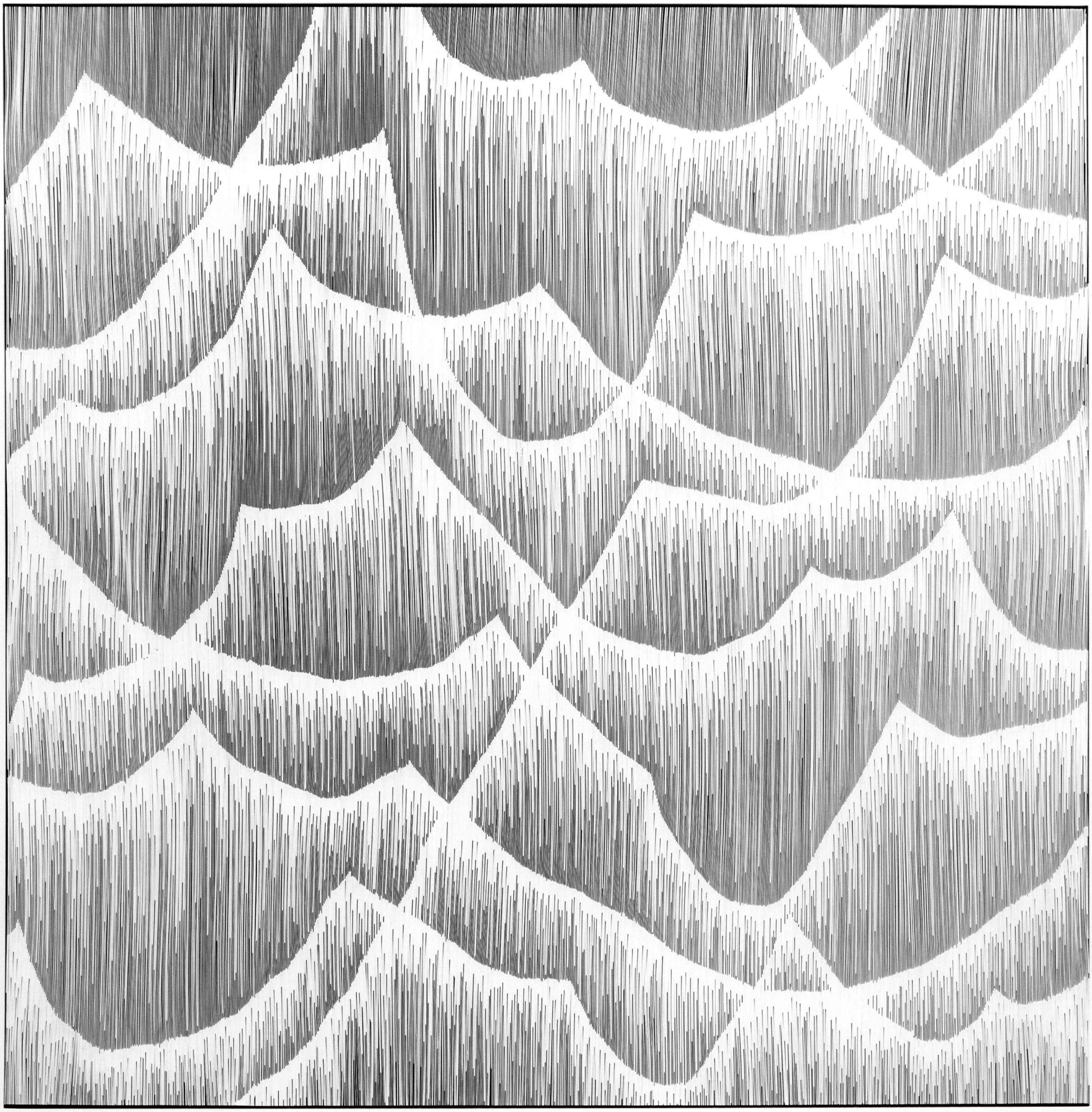

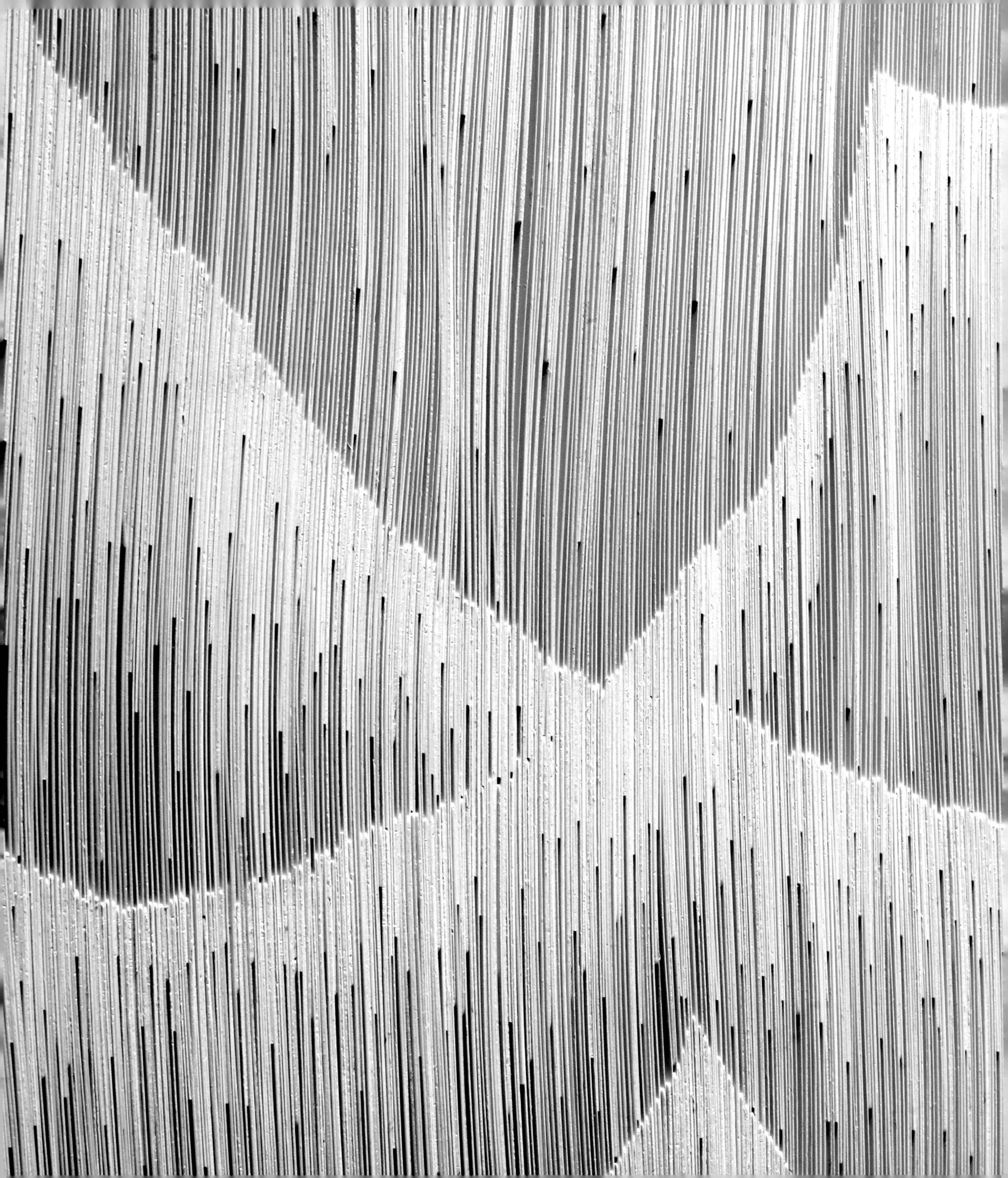

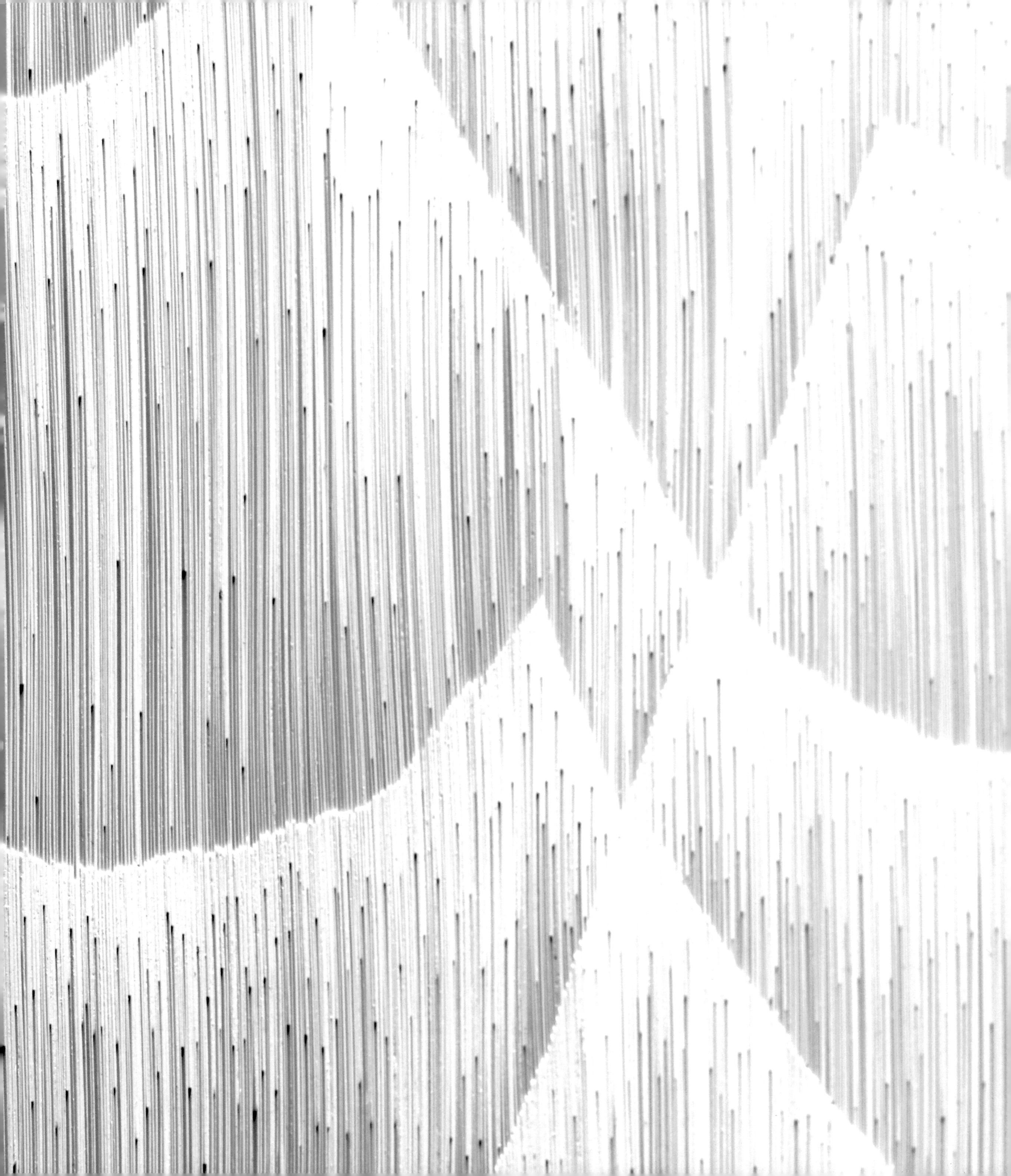

COMPOSITION (CARDS) 2017 39 ¼ x 39 ¼ x 4" | 99.7 x 99.7 x 10.2 cm

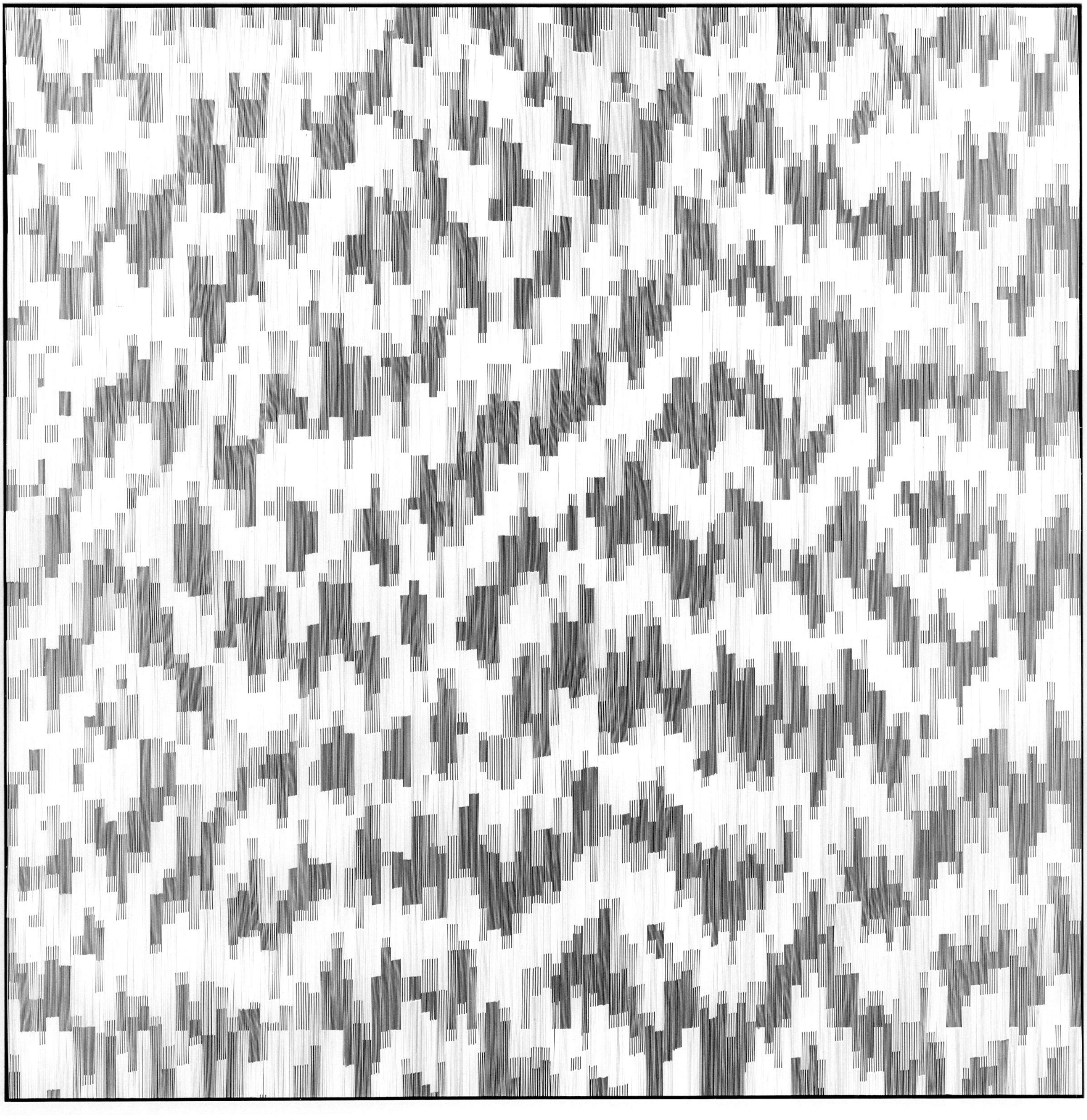

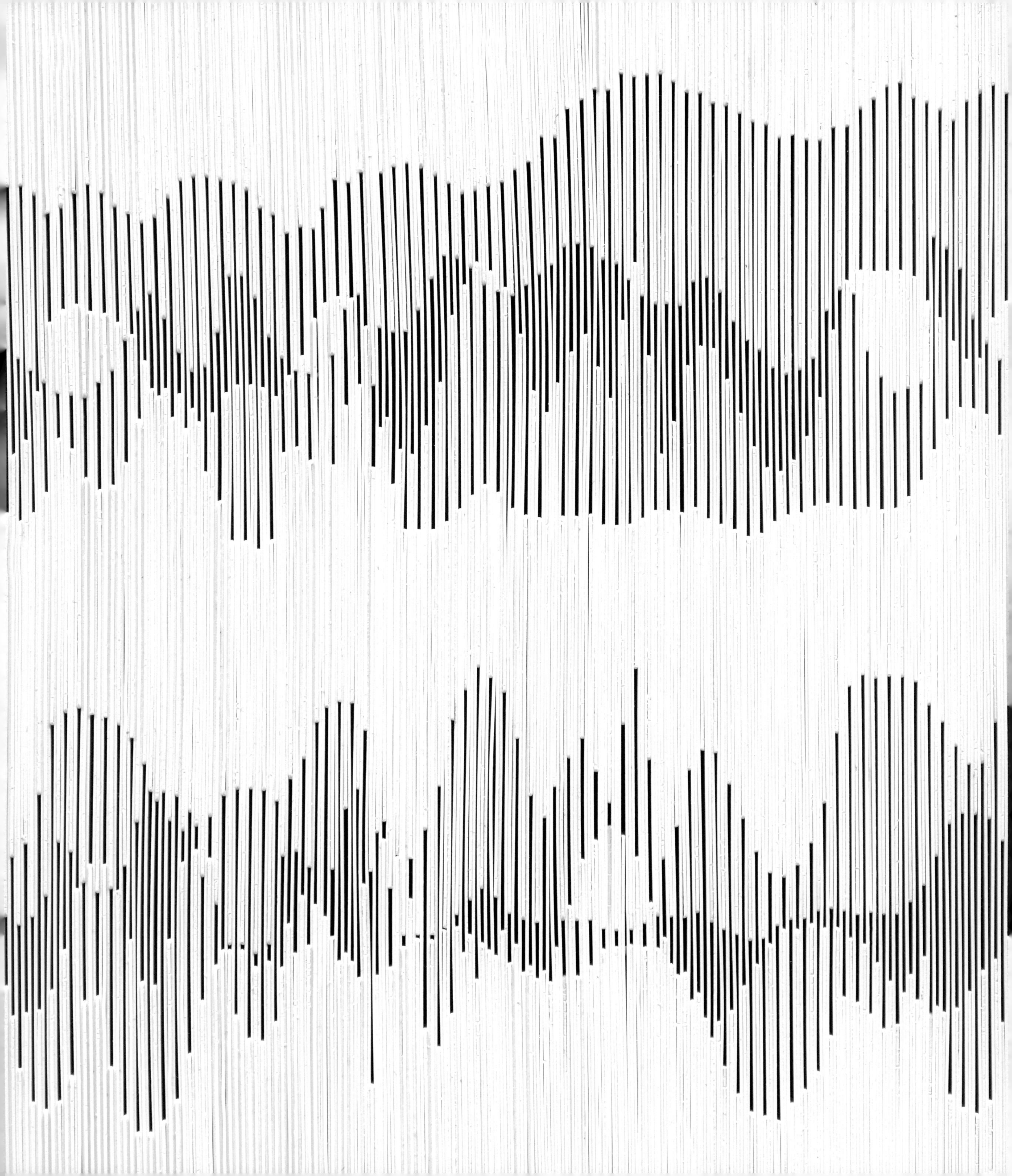

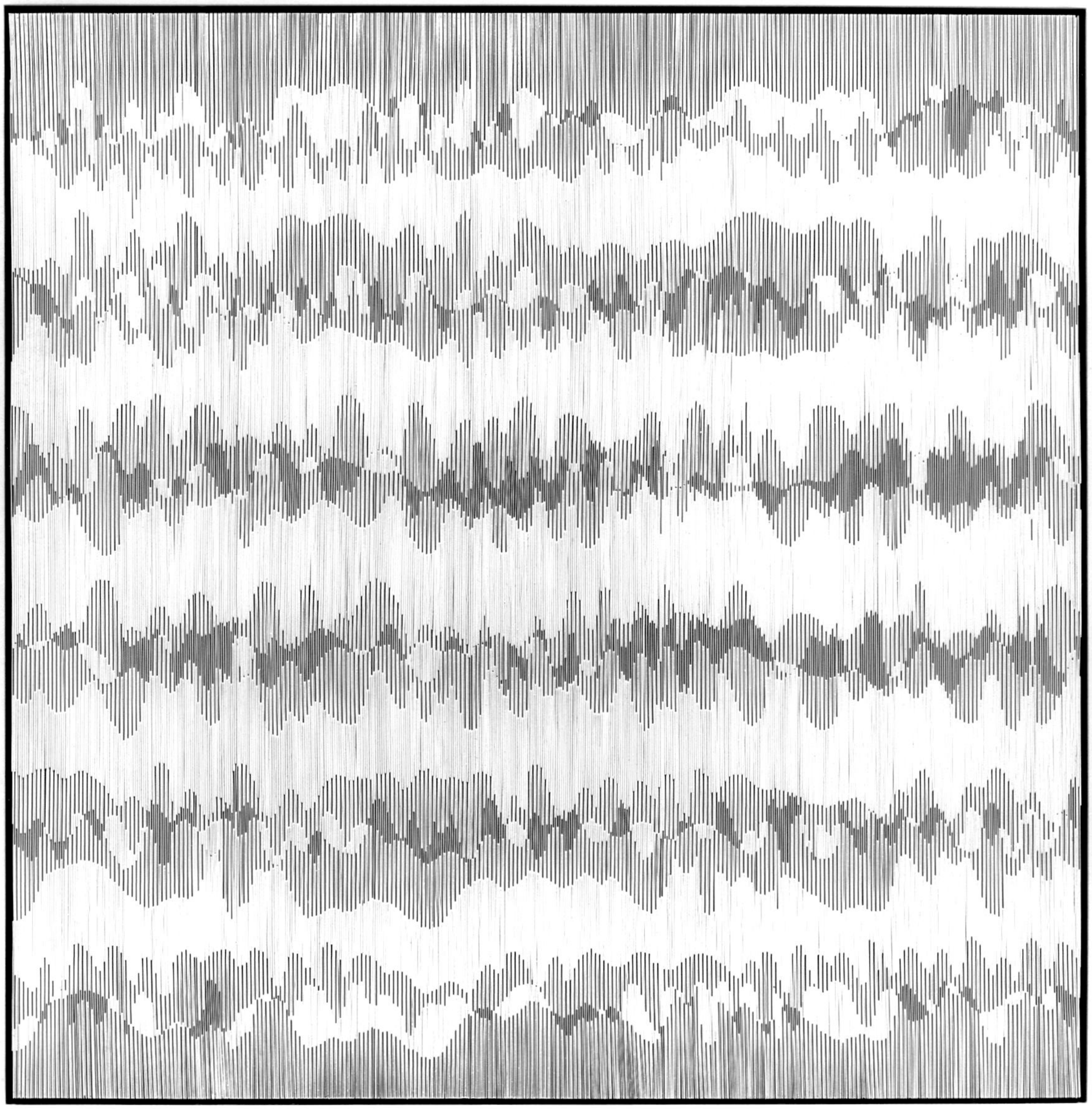

COMPOSITION (CARDS) 2017 22 ¼ x 22 ¼ x 4" | 56.5 x 56.5 x 10.2 cm

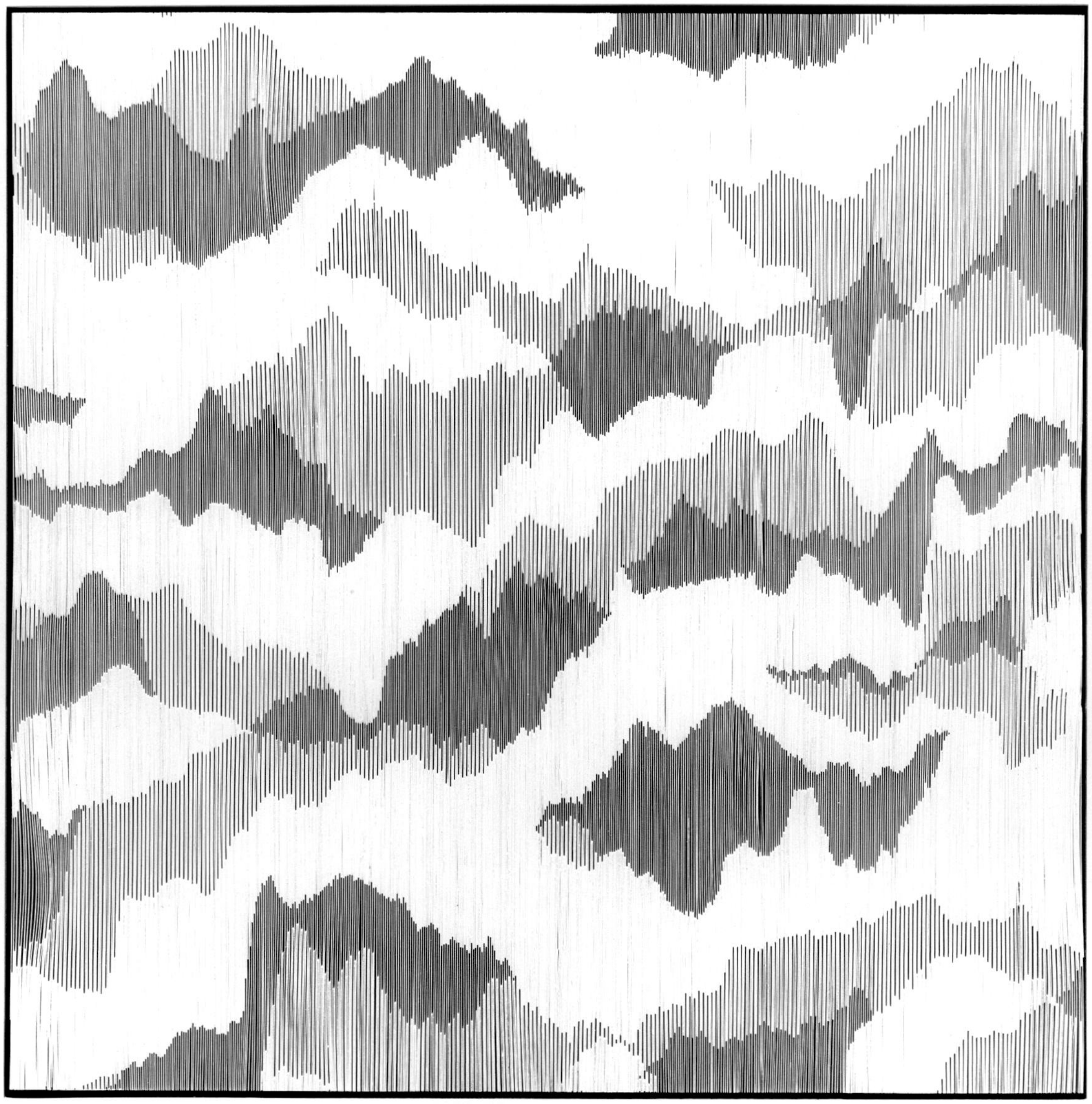

COMPOSITION (CARDS) 2017 22 ¼ x 22 ¼ x 4" | 56.5 x 56.5 x 10.2 cm

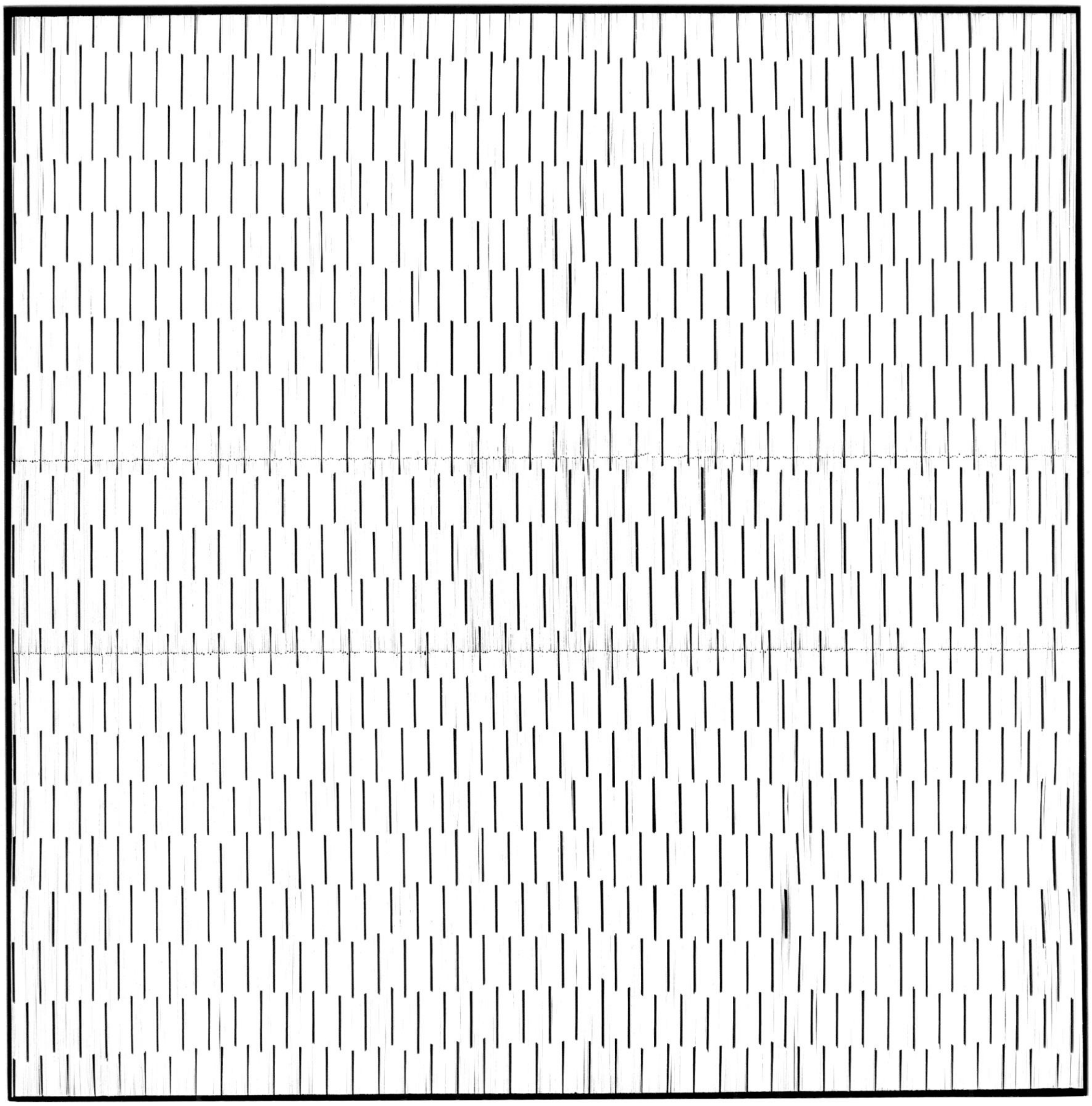

COMPOSITION (CARDS) 2017   22 ¼ x 22 ¼ x 4" | 56.5 x 56.5 x 10.2 cm

COMPOSITION (CARDS) 2017 39 ¼ x 39 ¼ x 4" | 99.7 x 99.7 x 10.2 cm

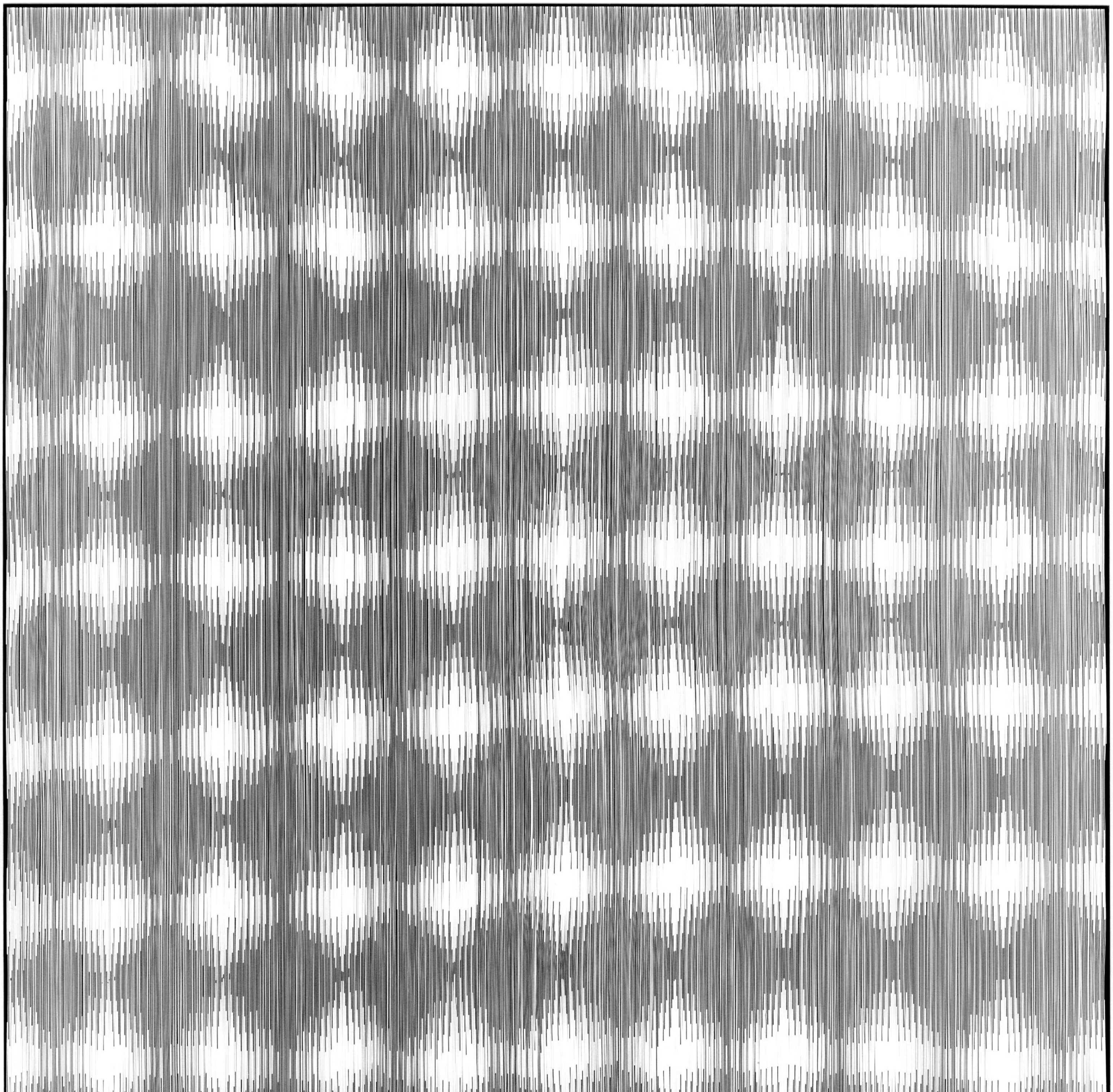

COMPOSITION (CARDS) 2017 39 ¼ x 39 ¼ x 4" | 99.7 x 99.7 x 10.2 cm

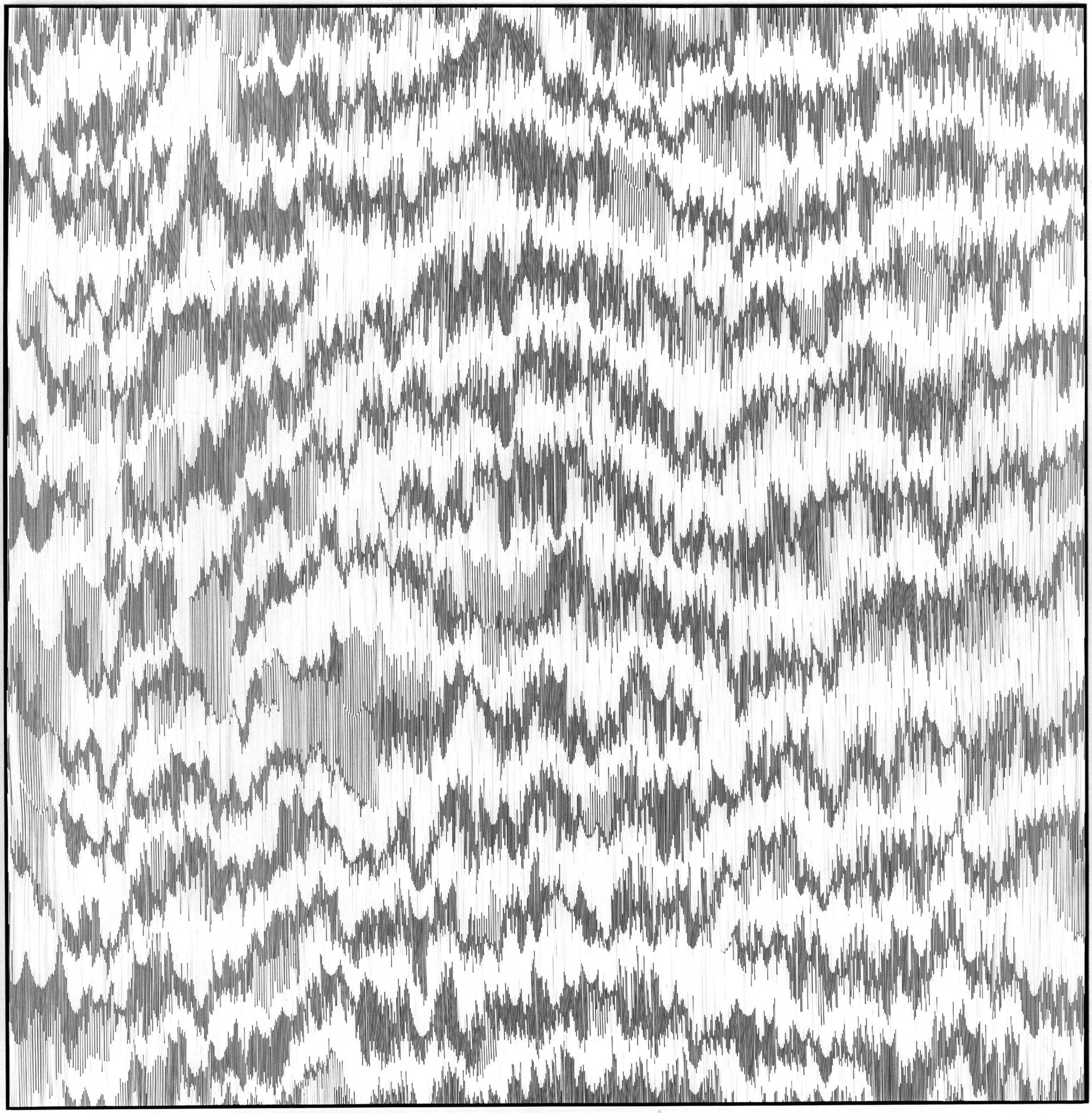

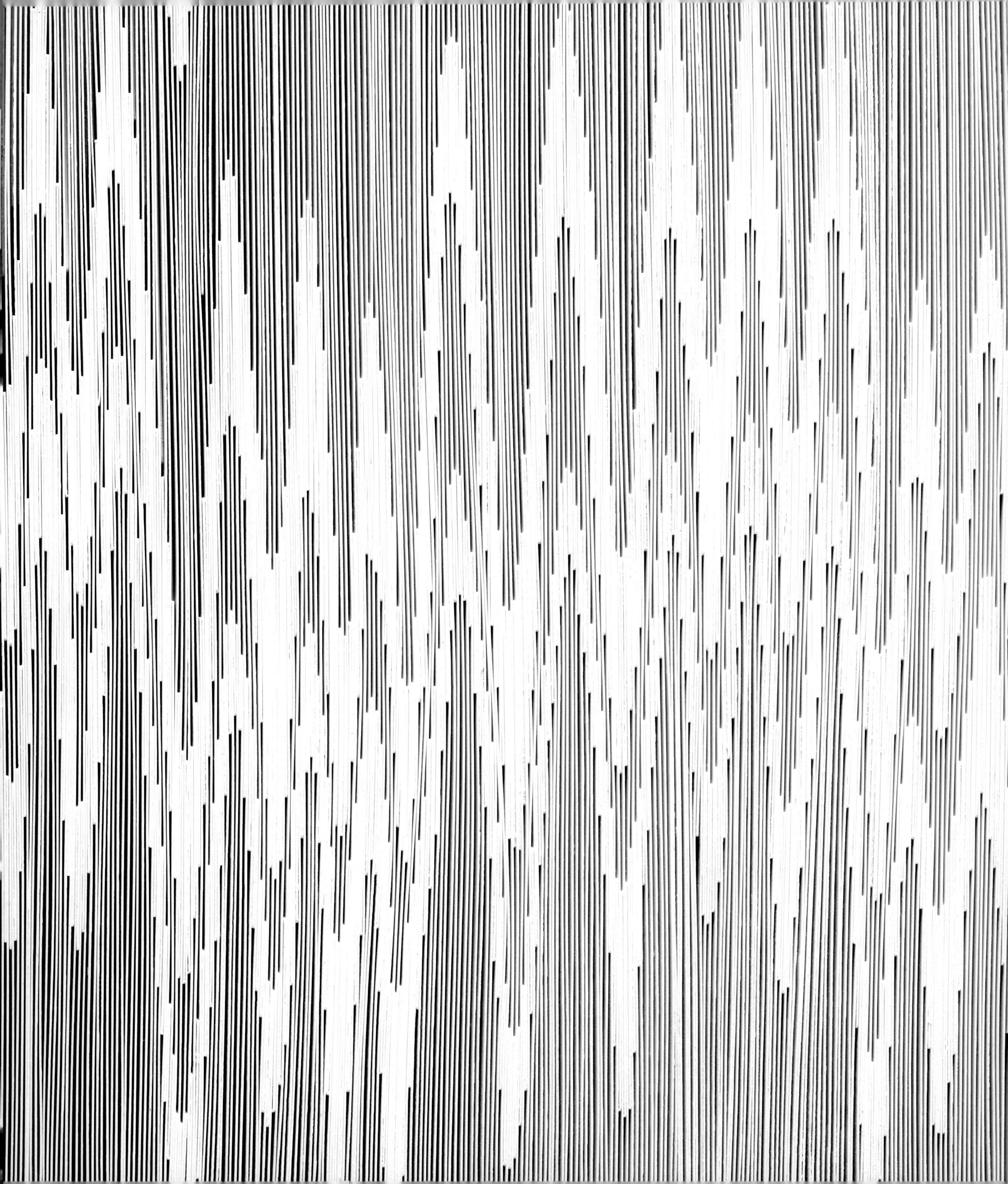

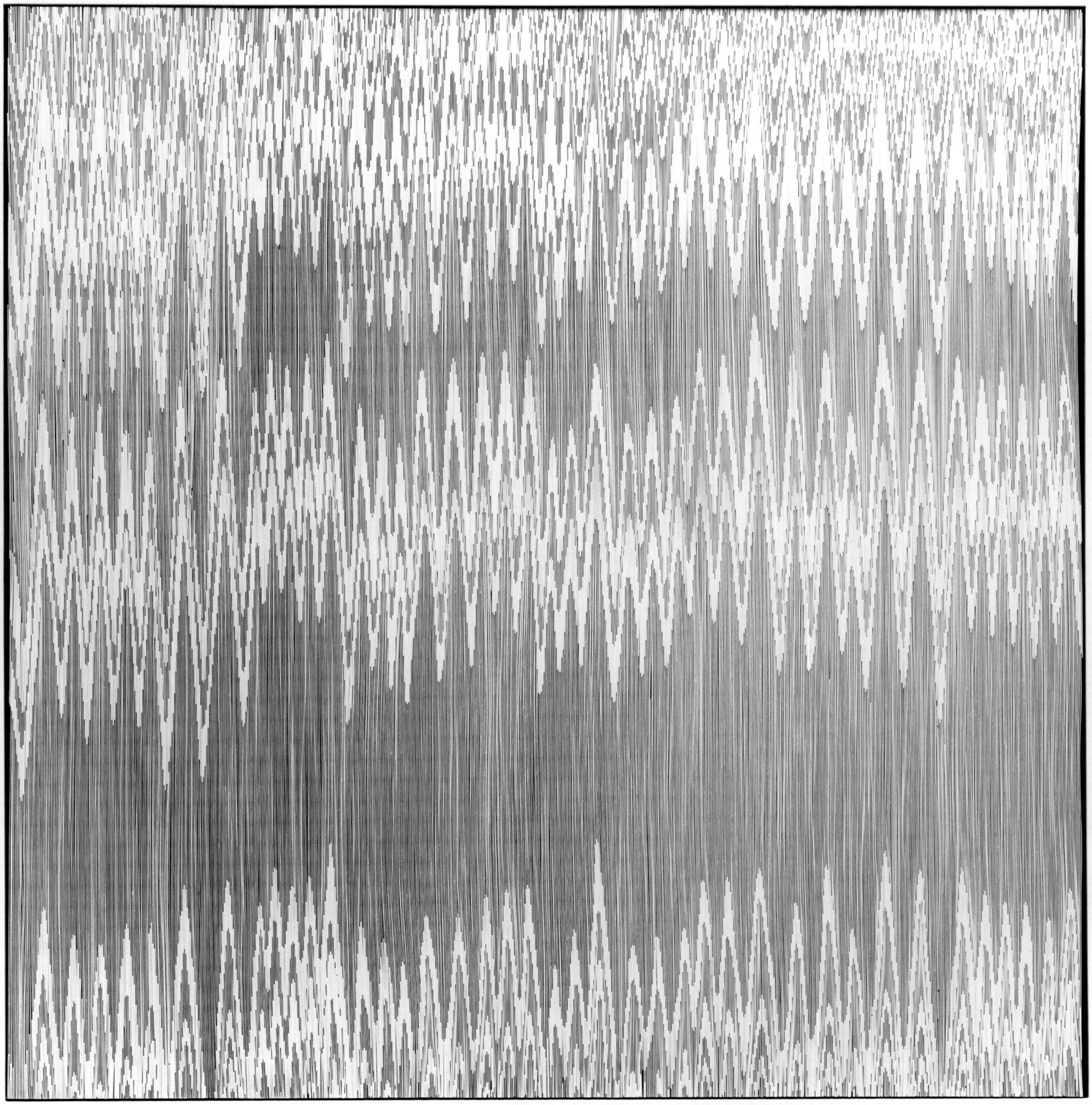

COMPOSITION (CARDS) 2017   36 ¼ x 36 ¼ x 4" | 92.1 x 92.1 x 10.2 cm

COMPOSITION (CARDS) 2017 39 ¼ x 39 ¼ x 4" | 99.7 x 99.7 x 10.2 cm

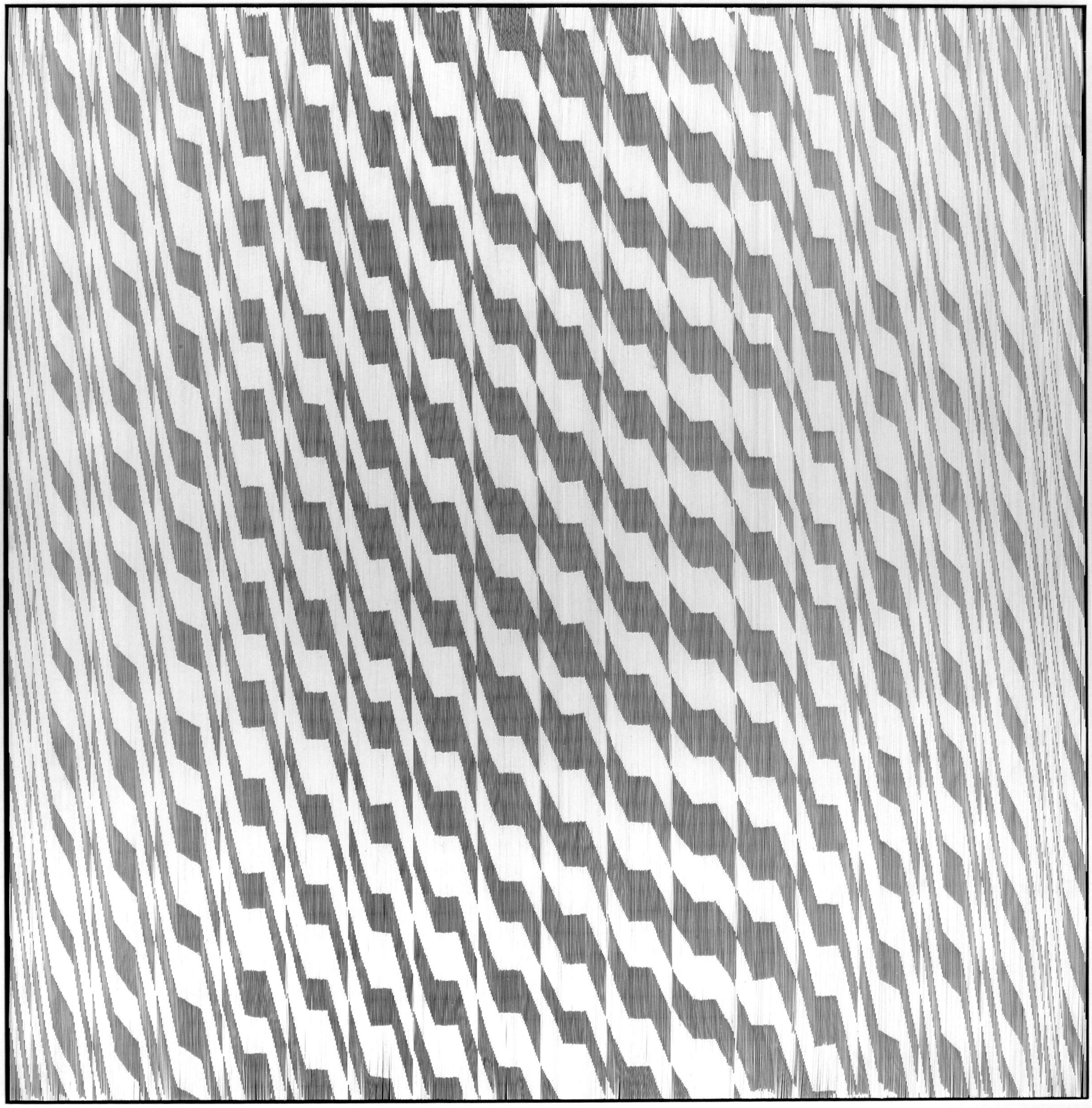

COMPOSITION (CARDS) 2017   39 ¼ x 39 ¼ x 4" | 99.7 x 99.7 x 10.2 cm

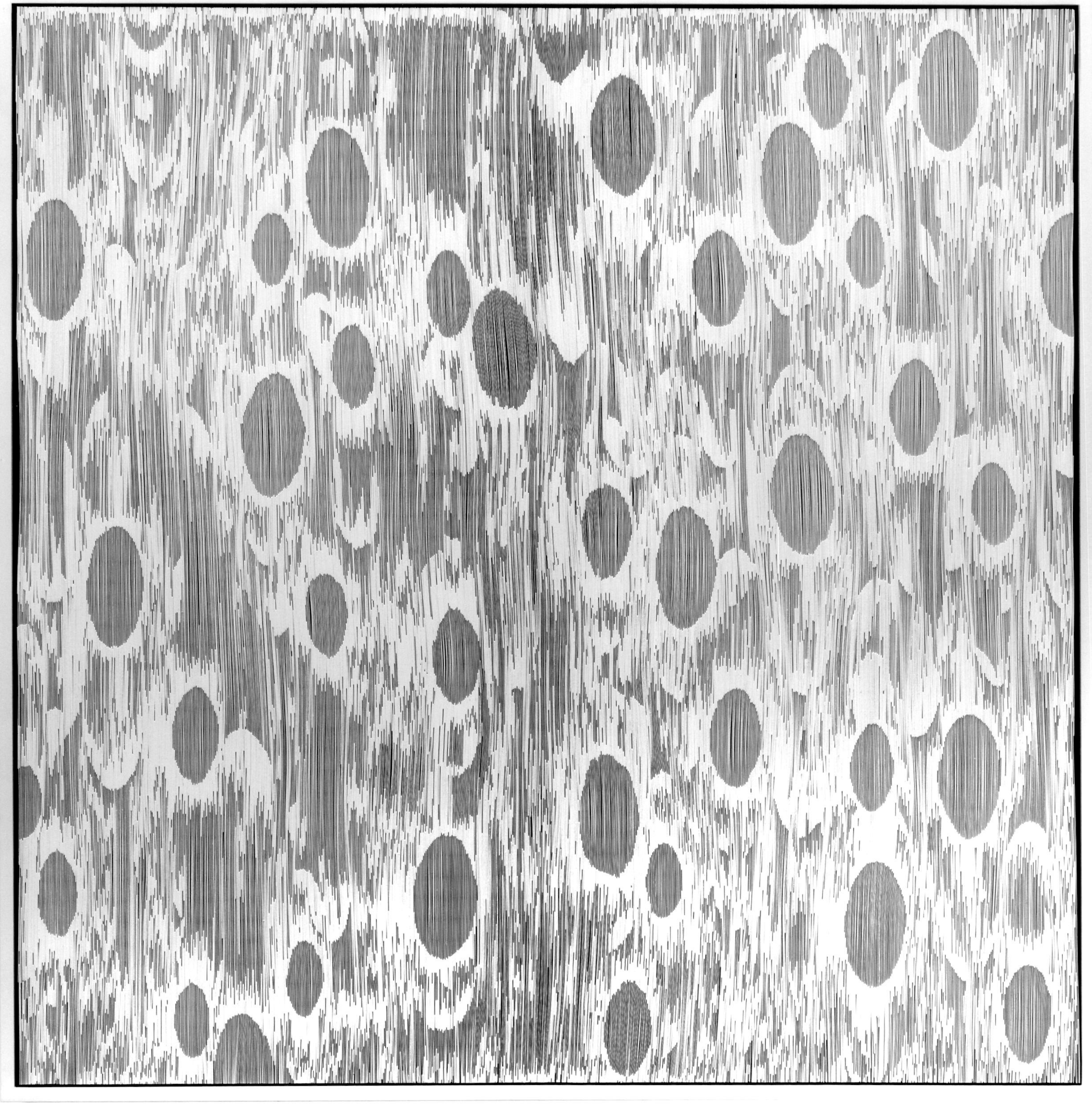

COMPOSITION (CARDS) 2017 39 ¼ x 39 ¼ x 4" | 99.7 x 99.7 x 10.2 cm

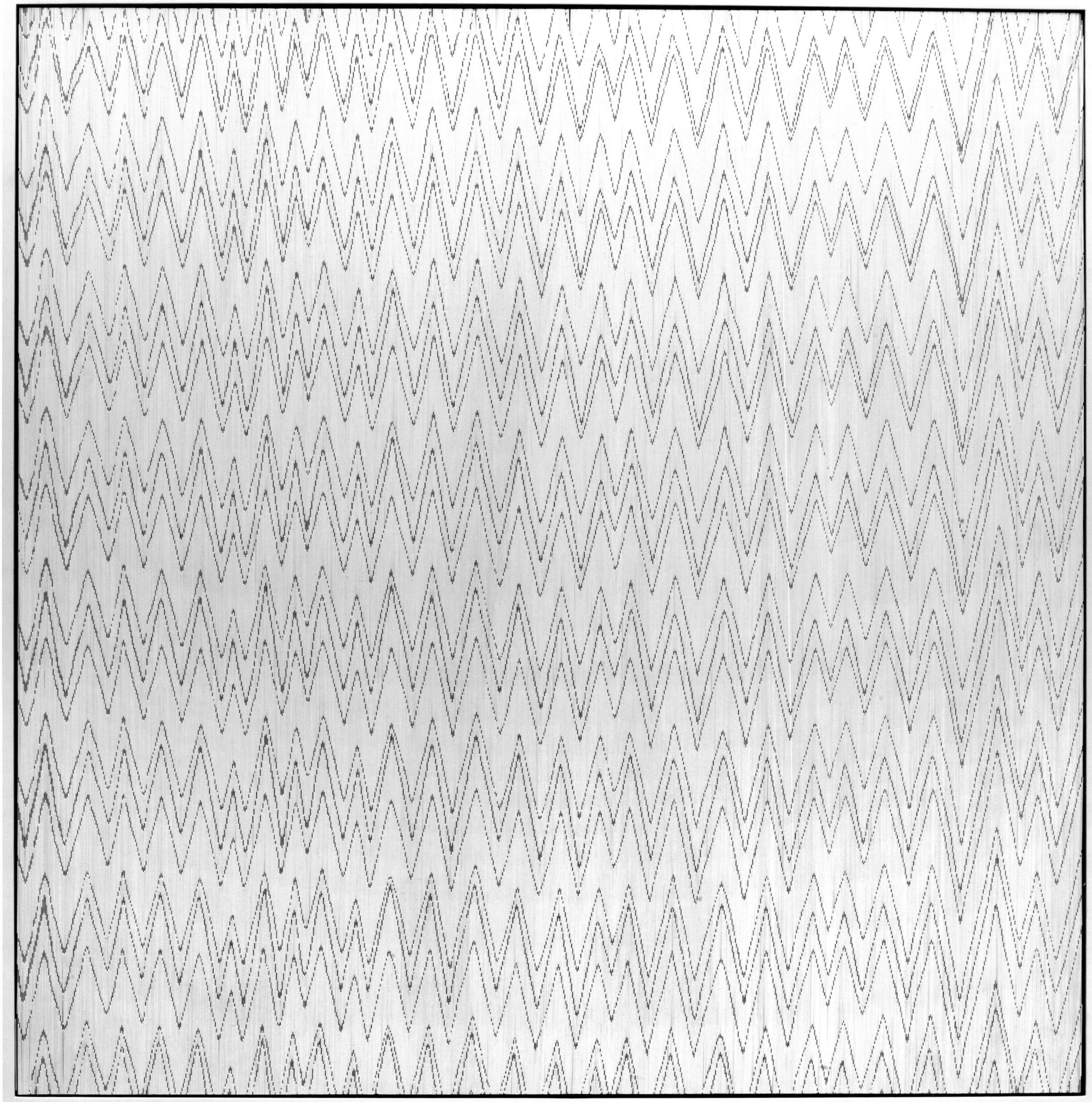

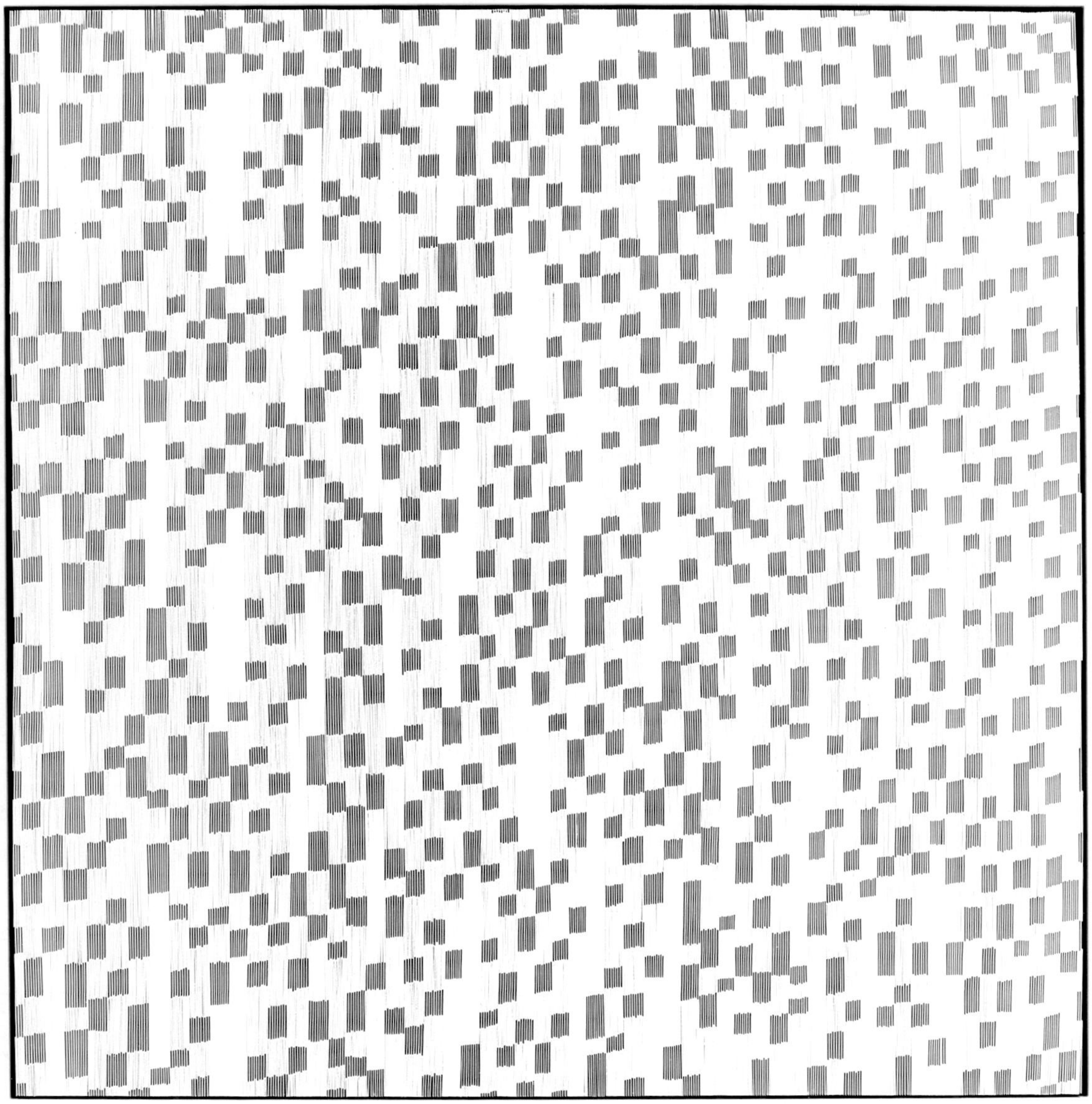

COMPOSITION (CARDS) 2017 22 ¼ x 22 ¼ x 4" | 56.5 x 56.5 x 10.2 cm

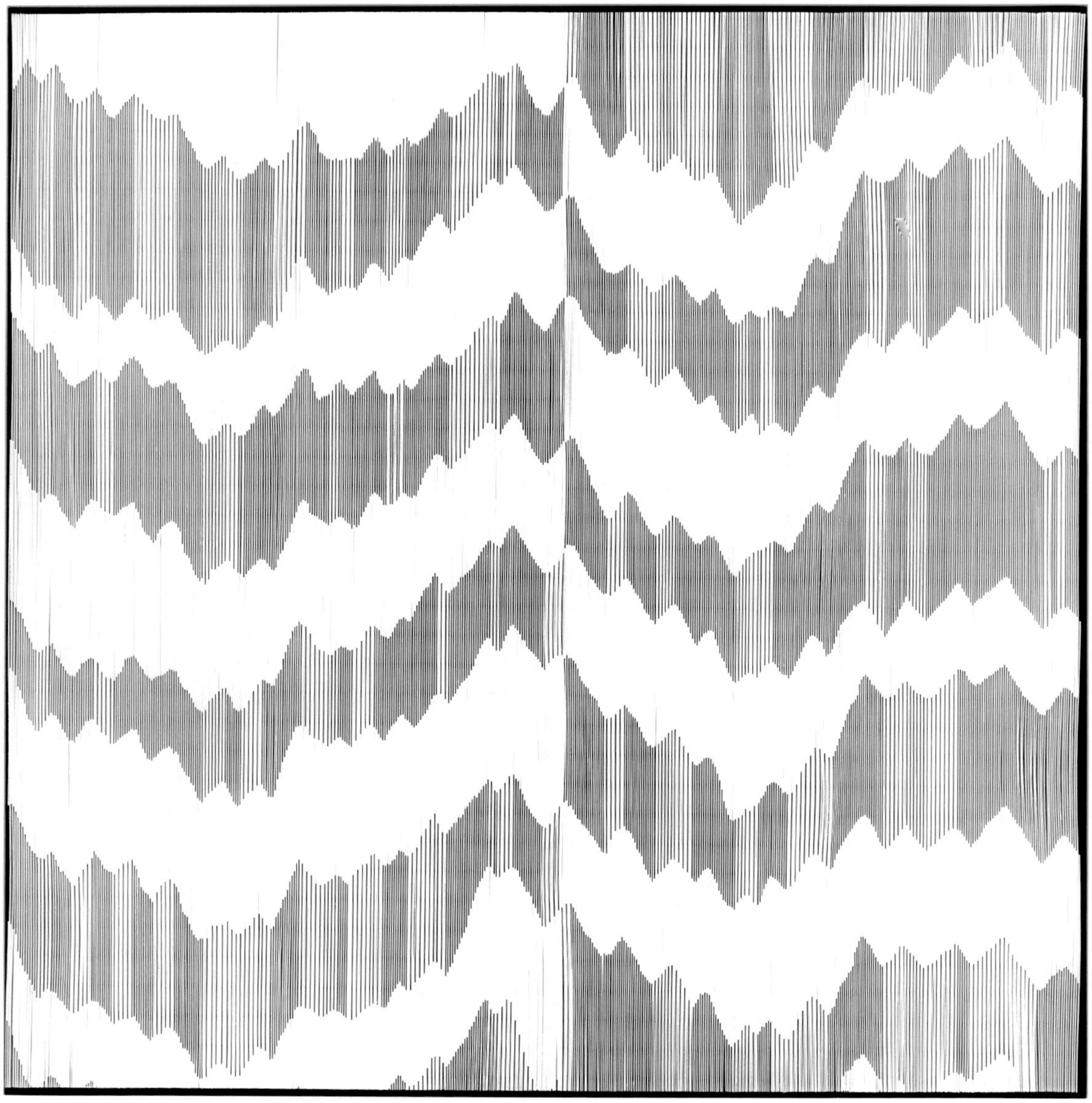

COMPOSITION (CARDS) 2017 22 ¼ x 22 ¼ x 4" | 56.5 x 56.5 x 10.2 cm

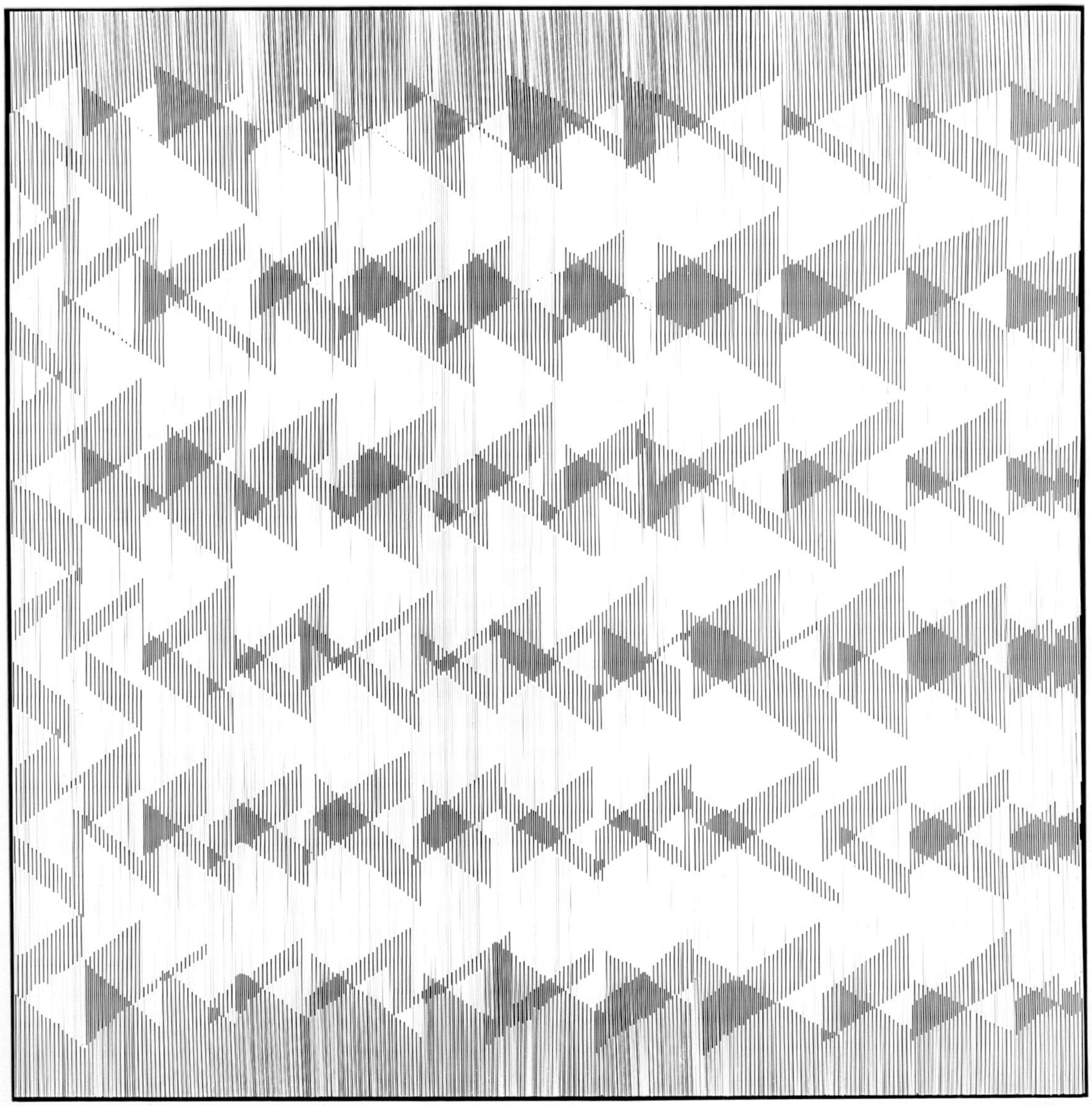

COMPOSITION (CARDS) 2017 22 ¼ x 22 ¼ x 4" | 56.5 x 56.5 x 10.2 cm

COMPOSITION (CARDS) 2017 39 ¼ x 39 ¼ x 4" | 99.7 x 99.7 x 10.2 cm

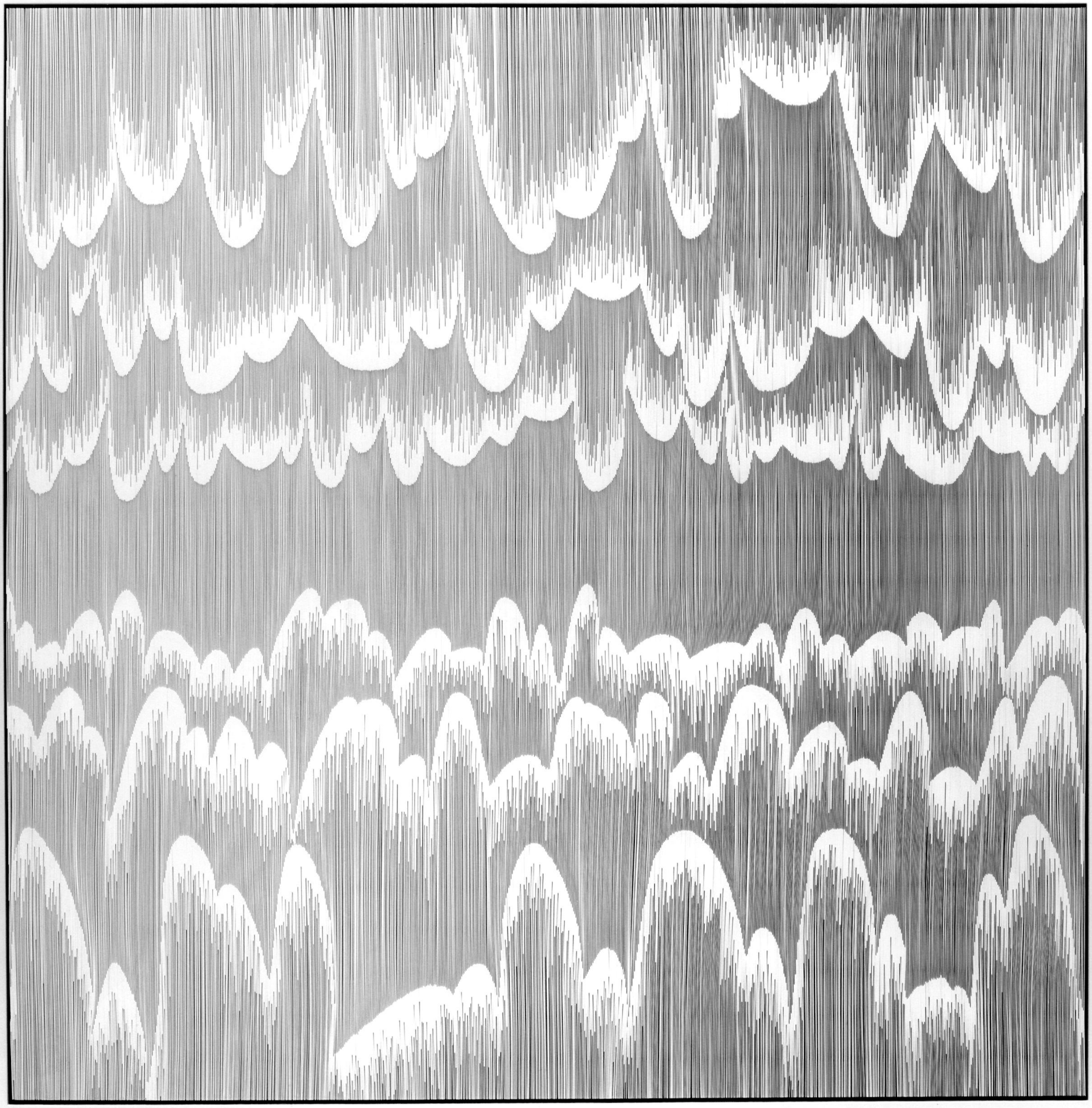

COMPOSITION (CARDS) 2017 39 ¼ x 39 ¼ x 4" | 99.7 x 99.7 x 10.2 cm

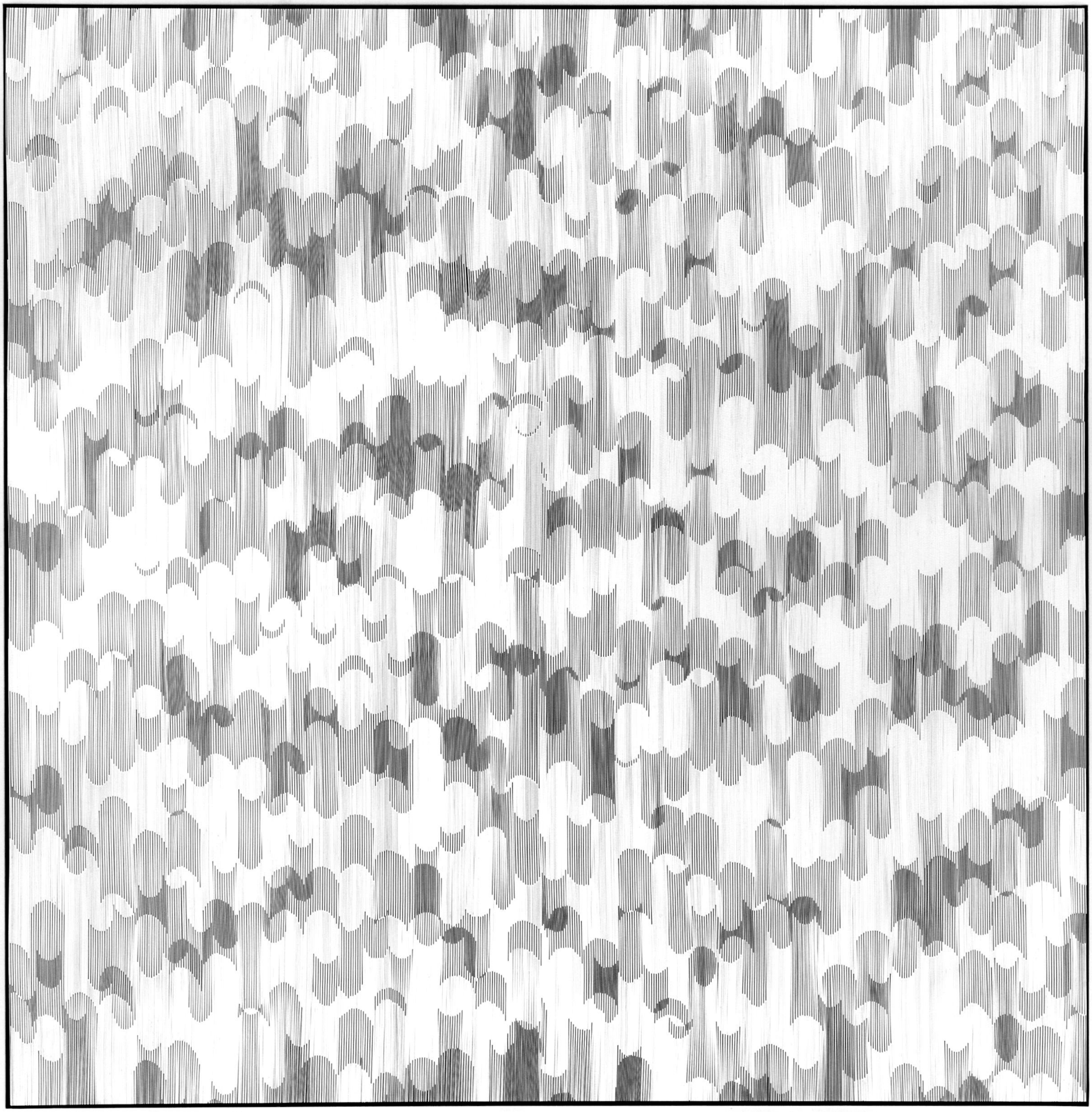

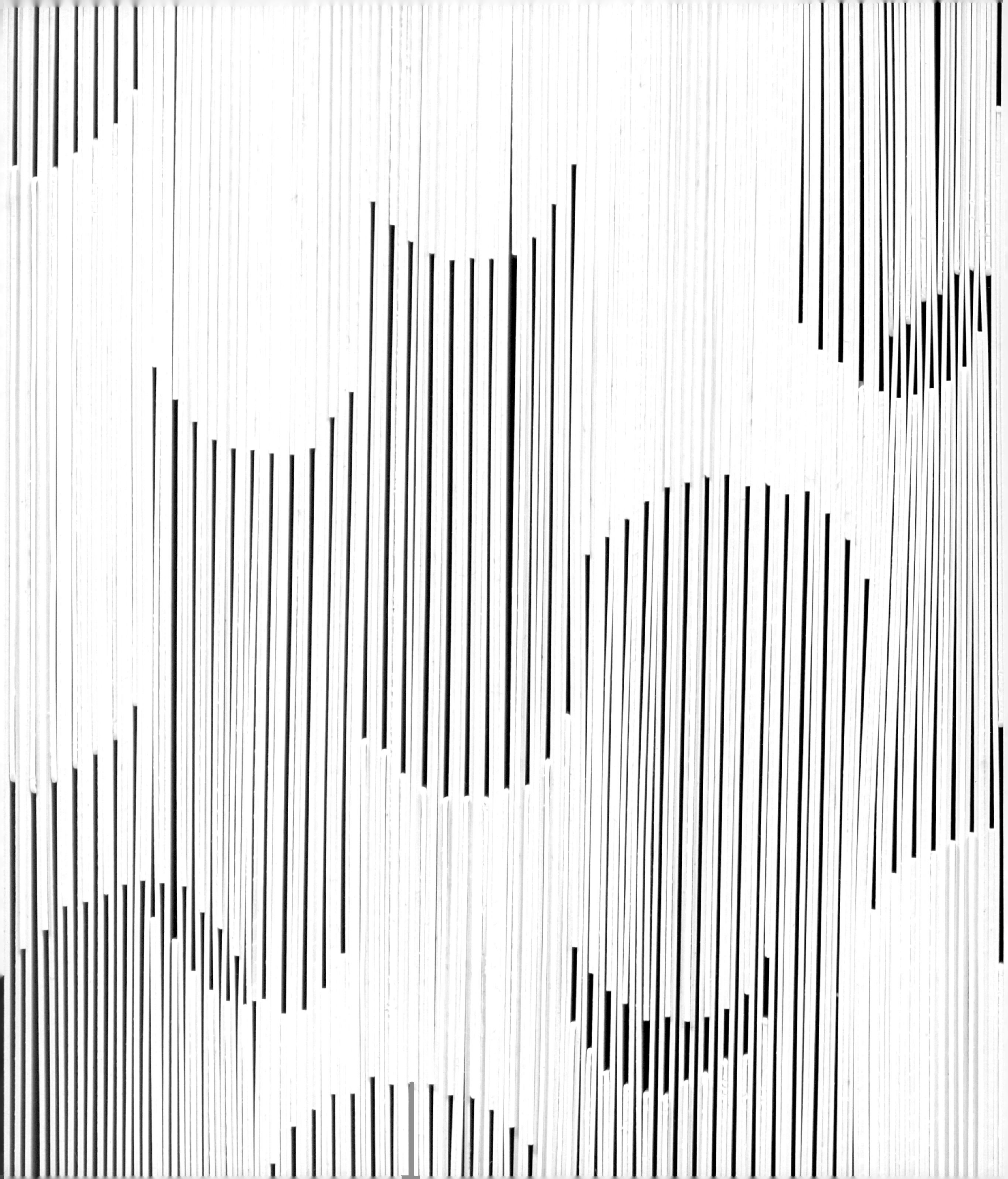

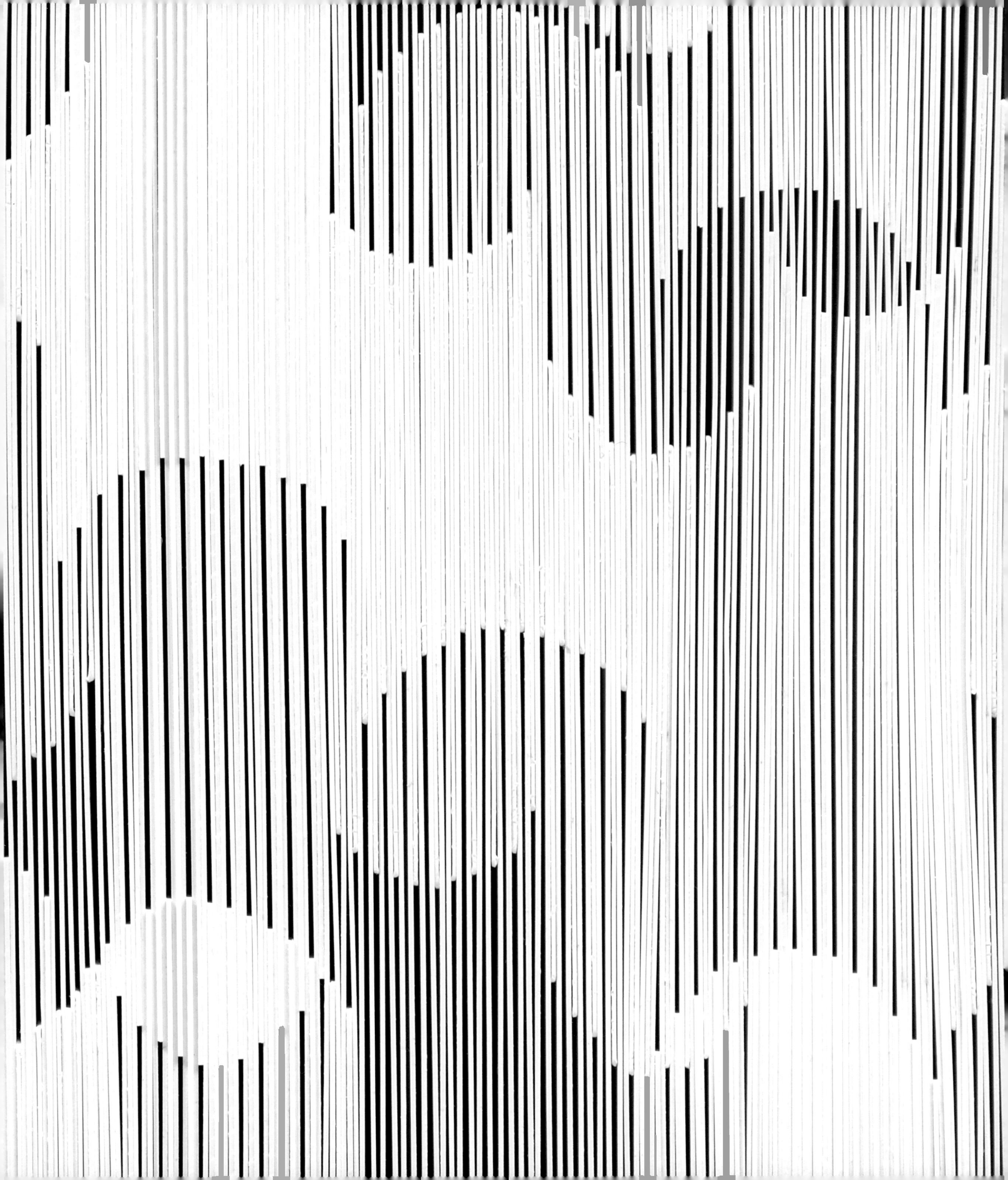

COMPOSITION (CARDS) 2017   36 ¼ x 36 ¼ x 4" | 92.1 x 92.1 x 10.2 cm

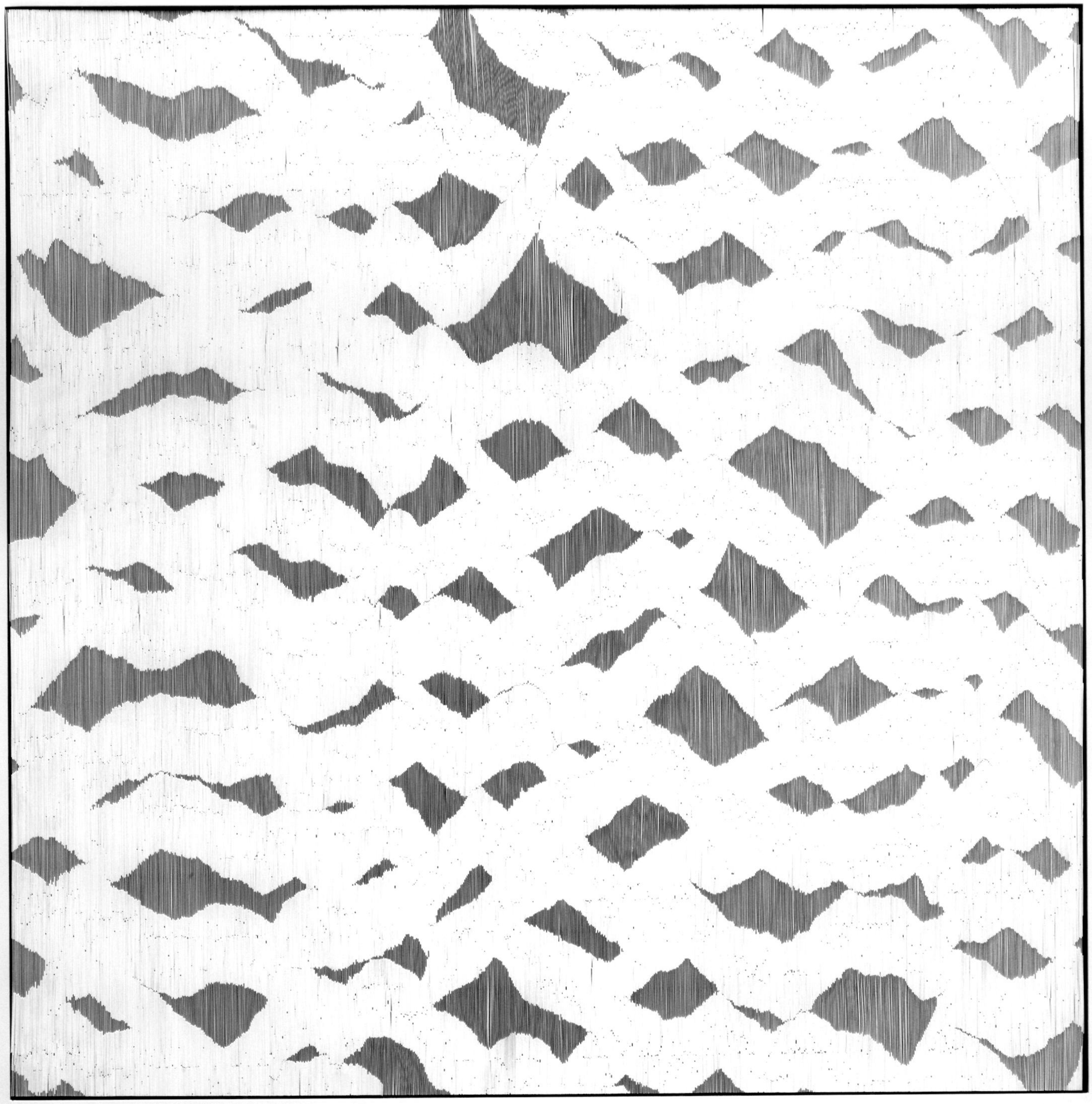

COMPOSITION (CARDS) 2017 39 ¼ x 39 ¼ x 4" | 99.7 x 99.7 x 10.2 cm

COMPOSITION (CARDS) 2017 39 ¼ x 39 ¼ x 4" | 99.7 x 99.7 x 10.2 cm

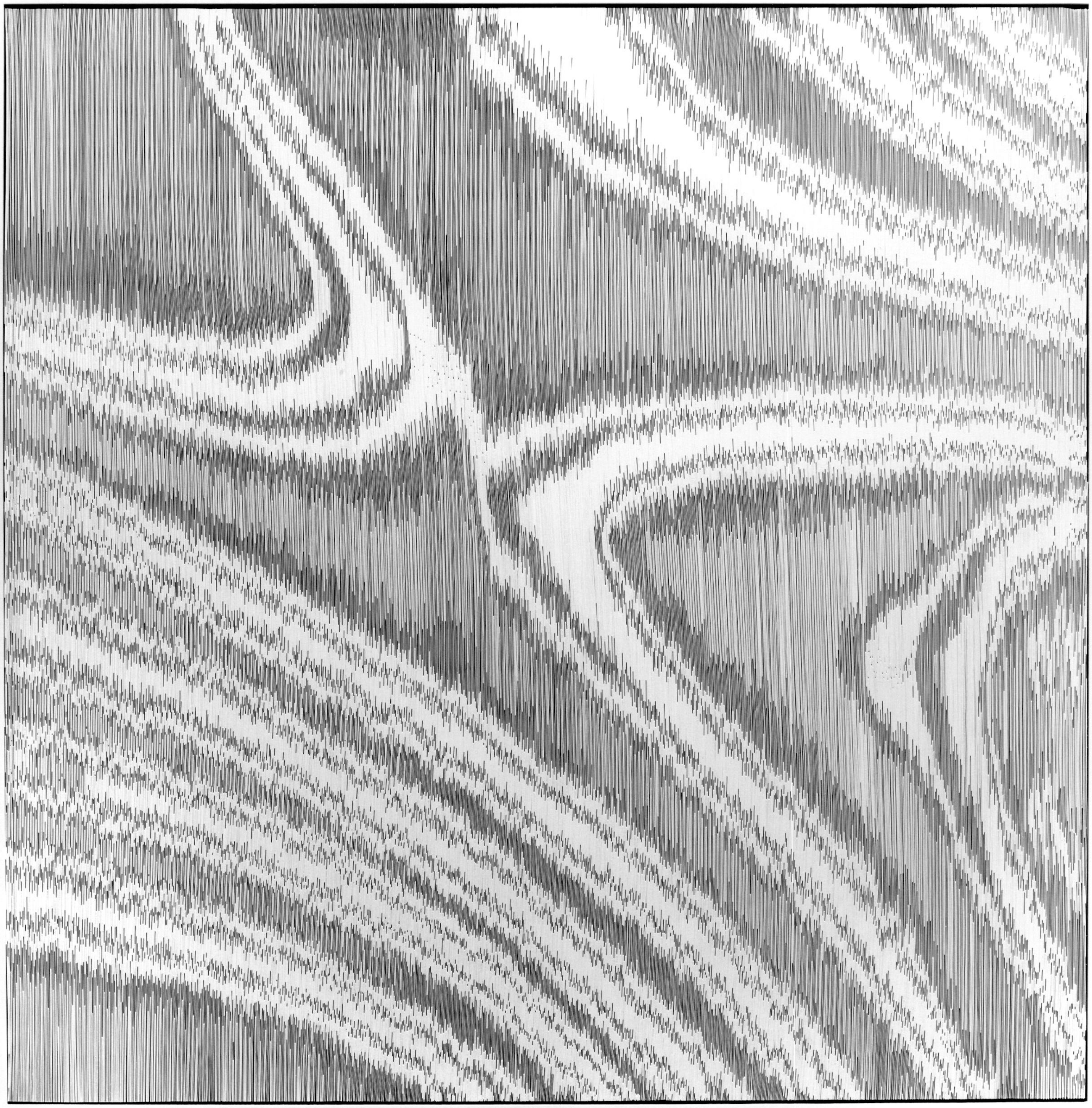

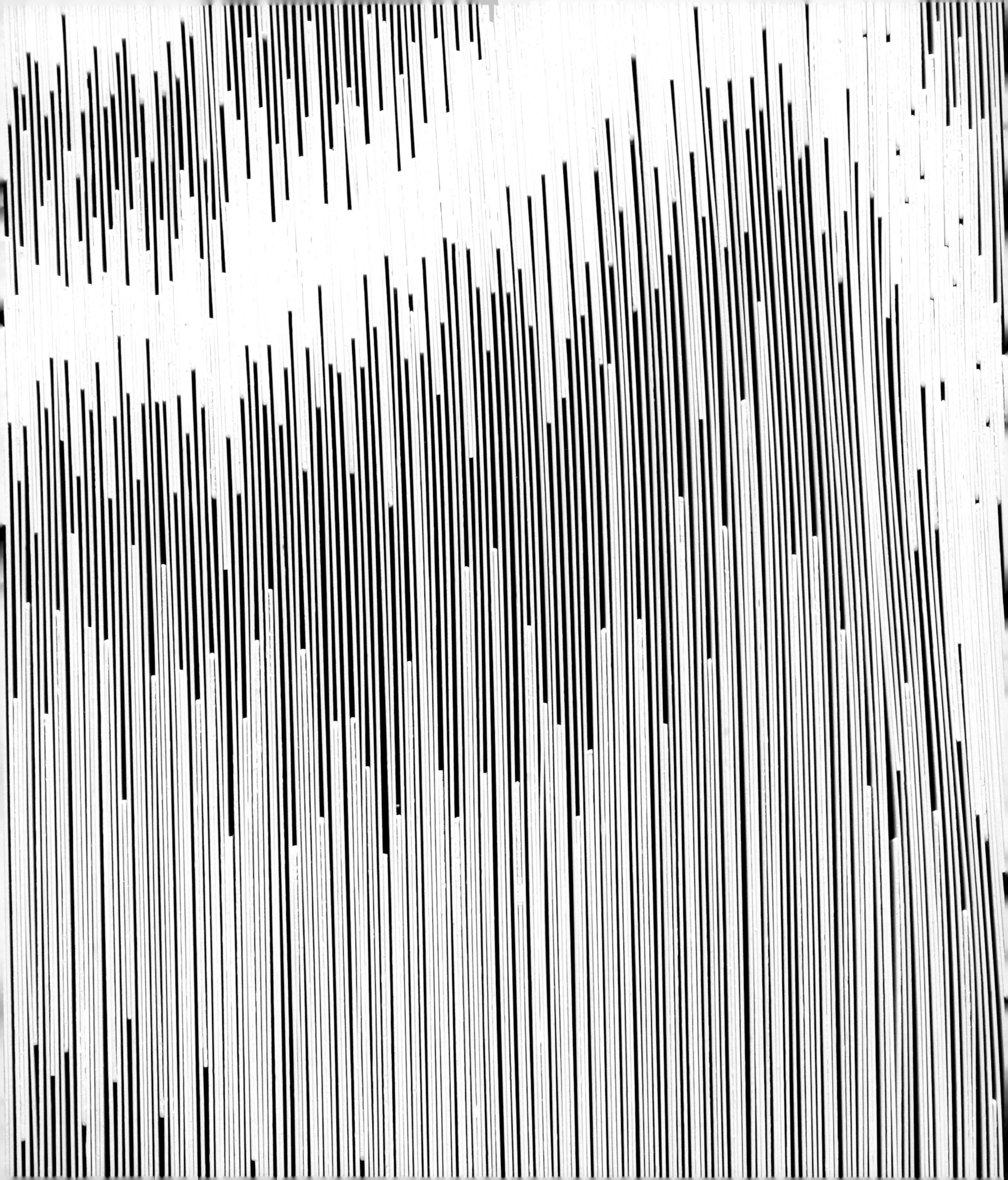

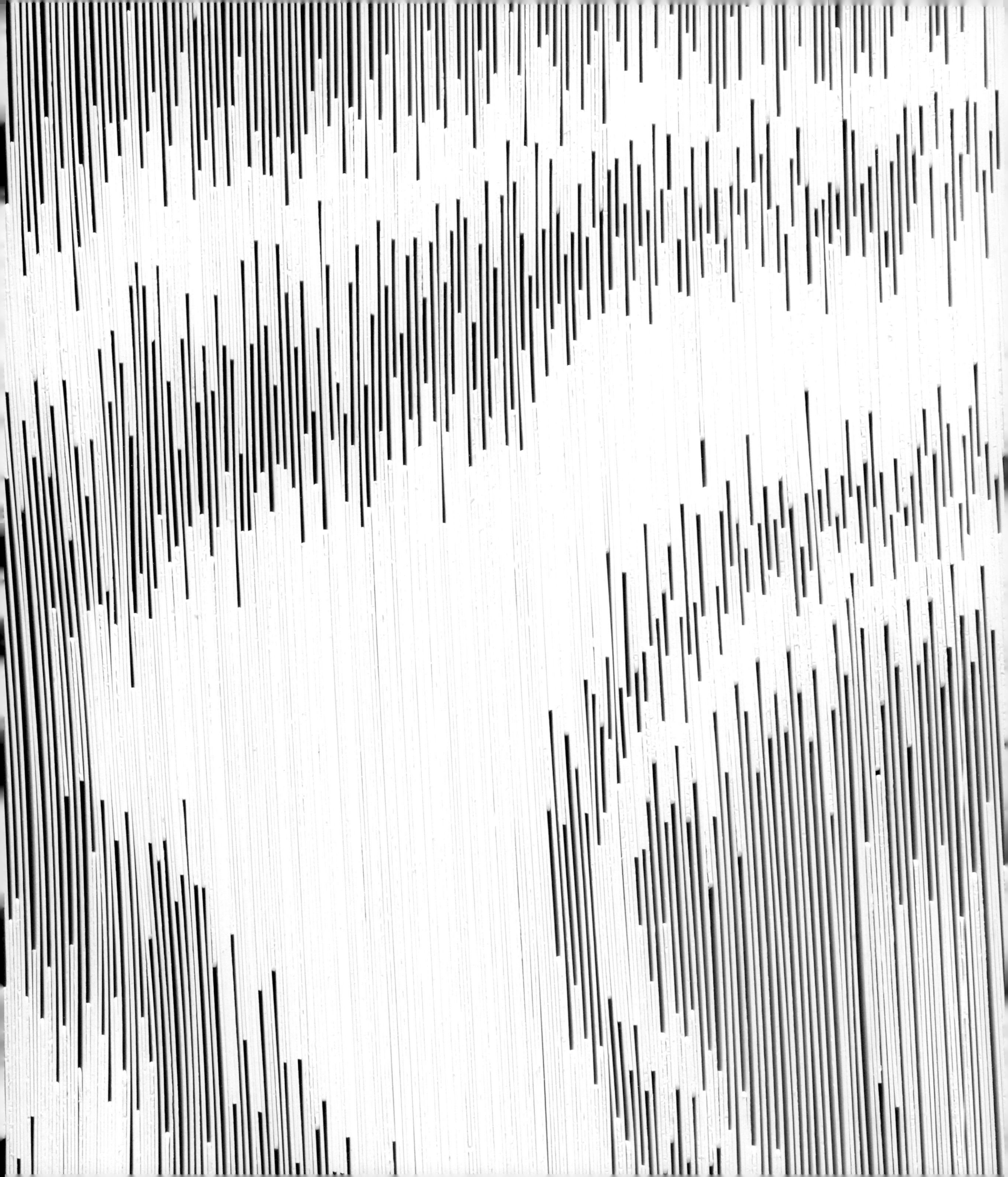

COMPOSITION (CARDS) 2017 39 ¼ x 39 ¼ x 4" | 99.7 x 99.7 x 10.2 cm

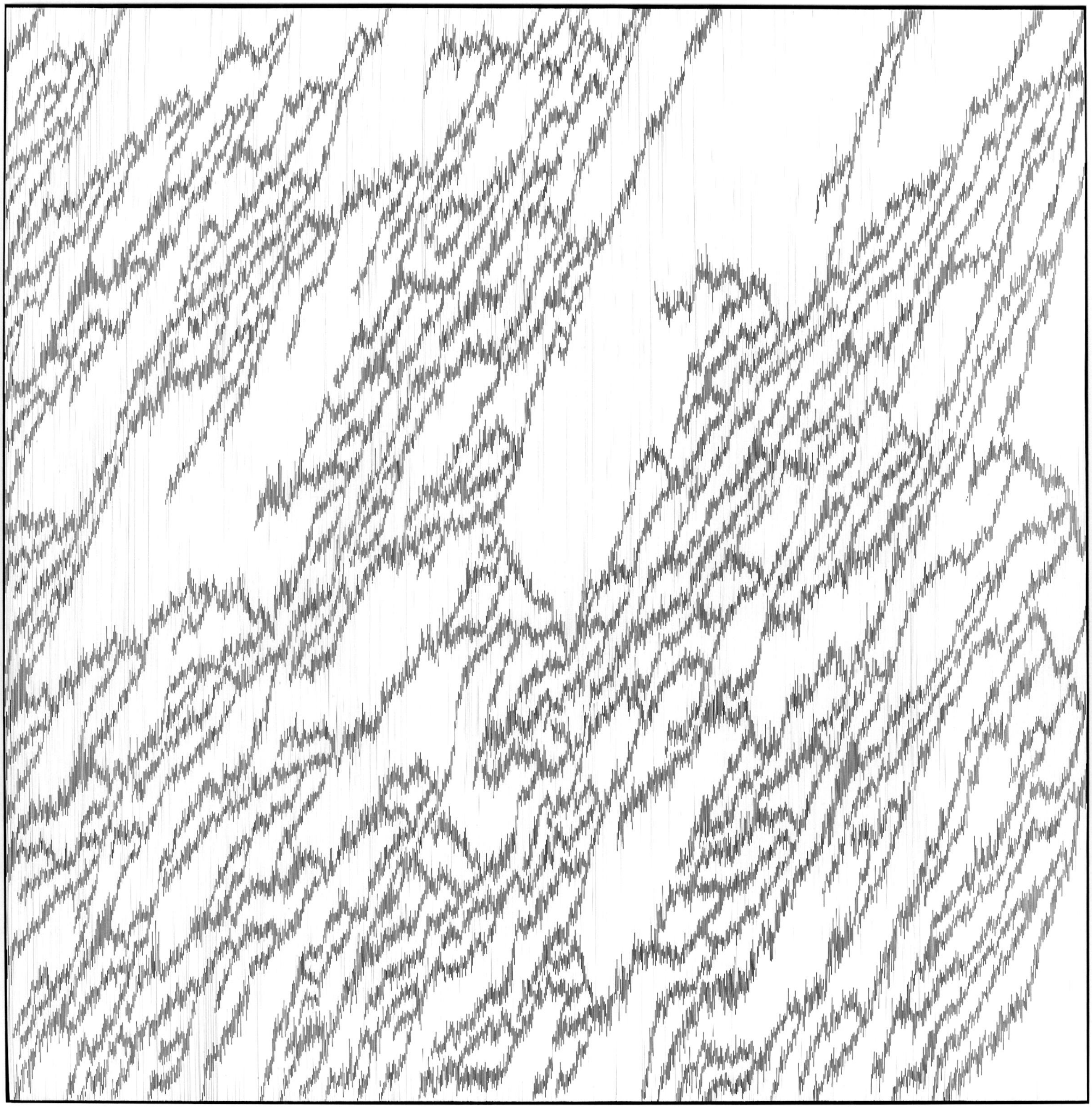

COMPOSITION (CARDS) 2017 39 ¼ x 39 ¼ x 4" | 99.7 x 99.7 x 10.2 cm

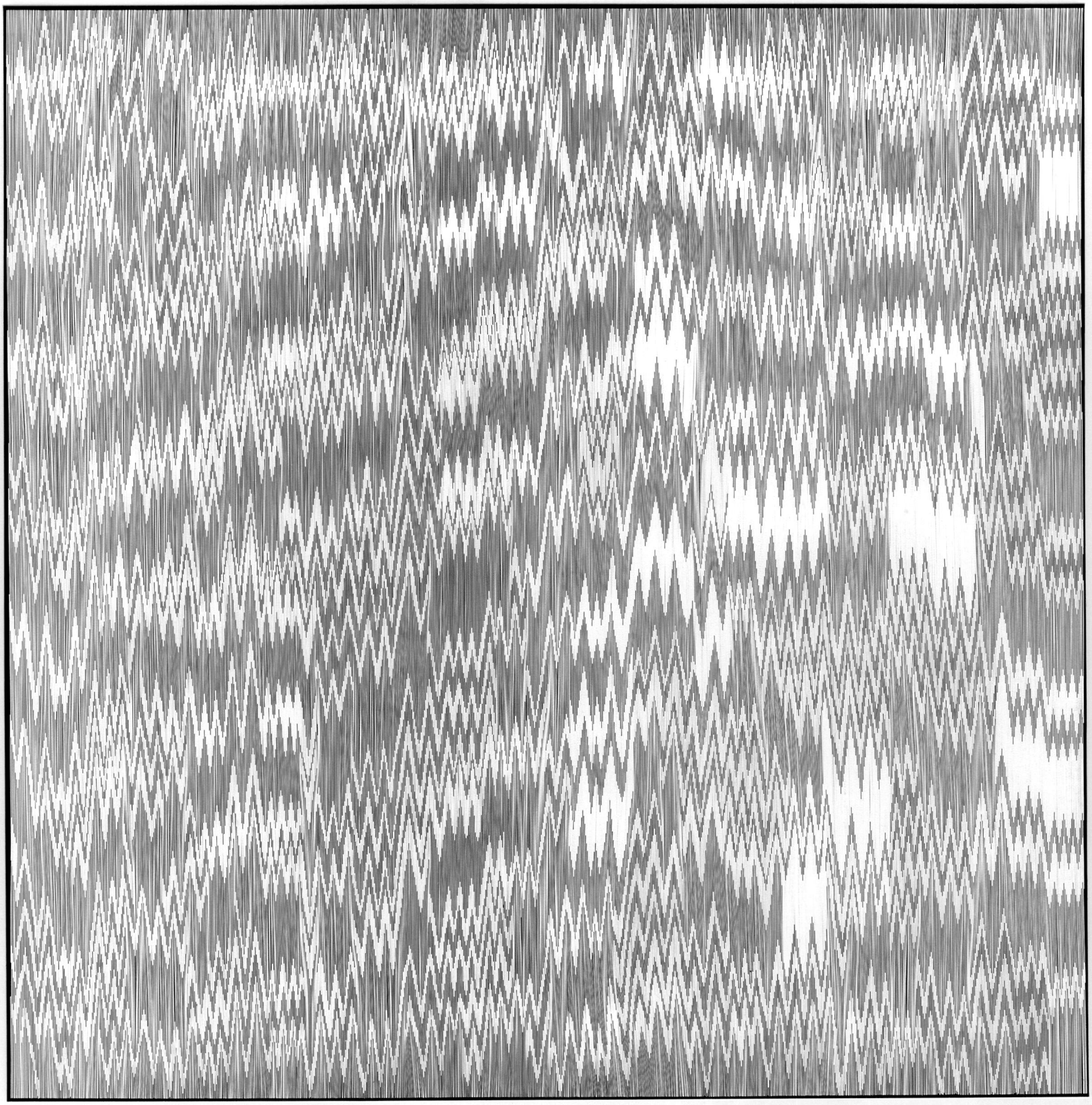

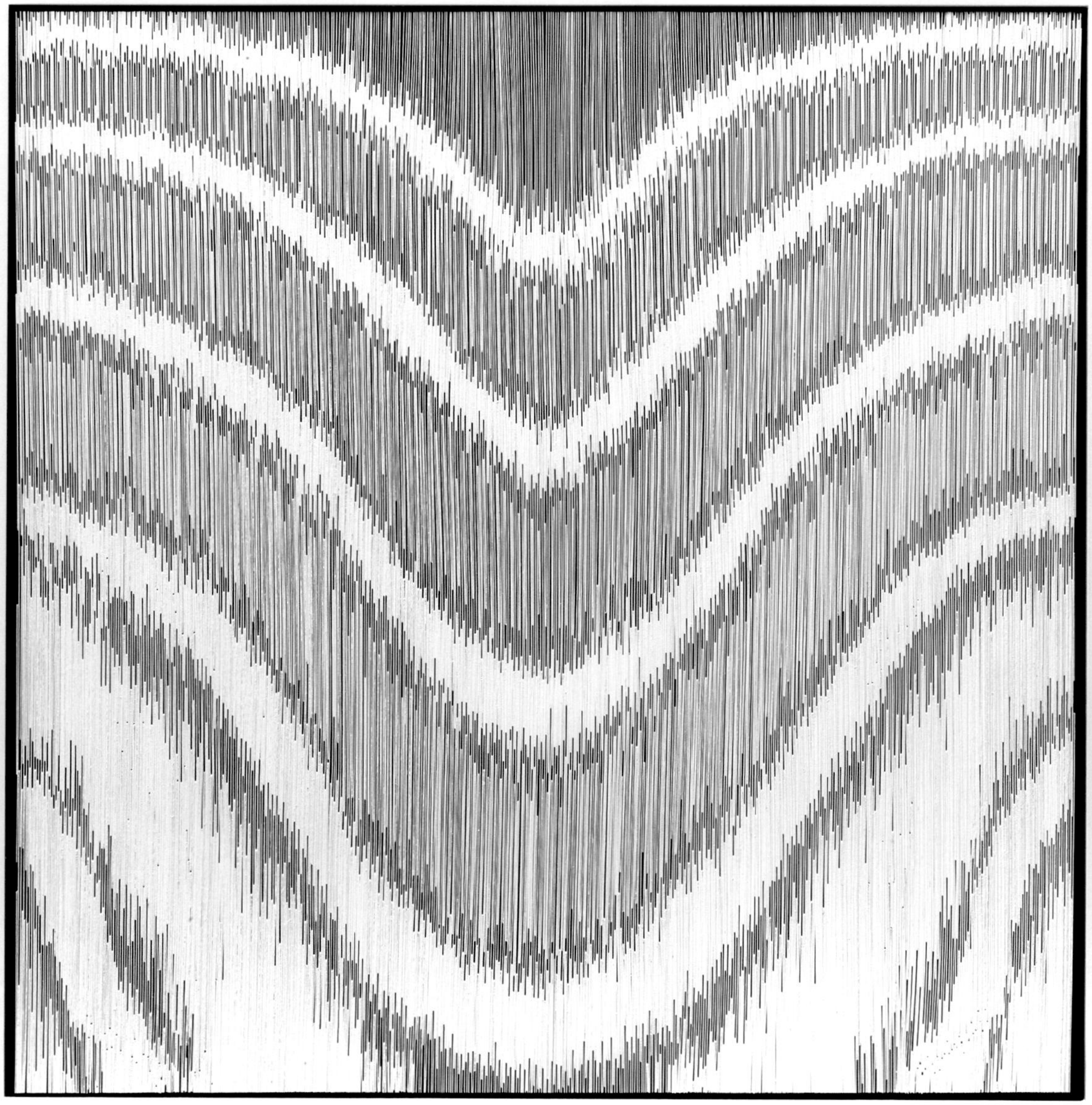

COMPOSITION (CARDS) 2017 22 ¼ x 22 ¼ x 4" | 56.5 x 56.5 x 10.2 cm

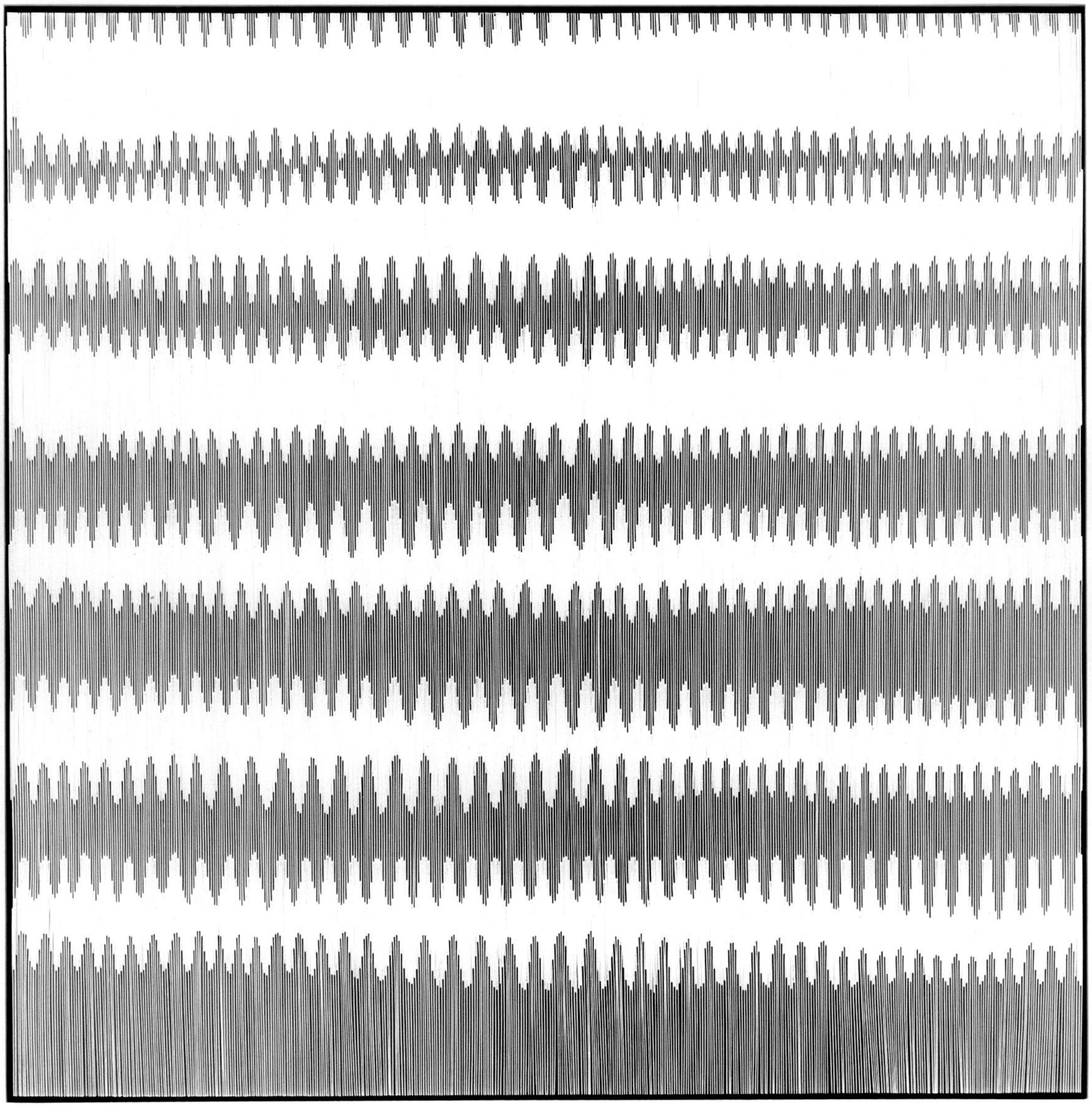

COMPOSITION (CARDS) 2017 22 ¼ x 22 ¼ x 4" | 56.5 x 56.5 x 10.2 cm

COMPOSITION (CARDS) 2017 39 ¼ x 39 ¼ x 4" | 99.7 x 99.7 x 10.2 cm

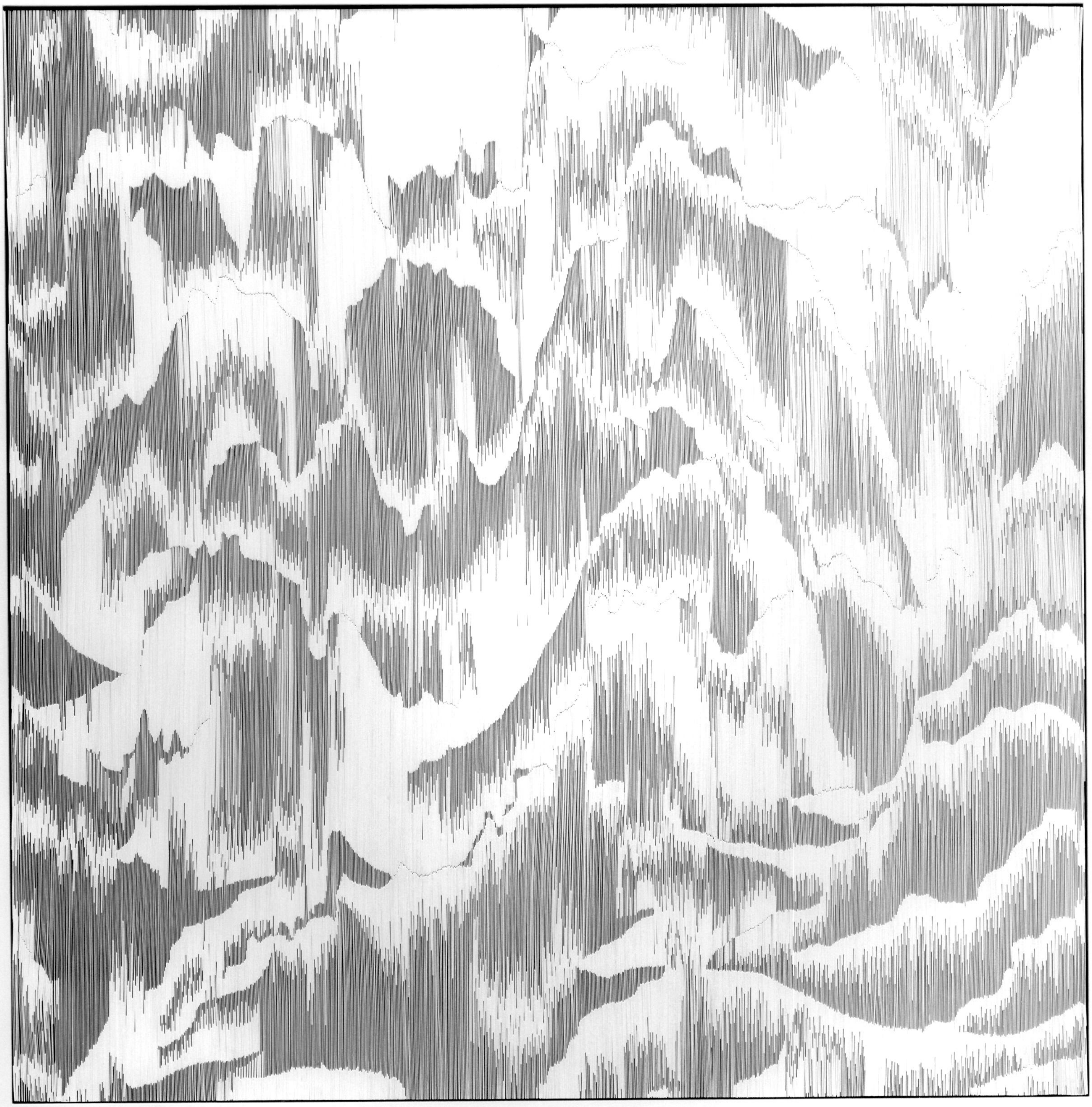

COMPOSITION (CARDS) 2017 39 ¼ x 39 ¼ x 4" | 99.7 x 99.7 x 10.2 cm

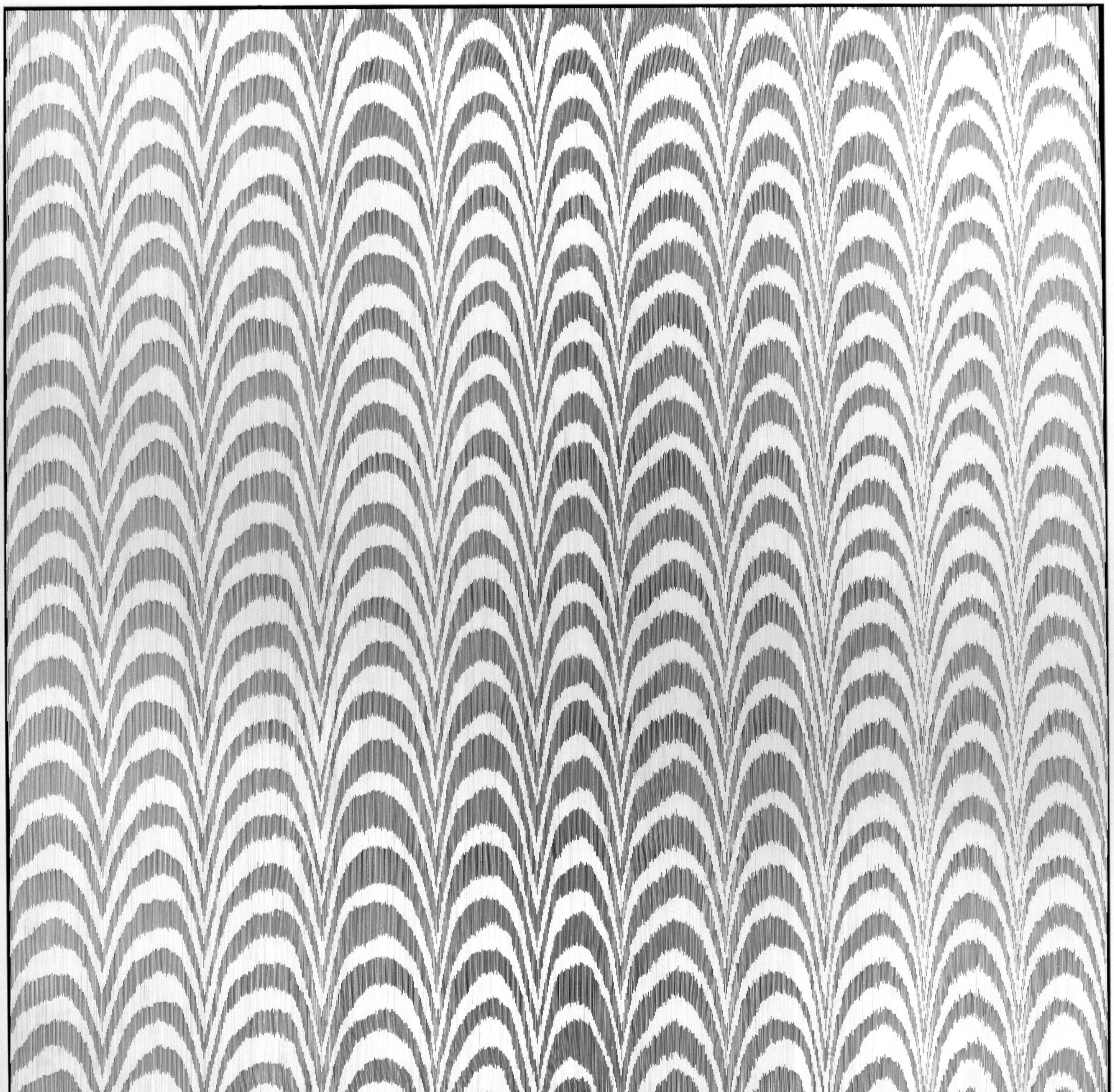

COMPOSITION (CARDS) 2017 39 ¼ x 39 ¼ x 4" | 99.7 x 99.7 x 10.2 cm

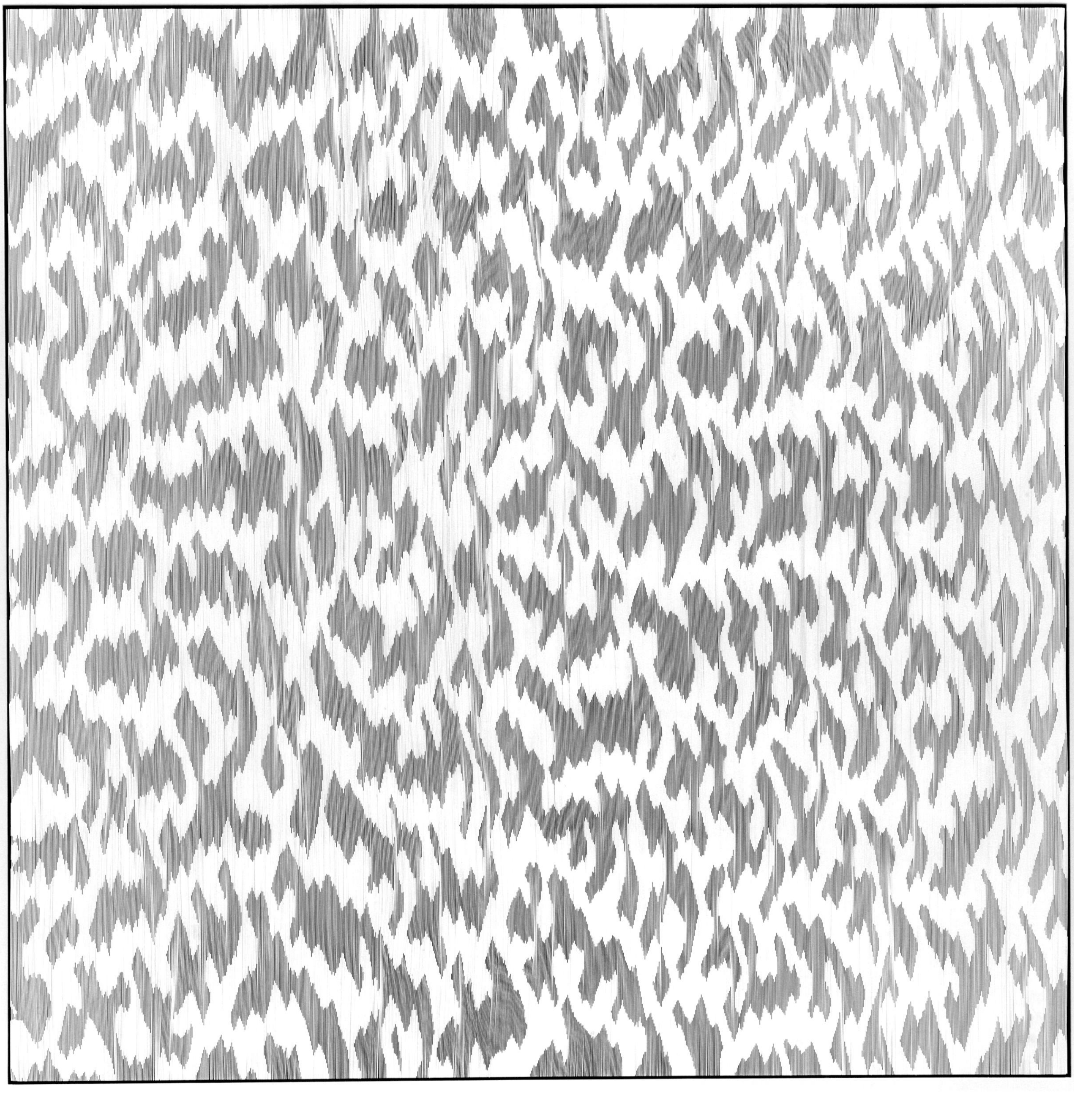

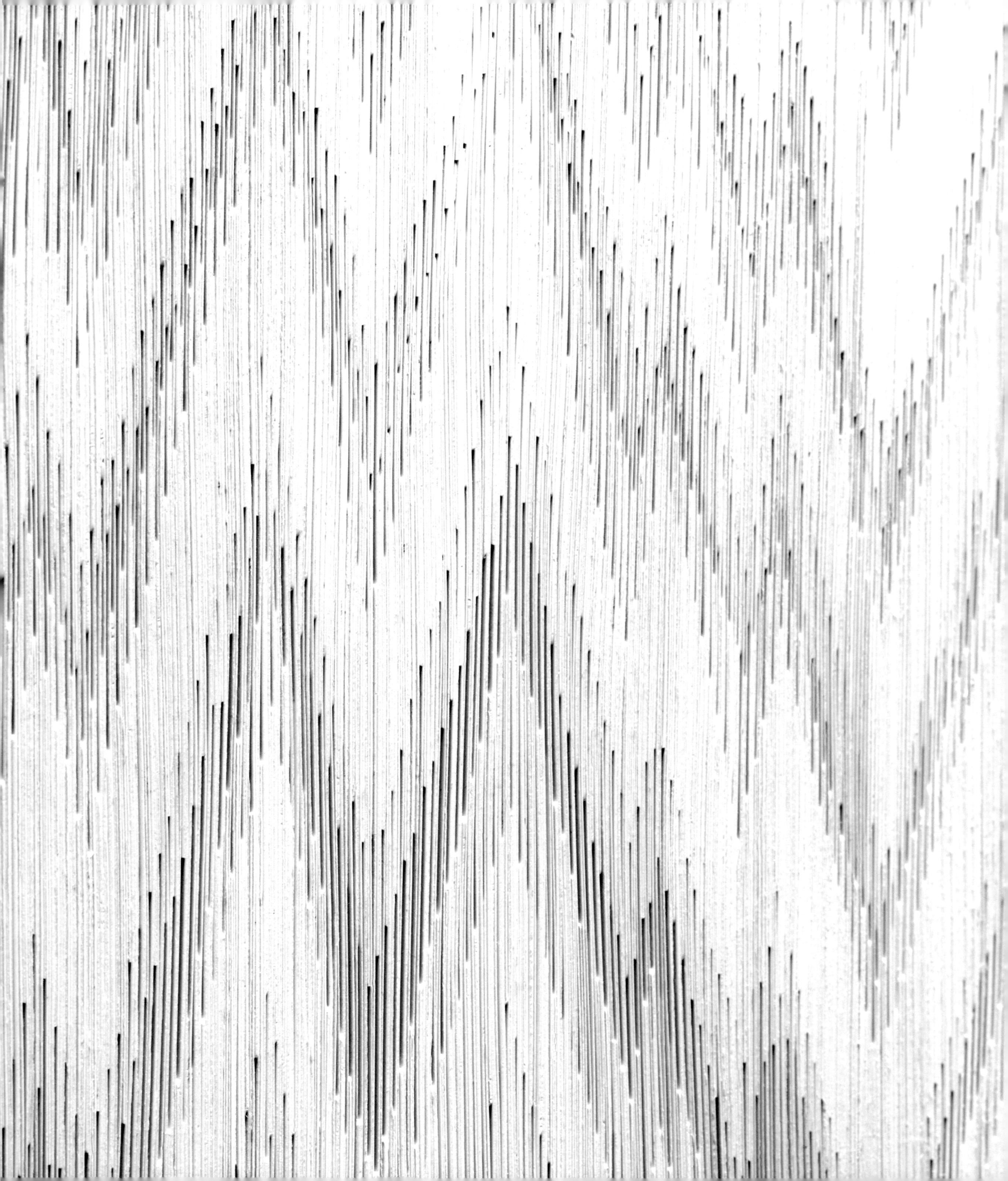

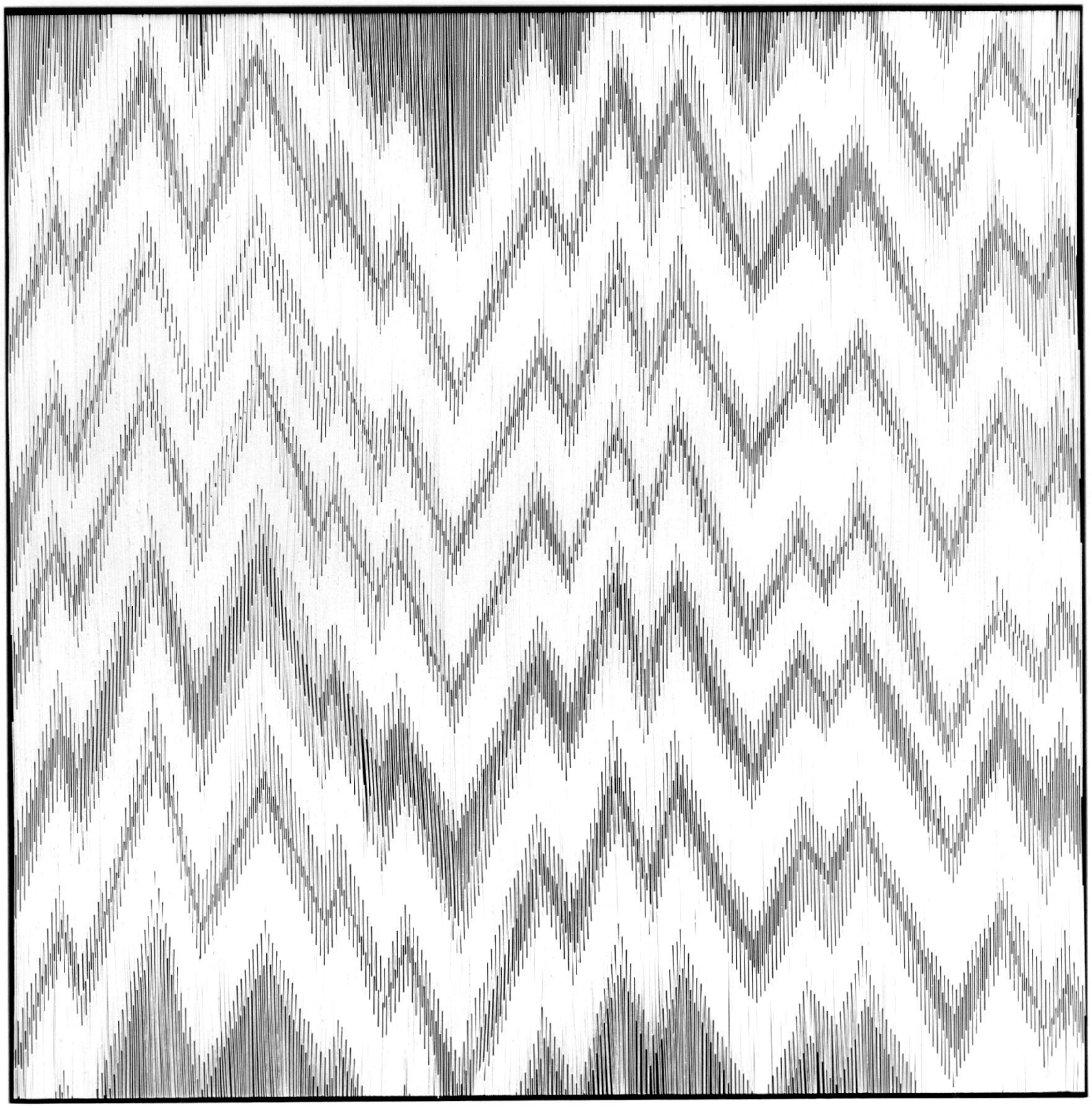

COMPOSITION (CARDS) 2017 22 ¼ x 22 ¼ x 4" | 56.5 x 56.5 x 10.2 cm

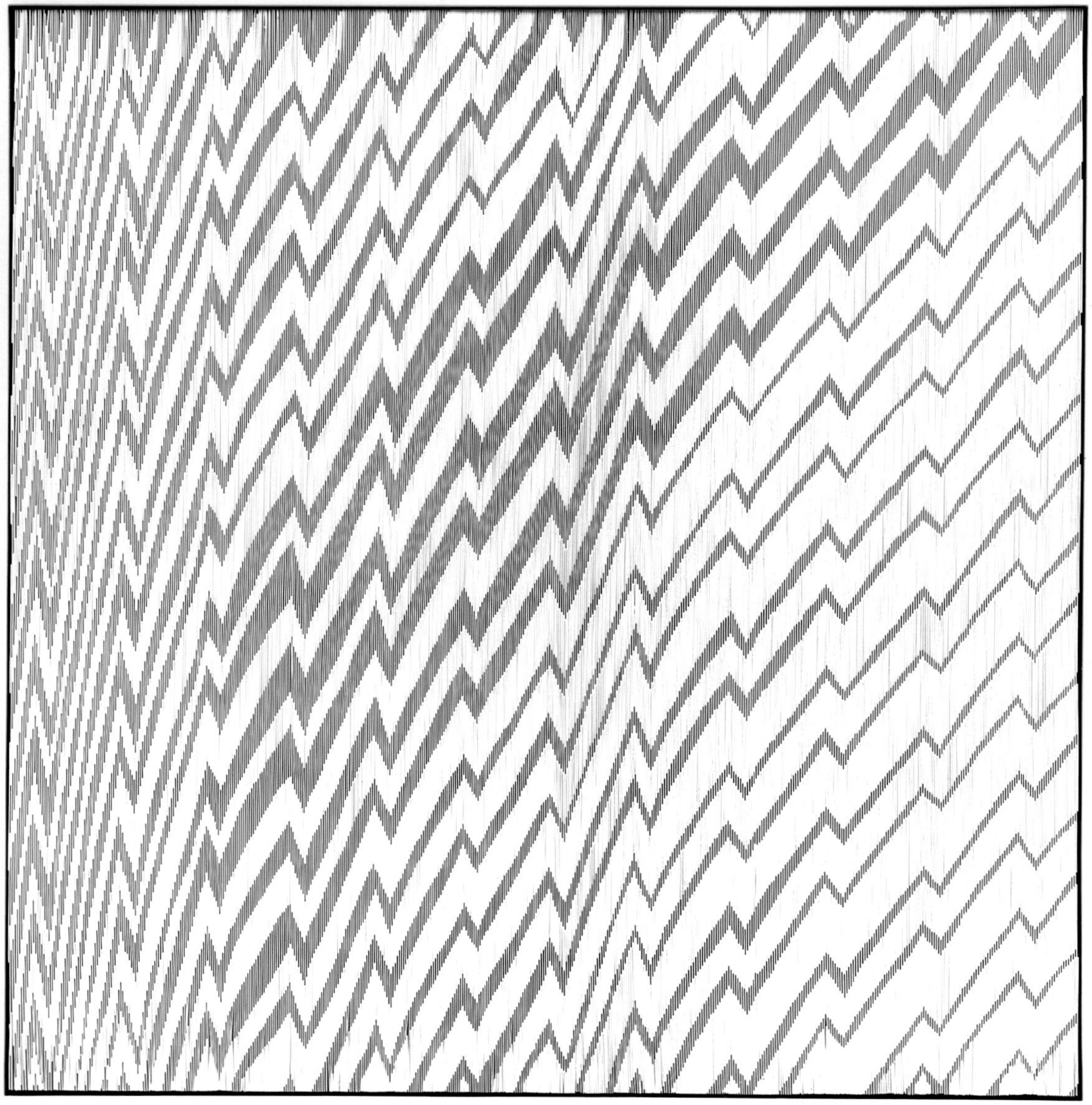

 COMPOSITION (CARDS) 2017 22 ¼ x 22 ¼ x 4" | 56.5 x 56.5 x 10.2 cm

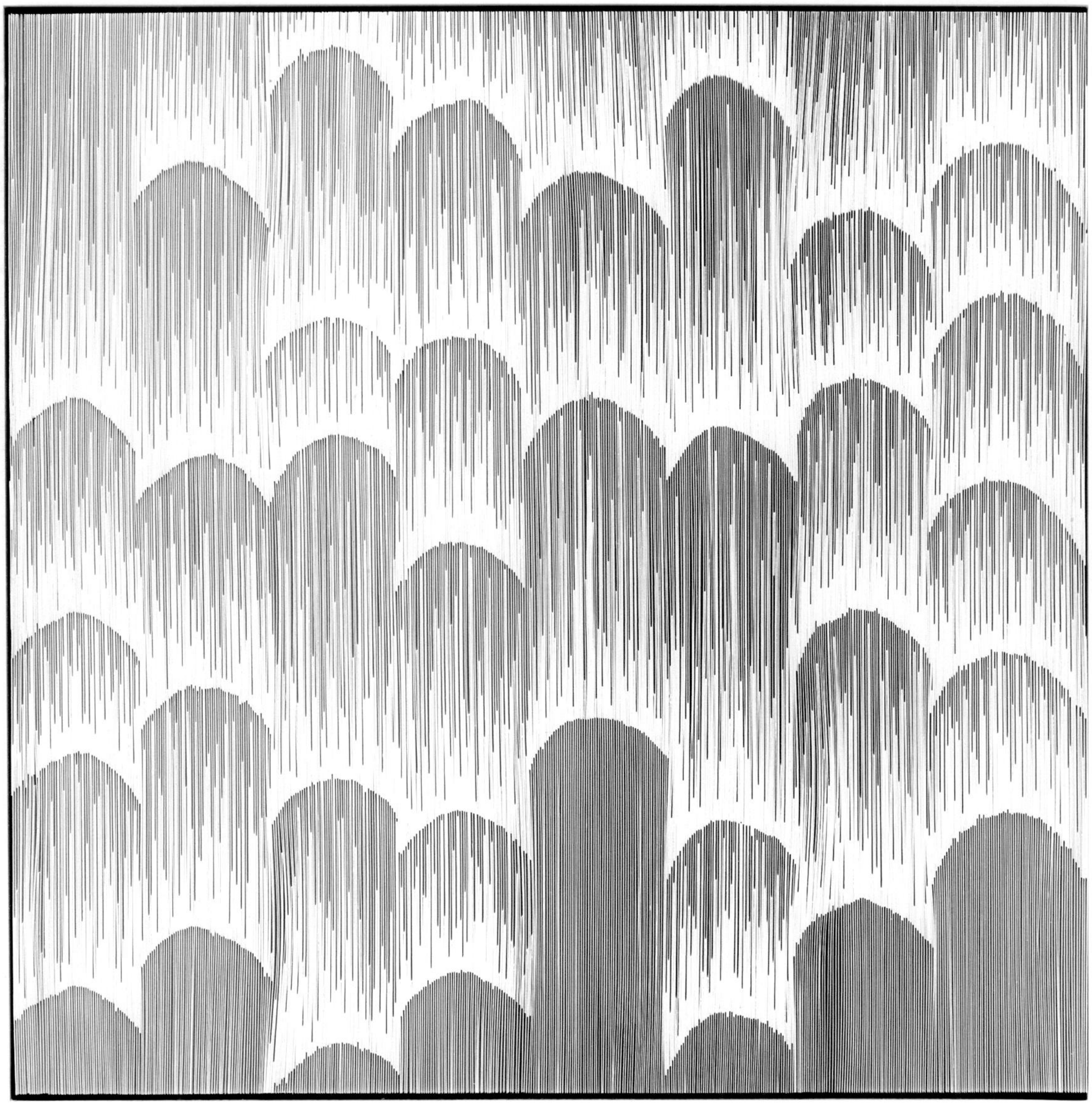

COMPOSITION (CARDS) 2017 22 ¼ x 22 ¼ x 4" | 56.5 x 56.5 x 10.2 cm

COMPOSITION (CARDS) 2017 39 ¼ x 39 ¼ x 4" | 99.7 x 99.7 x 10.2 cm

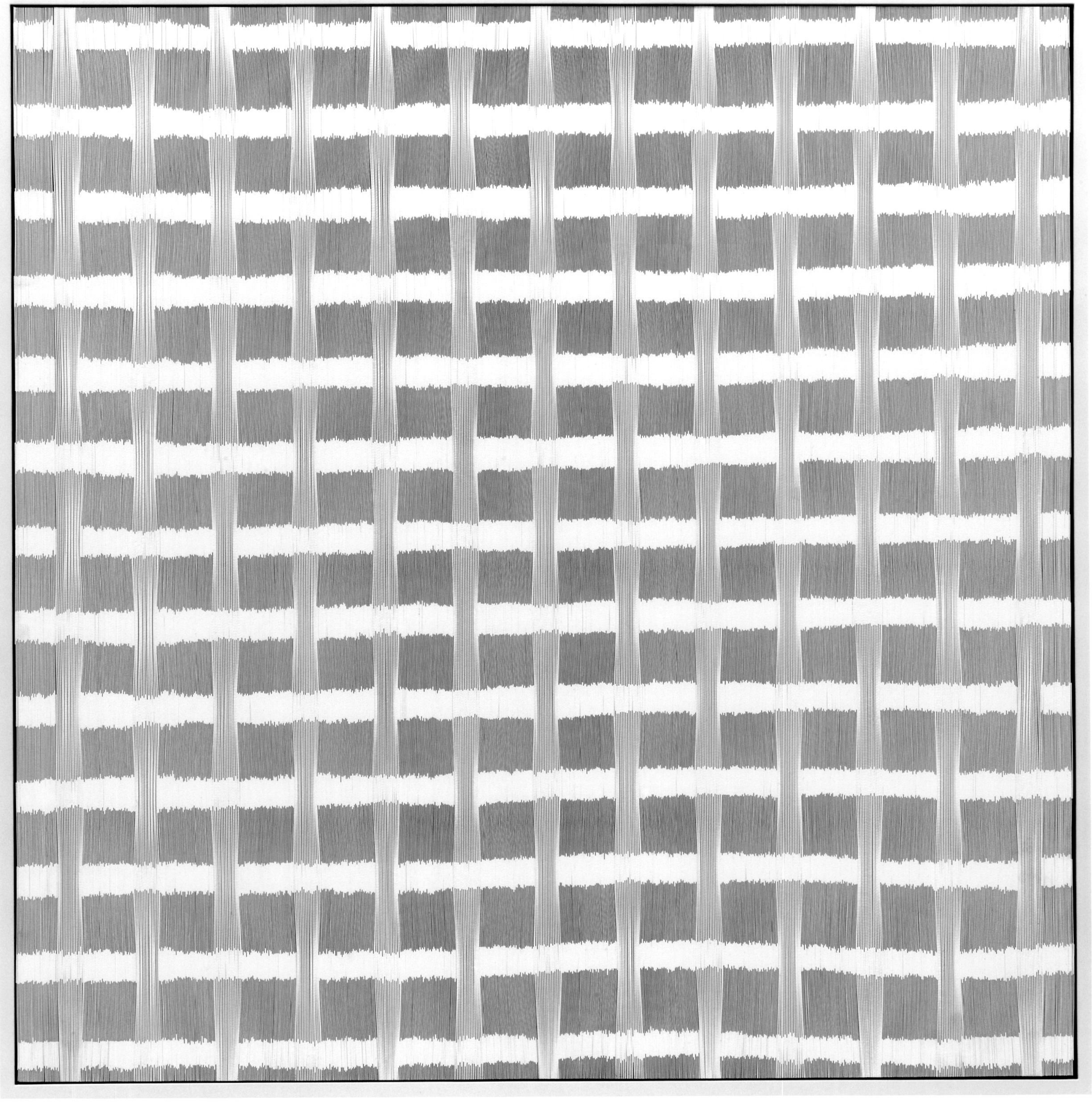

COMPOSITION (CARDS) 2017 39 ¼ x 39 ¼ x 4" | 99.7 x 99.7 x 10.2 cm

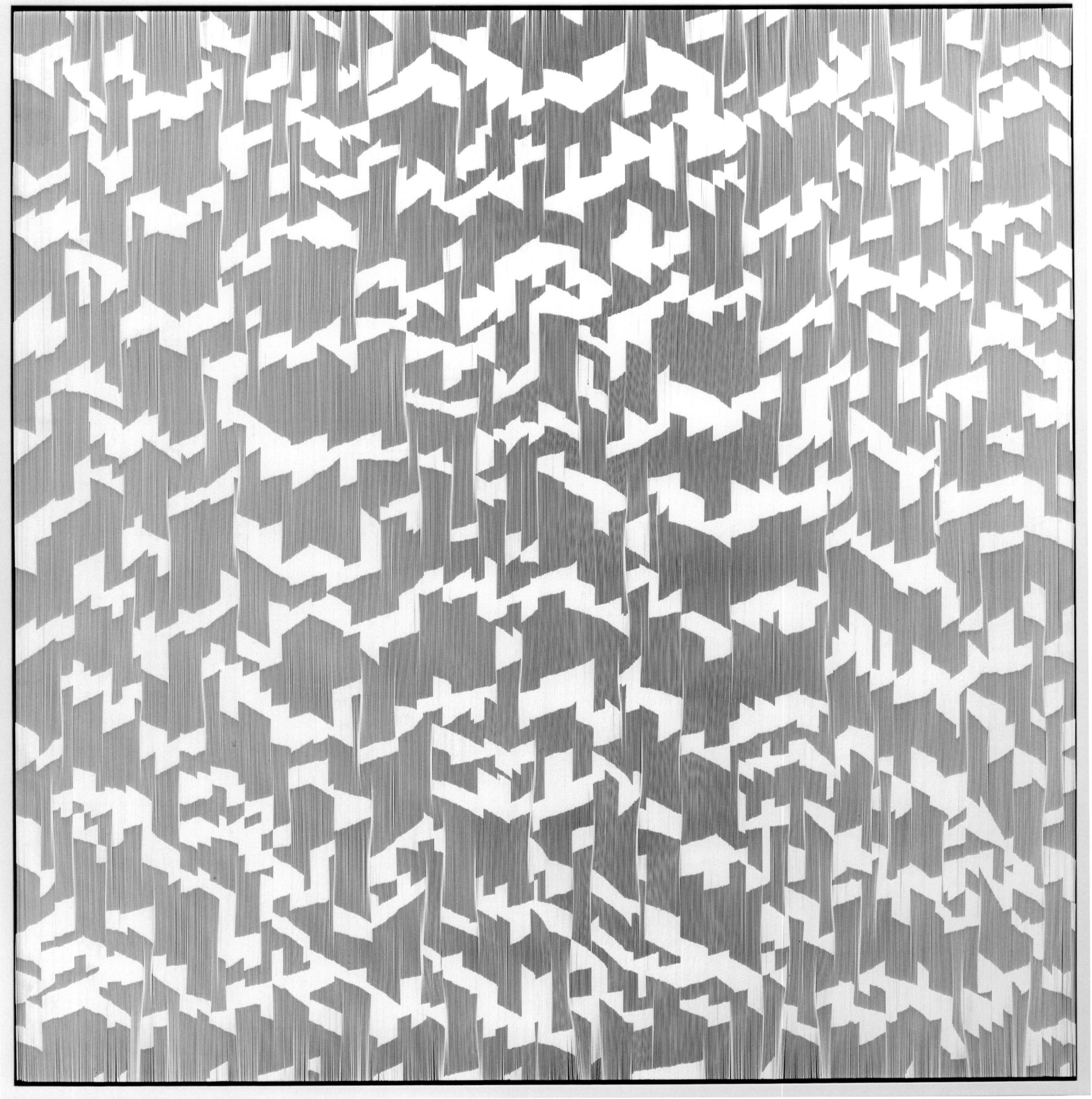

COMPOSITION (CARDS) 2017 39 ¼ x 39 ¼ x 4" | 99.7 x 99.7 x 10.2 cm

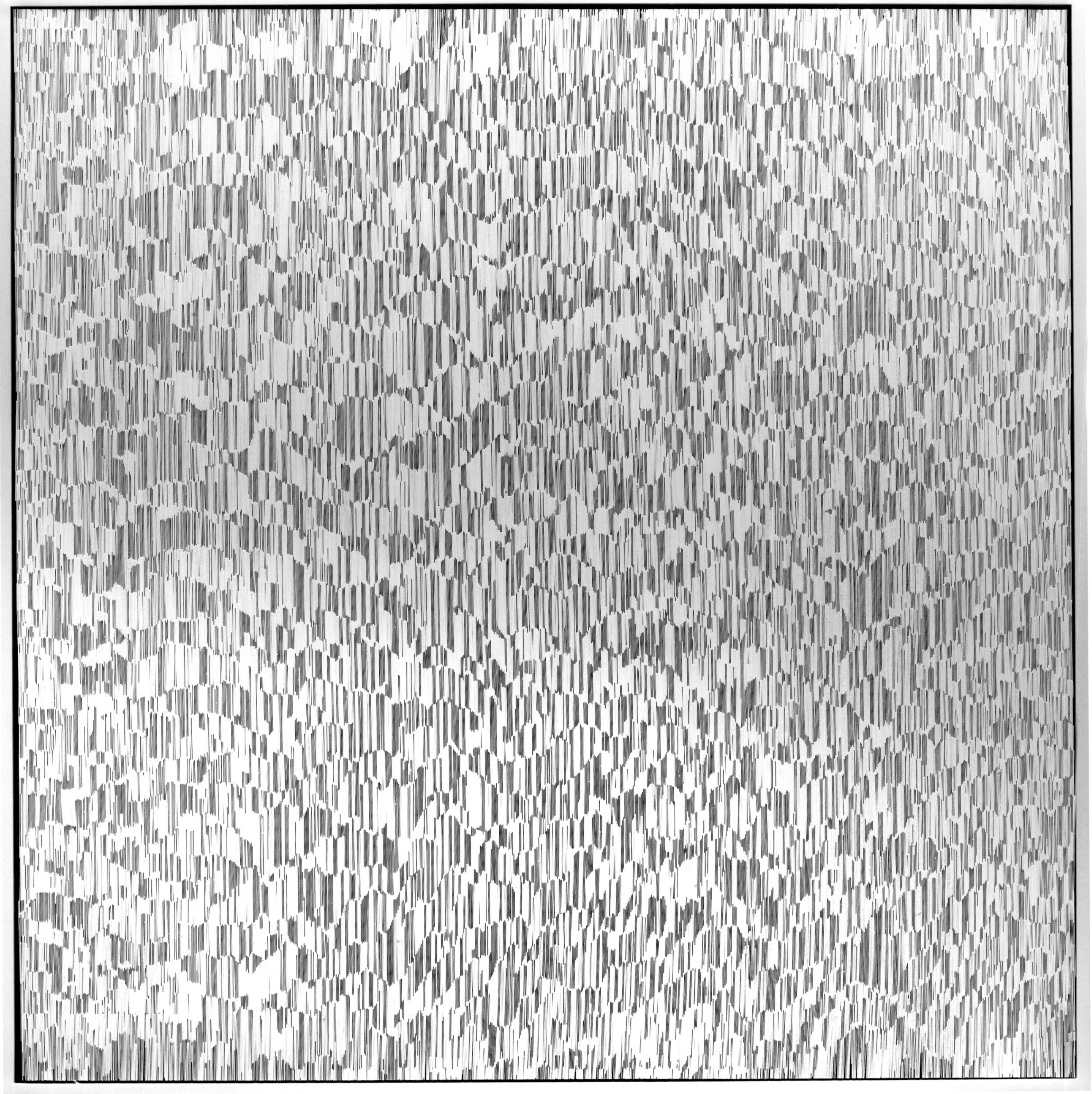

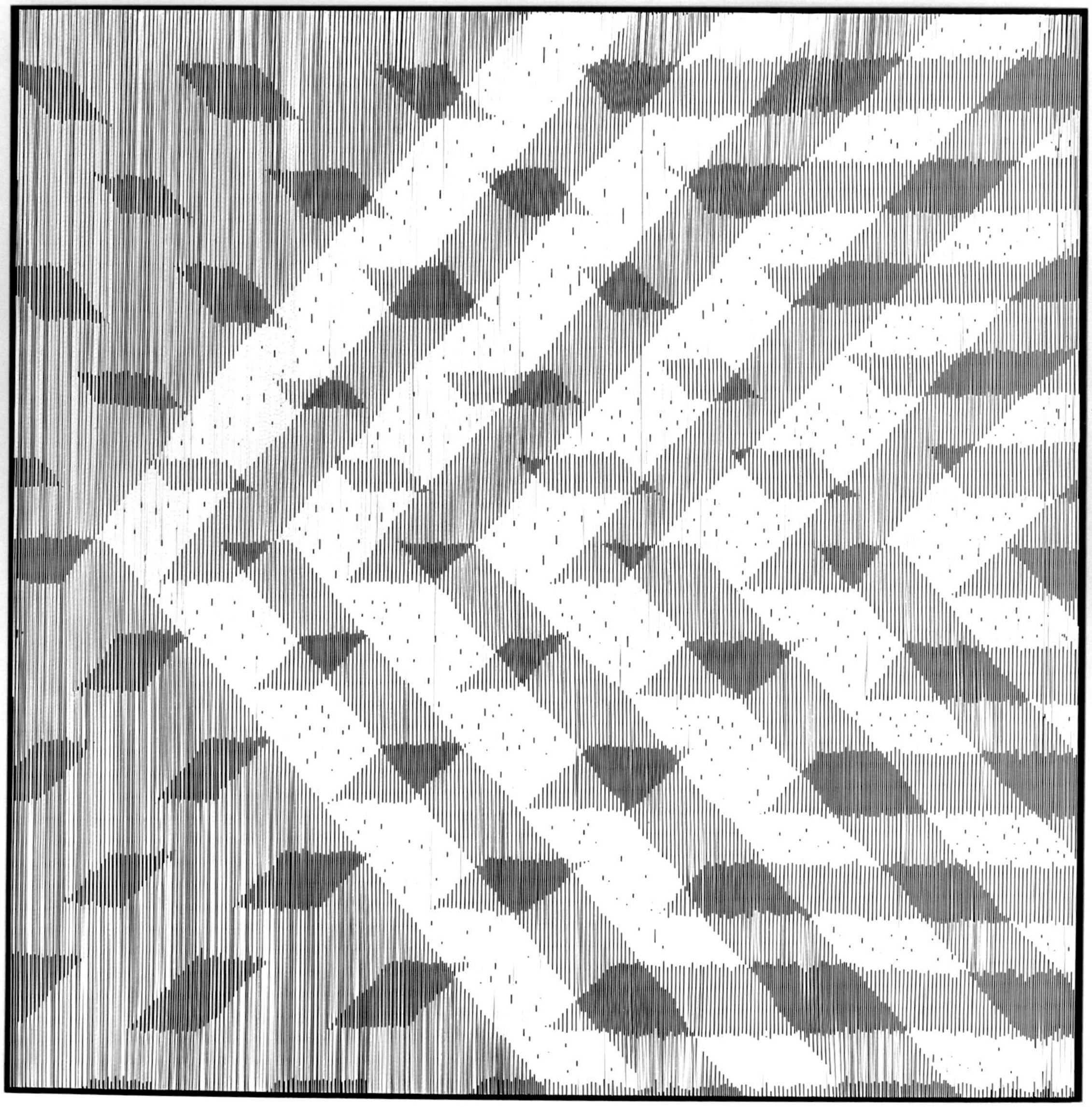

COMPOSITION (CARDS) 2017 22 ¼ x 22 ¼ x 4" | 56.5 x 56.5 x 10.2 cm

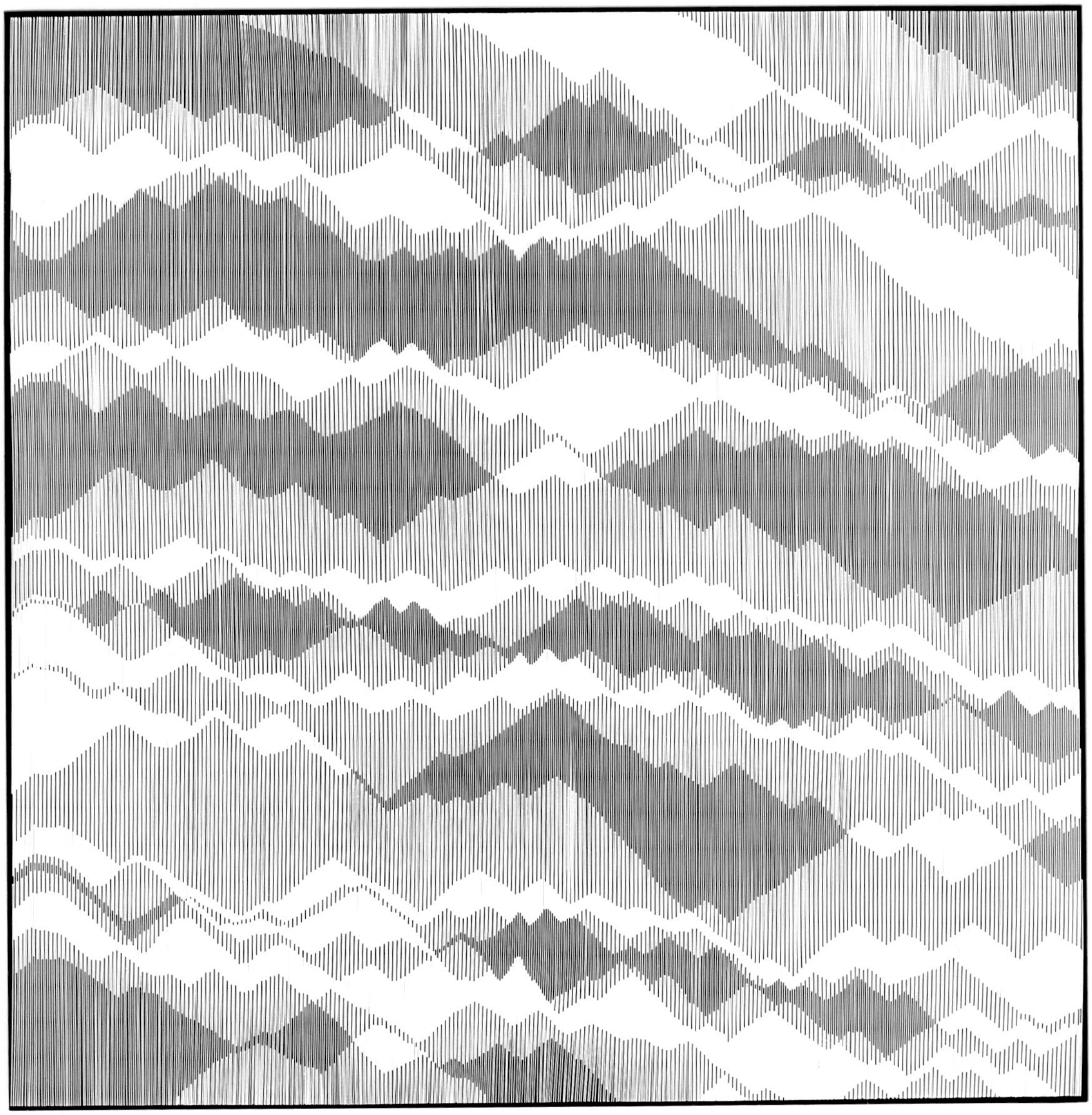

COMPOSITION (CARDS) 2017 22 ¼ x 22 ¼ x 4" | 56.5 x 56.5 x 10.2 cm

COMPOSITION (CARDS) 2017 39 ¼ x 39 ¼ x 4" | 99.7 x 99.7 x 10.2 cm

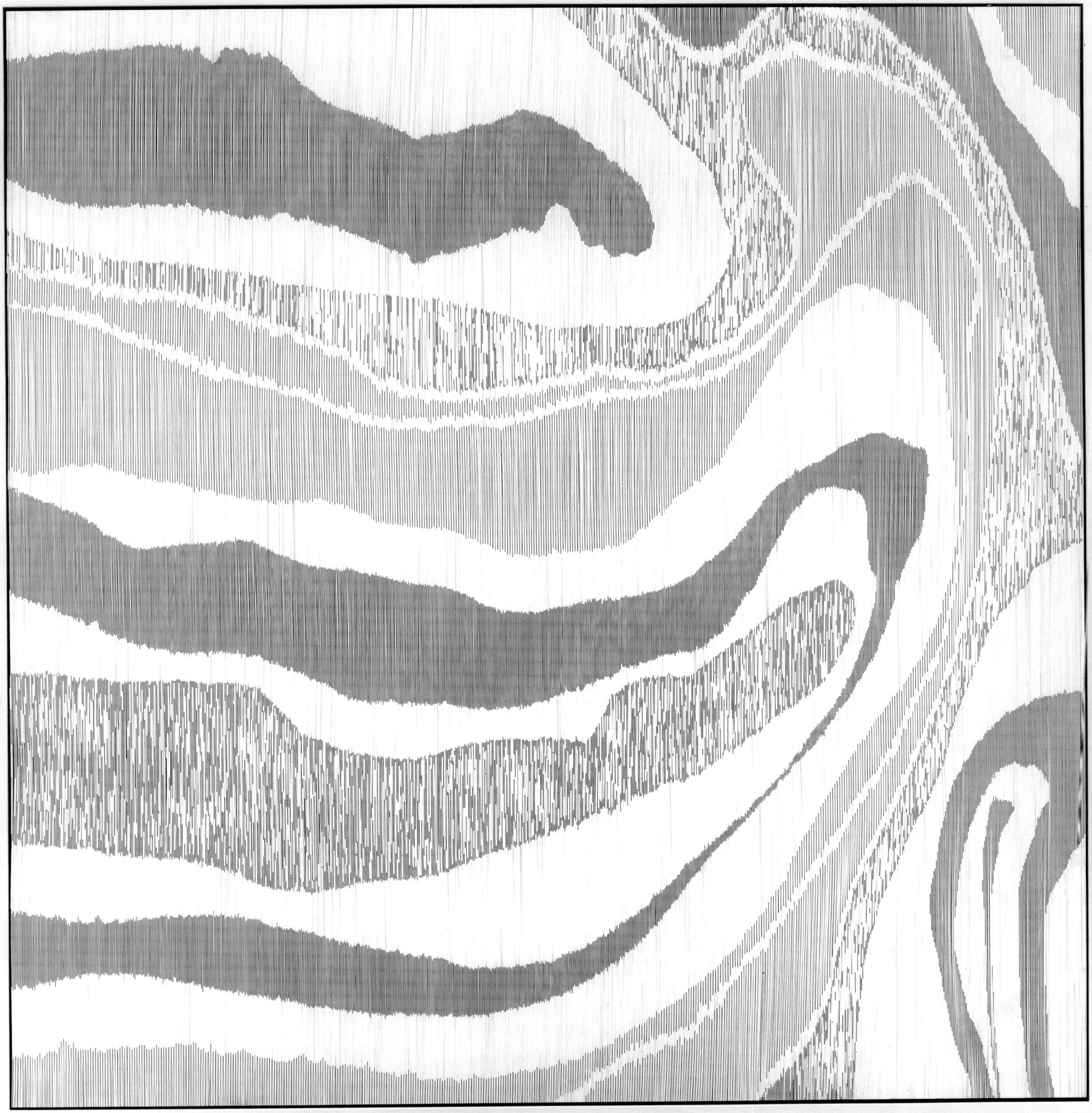

COMPOSITION (CARDS) 2017 36 ¼ x 36 ¼ x 4" | 92.1 x 92.1 x 10.2 cm

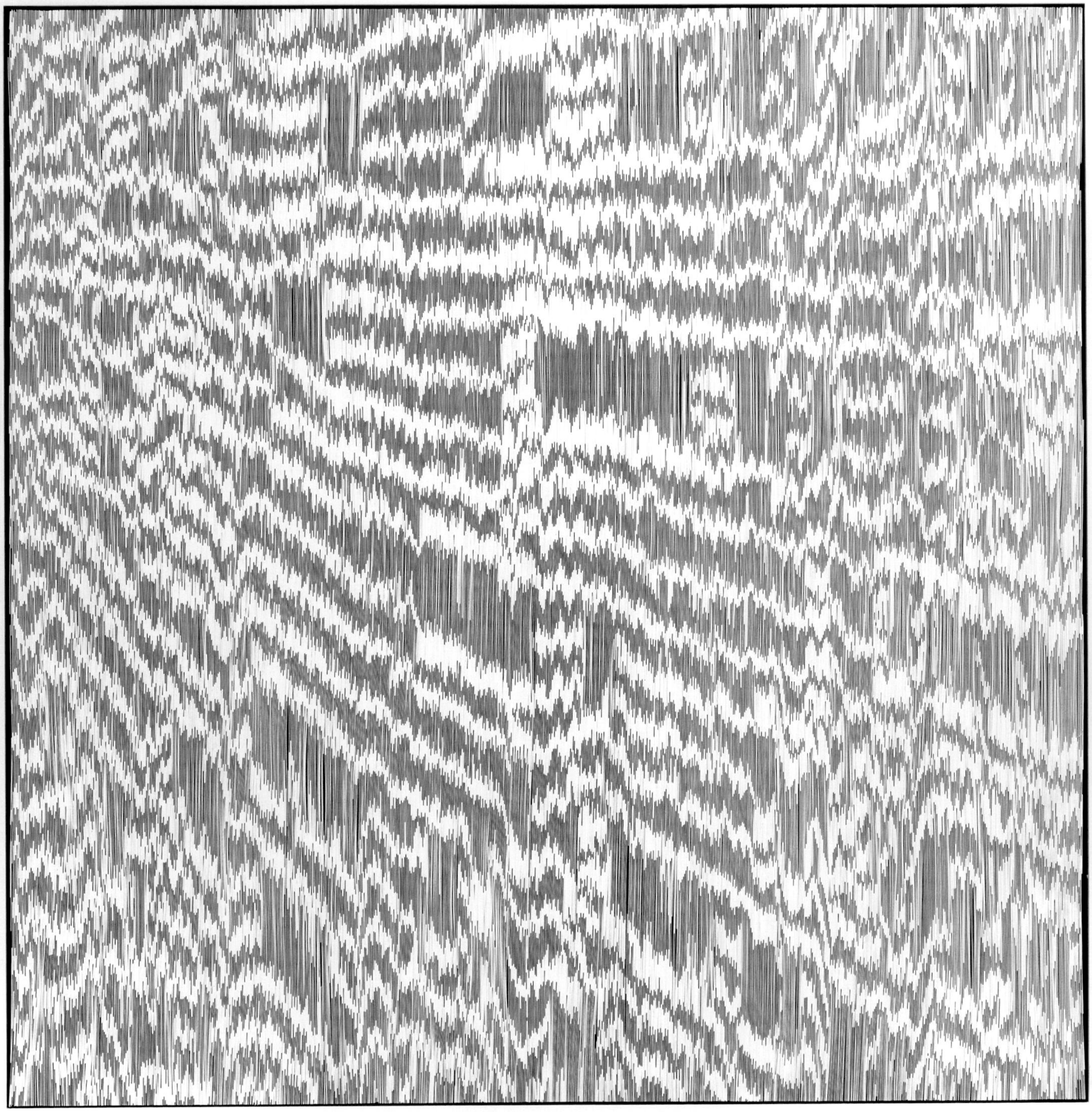

COMPOSITION (CARDS) 2017   39 ¼ x 39 ¼ x 4" | 99.7 x 99.7 x 10.2 cm

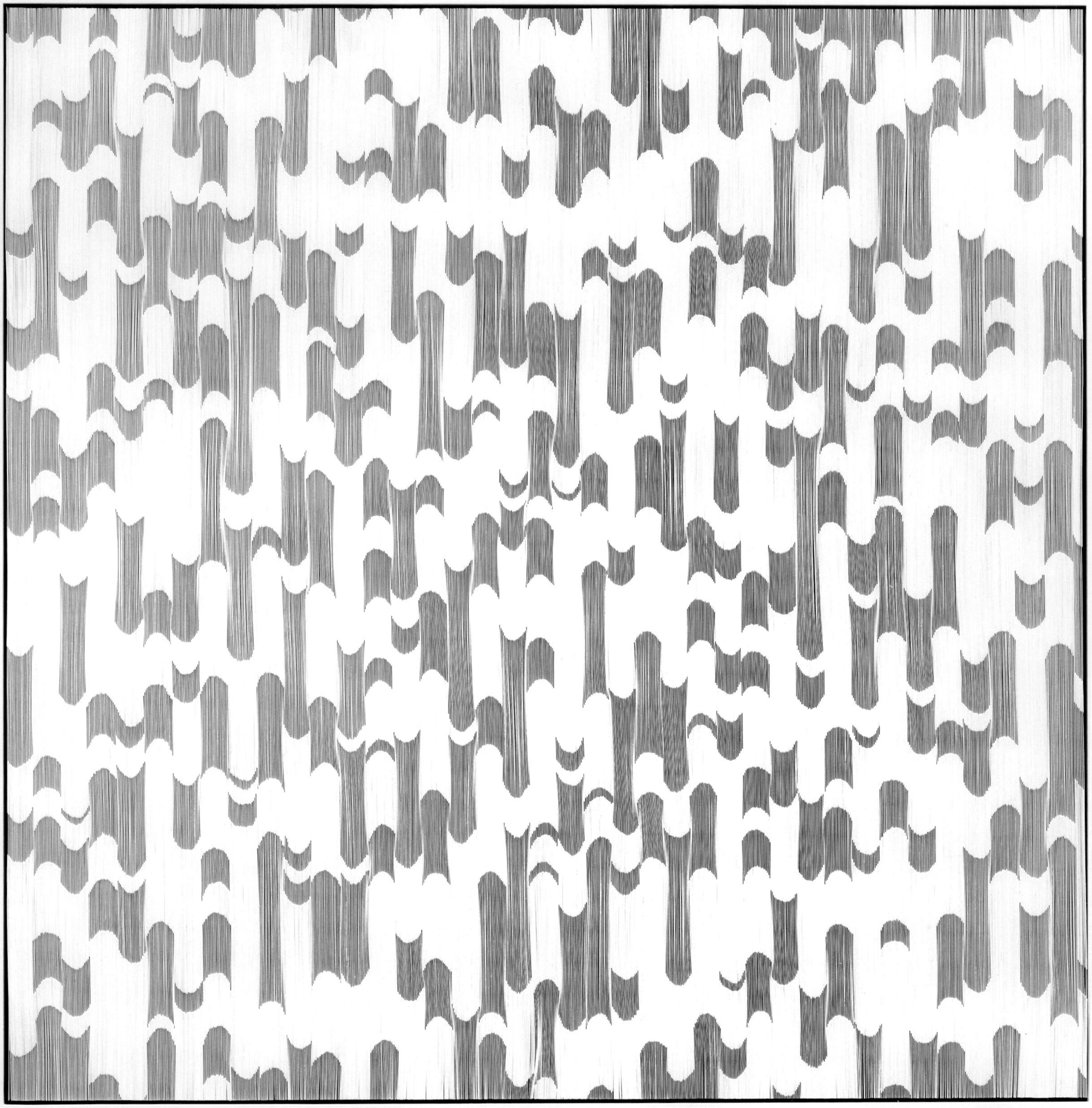

COMPOSITION (CARDS) 2017 39 ¼ x 39 ¼ x 4" | 99.7 x 99.7 x 10.2 cm

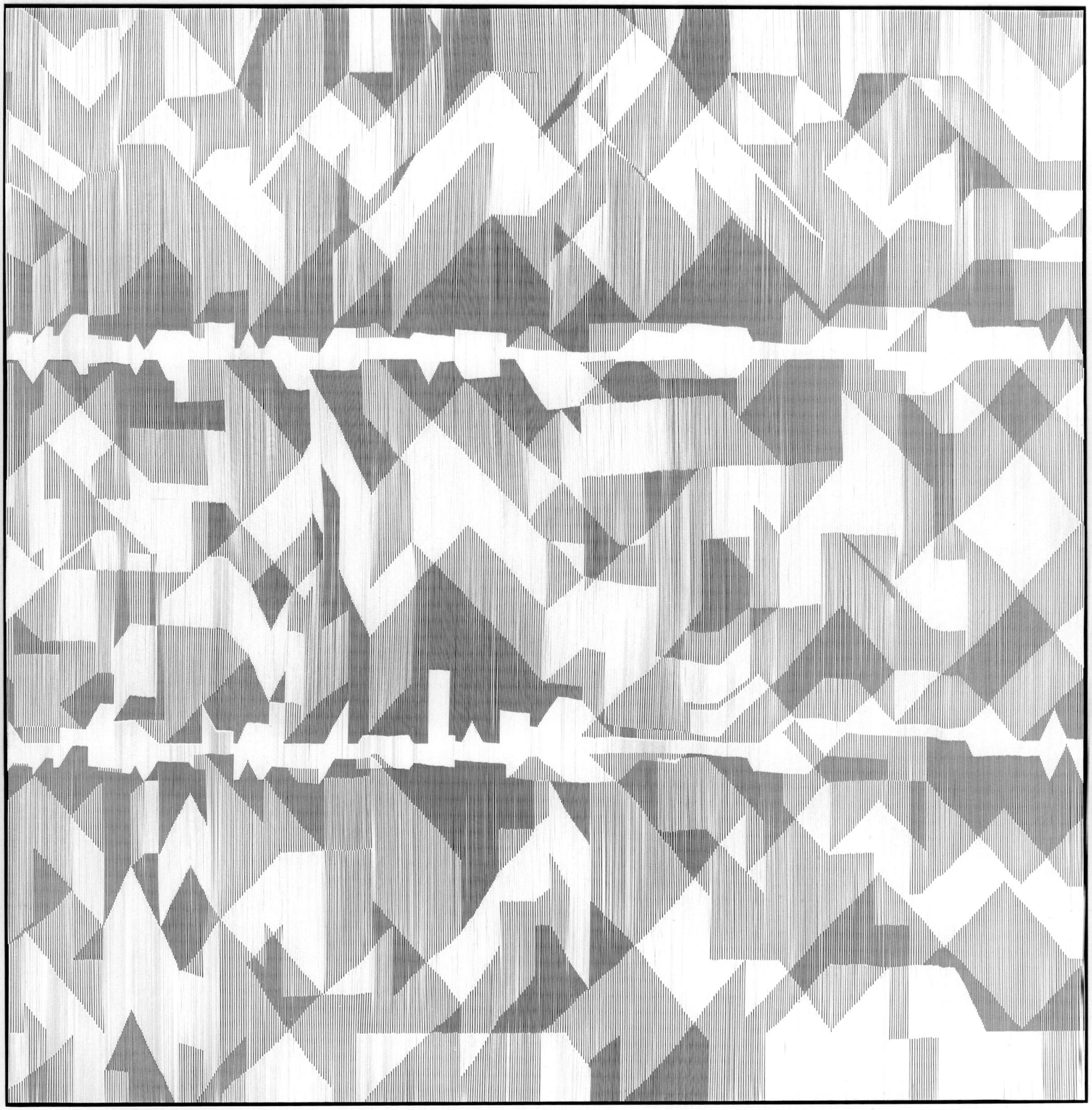

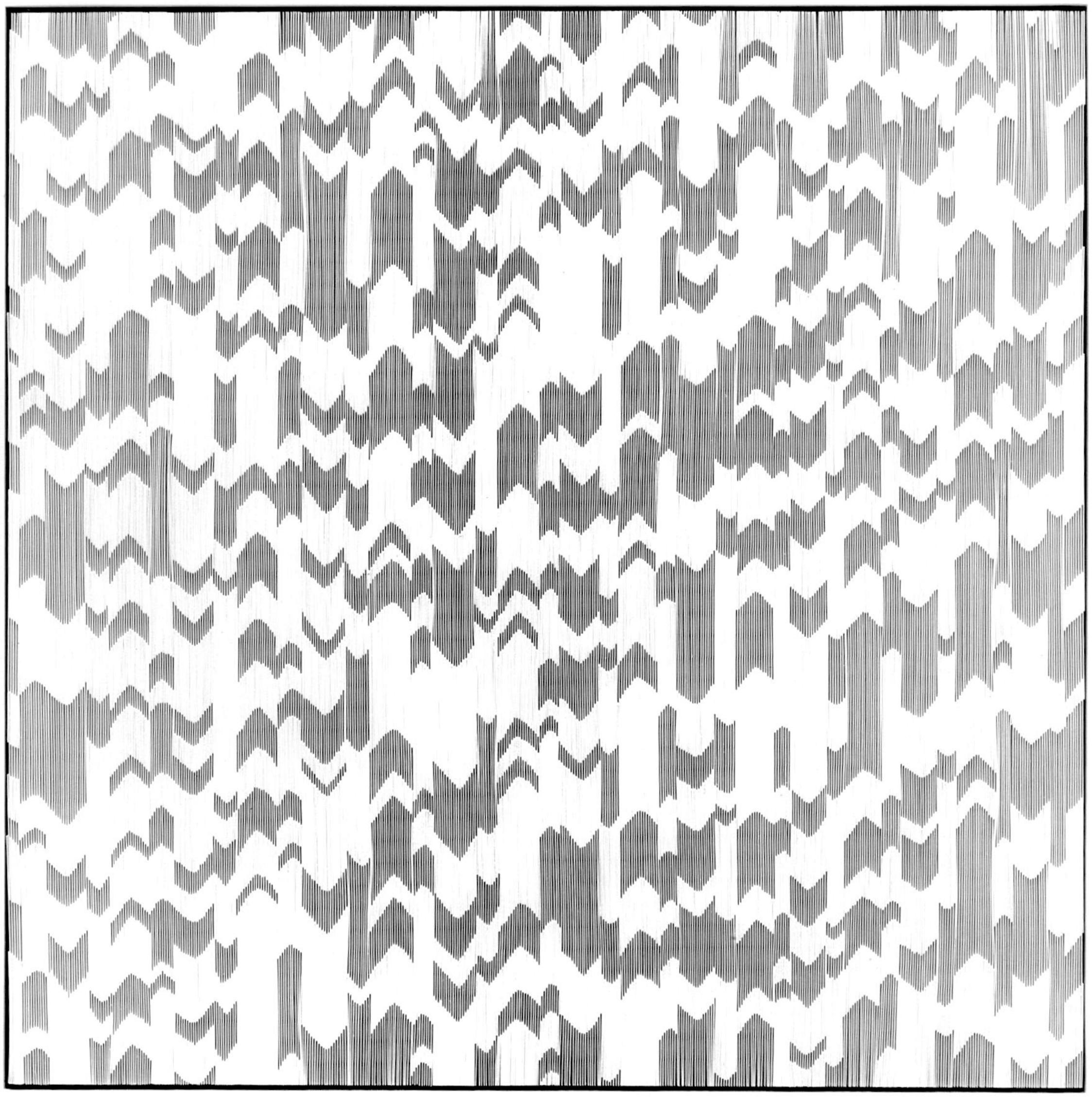

COMPOSITION (CARDS) 2017 22 ¼ x 22 ¼ x 4" | 56.5 x 56.5 x 10.2 cm

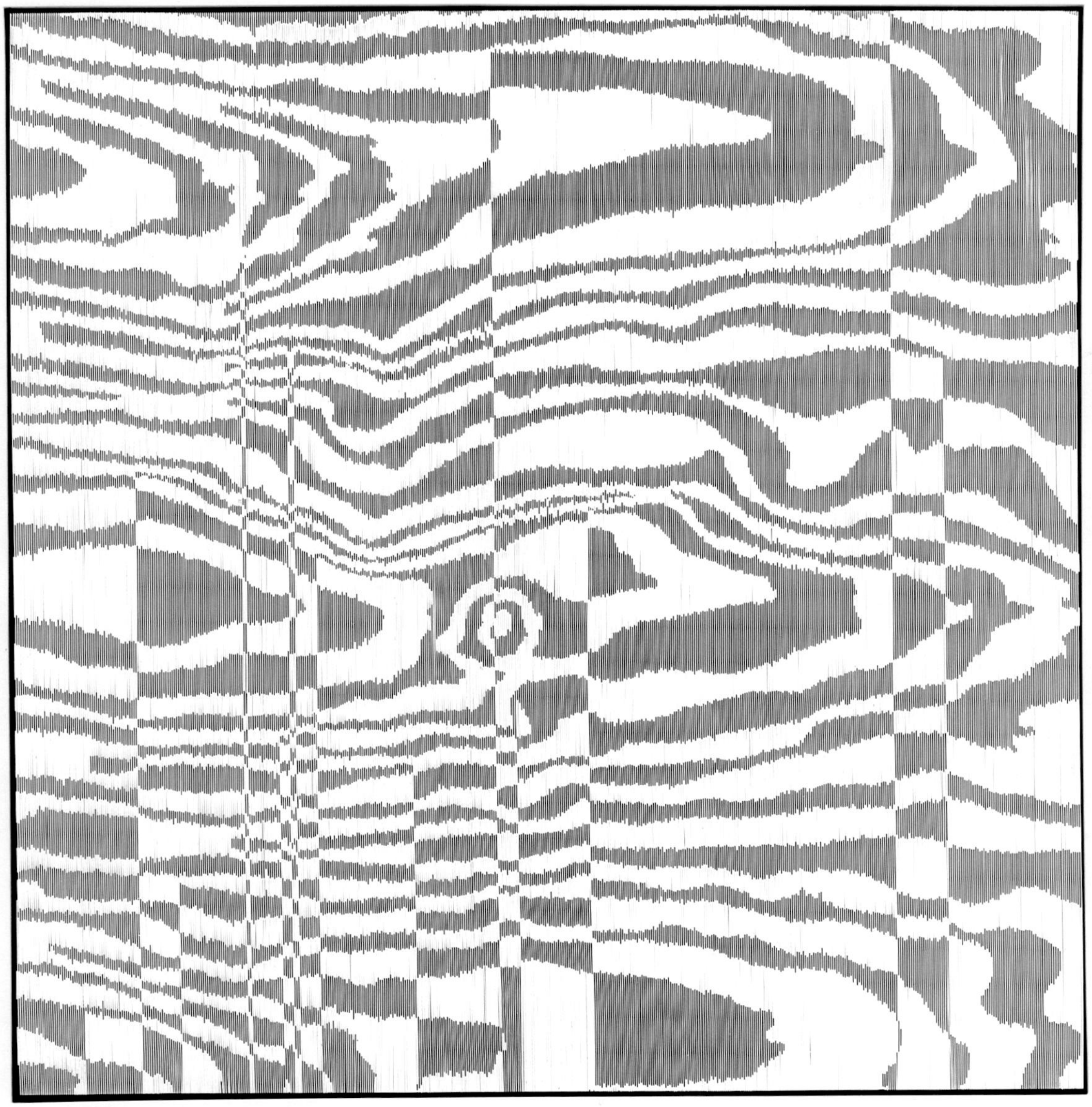

COMPOSITION (CARDS) 2017 22 ¼ x 22 ¼ x 4" | 56.5 x 56.5 x 10.2 cm

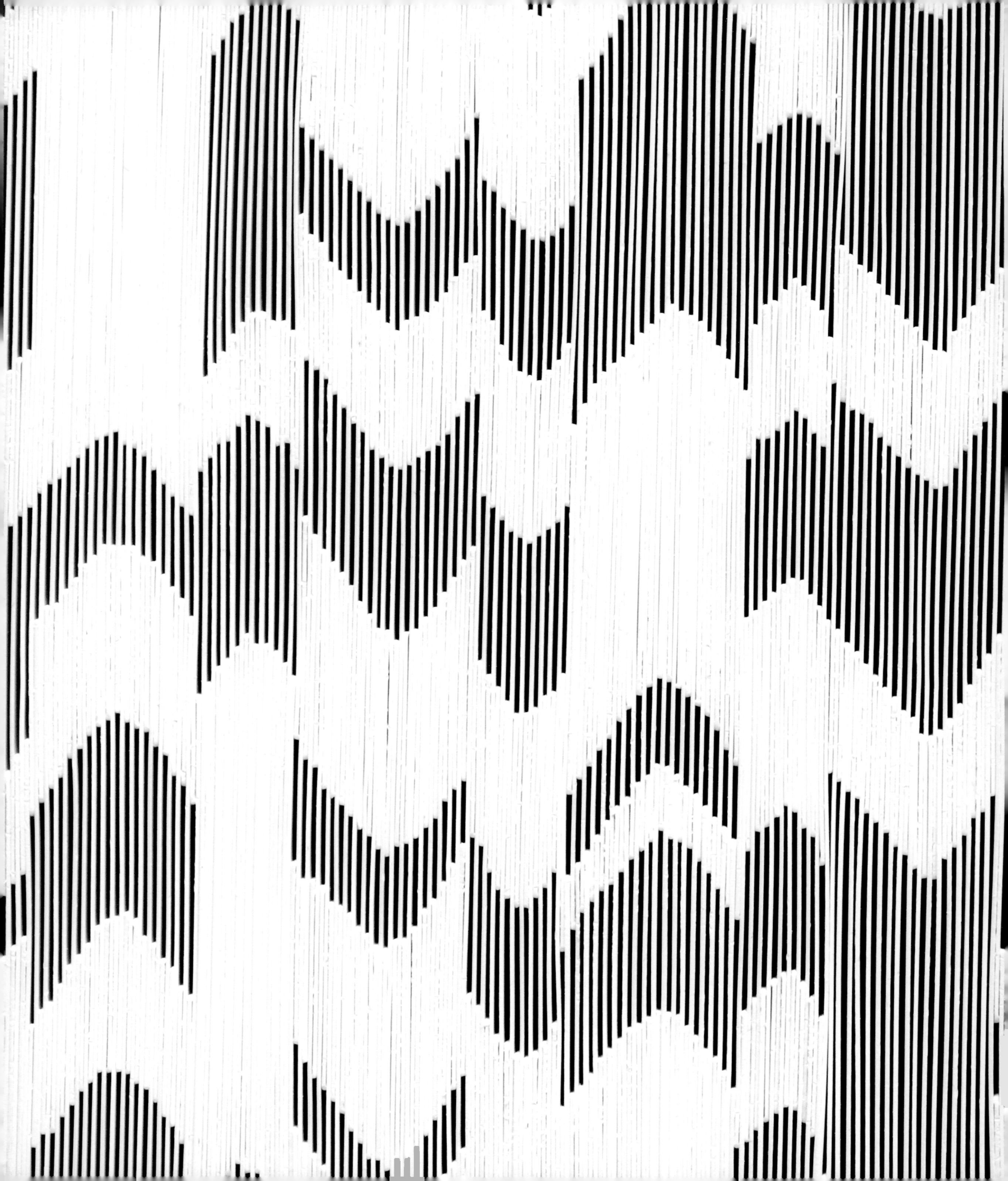

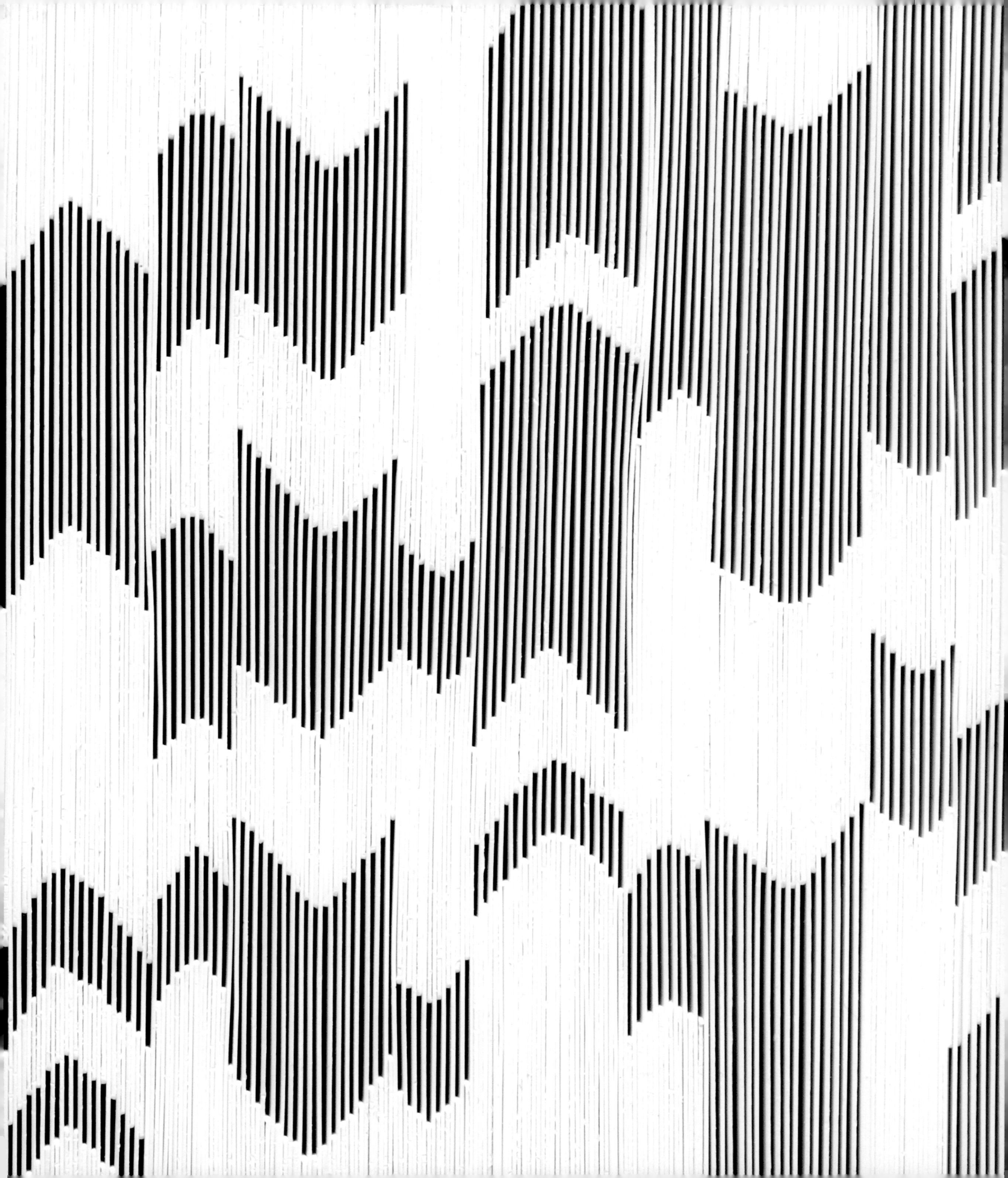

16 COMPOSITION (CARDS) 2017
styrene cards and glue
39 ¼ x 39 ¼ x 4" | 99.7 x 99.7 x 10.2 cm

18 COMPOSITION (CARDS) 2017
styrene cards and glue
39 ¼ x 39 ¼ x 4" | 99.7 x 99.7 x 10.2 cm

20 COMPOSITION (CARDS) 2017
styrene cards and glue
39 ¼ x 39 ¼ x 4" | 99.7 x 99.7 x 10.2 cm
Private collection

22 COMPOSITION (CARDS) 2017
styrene cards and glue
39 ¼ x 39 ¼ x 4" | 99.7 x 99.7 x 10.2 cm
Private collection

24 COMPOSITION (CARDS) 2017
styrene cards and glue
22 ¼ x 22 ¼ x 4" | 56.5 x 56.5 x 10.2 cm

25 COMPOSITION (CARDS) 2017
styrene cards and glue
22 ¼ x 22 ¼ x 4" | 56.5 x 56.5 x 10.2 cm

26 COMPOSITION (CARDS) 2017
styrene cards and glue
22 ¼ x 22 ¼ x 4" | 56.5 x 56.5 x 10.2 cm

27 COMPOSITION (CARDS) 2017
styrene cards and glue
22 ¼ x 22 ¼ x 4" | 56.5 x 56.5 x 10.2 cm

28 COMPOSITION (CARDS) 2017
styrene cards and glue
39 ¼ x 39 ¼ x 4" | 99.7 x 99.7 x 10.2 cm
Collection of Peter Marino

32 COMPOSITION (CARDS) 2017
styrene cards and glue
39 ¼ x 39 ¼ x 4" | 99.7 x 99.7 x 10.2 cm
Private collection

34 COMPOSITION (CARDS) 2017
styrene cards and glue
22 ¼ x 22 ¼ x 4" | 56.5 x 56.5 x 10.2 cm
Collection of Jack and Joy

35 COMPOSITION (CARDS) 2017
styrene cards and glue
22 ¼ x 22 ¼ x 4" | 56.5 x 56.5 x 10.2 cm

36 COMPOSITION (CARDS) 2017
styrene cards and glue
22 ¼ x 22 ¼ x 4" | 56.5 x 56.5 x 10.2 cm

37 COMPOSITION (CARDS) 2017
styrene cards and glue
22 ¼ x 22 ¼ x 4" | 56.5 x 56.5 x 10.2 cm

38 COMPOSITION (CARDS) 2017
styrene cards and glue
39 ¼ x 39 ¼ x 4" | 99.7 x 99.7 x 10.2 cm

40 COMPOSITION (CARDS) 2017
styrene cards and glue
39 ¼ x 39 ¼ x 4" | 99.7 x 99.7 x 10.2 cm

42 COMPOSITION (CARDS) 2017
styrene cards and glue
39 ¼ x 39 ¼ x 4" | 99.7 x 99.7 x 10.2 cm

46 COMPOSITION (CARDS) 2016
styrene cards and glue
39 ¼ x 39 ¼ x 4" | 99.7 x 99.7 x 10.2 cm
Private collection

48 COMPOSITION (CARDS) 2017
styrene cards and glue
39 ¼ x 39 ¼ x 4" | 99.7 x 99.7 x 10.2 cm
Private collection

50 COMPOSITION (CARDS) 2017
styrene cards and glue
22 ¼ x 22 ¼ x 4" | 56.5 x 56.5 x 10.2 cm

51 COMPOSITION (CARDS) 2017
styrene cards and glue
22 ¼ x 22 ¼ x 4" | 56.5 x 56.5 x 10.2 cm
Private collection

52 COMPOSITION (CARDS) 2017
styrene cards and glue
39 ¼ x 39 ¼ x 4" | 99.7 x 99.7 x 10.2 cm
Collection of GoldenTree Asset Management

54 COMPOSITION (CARDS) 2017
styrene cards and glue
39 ¼ x 39 ¼ x 4" | 99.7 x 99.7 x 10.2 cm

56 COMPOSITION (CARDS) 2017
styrene cards and glue
39 ¼ x 39 ¼ x 4" | 99.7 x 99.7 x 10.2 cm
Collection of Glori Cohen

58 COMPOSITION (CARDS) 2017
styrene cards and glue
22 ¼ x 22 ¼ x 4" | 56.5 x 56.5 x 10.2 cm
Collection of Pan Family

59 COMPOSITION (CARDS) 2017
styrene cards and glue
22 ¼ x 22 ¼ x 4" | 56.5 x 56.5 x 10.2 cm

60 COMPOSITION (CARDS) 2017
styrene cards and glue
22 ¼ x 22 ¼ x 4" | 56.5 x 56.5 x 10.2 cm

62 COMPOSITION (CARDS) 2017
styrene cards and glue
39 ¼ x 39 ¼ x 4" | 99.7 x 99.7 x 10.2 cm
Collection of Harris C. Mehos

64 COMPOSITION (CARDS) 2017
styrene cards and glue
39 ¼ x 39 ¼ x 4" | 99.7 x 99.7 x 10.2 cm

66 COMPOSITION (CARDS) 2016
styrene cards and glue
39 ¼ x 39 ¼ x 4" | 99.7 x 99.7 x 10.2 cm
Collection of Patrick and Kirsten McMahon

68 COMPOSITION (CARDS) 2017
styrene cards and glue
39 ¼ x 39 ¼ x 4" | 99.7 x 99.7 x 10.2 cm

72 COMPOSITION (CARDS) 2017
styrene cards and glue
39 ¼ x 39 ¼ x 4" | 99.7 x 99.7 x 10.2 cm

74 COMPOSITION (CARDS) 2017
styrene cards and glue
39 ¼ x 39 ¼ x 4" | 99.7 x 99.7 x 10.2 cm

76 COMPOSITION (CARDS) 2017
styrene cards and glue
22 ¼ x 22 ¼ x 4" | 56.5 x 56.5 x 10.2 cm

77 COMPOSITION (CARDS) 2017
styrene cards and glue
22 ¼ x 22 ¼ x 4" | 56.5 x 56.5 x 10.2 cm

79 COMPOSITION (CARDS) 2017
styrene cards and glue
22 ¼ x 22 ¼ x 4" | 56.5 x 56.5 x 10.2 cm

80 COMPOSITION (CARDS) 2017
styrene cards and glue
39 ¼ x 39 ¼ x 4" | 99.7 x 99.7 x 10.2 cm

82 COMPOSITION (CARDS) 2017
styrene cards and glue
39 ¼ x 39 ¼ x 4" | 99.7 x 99.7 x 10.2 cm
Private collection

84 COMPOSITION (CARDS) 2017
styrene cards and glue
45 ¼" x 9' 5 ¼" x 4" | 114.9 x 287.7 x 10.2 cm
Private collection

86 COMPOSITION (CARDS) 2017
styrene cards and glue
39 ¼ x 39 ¼ x 4" | 99.7 x 99.7 x 10.2 cm
Collection of Nanci and Gary Fredkin

88 COMPOSITION (CARDS) 2017
styrene cards and glue
36 ¼ x 36 ¼ x 4" | 92.1 x 92.1 x 10.2 cm

90 COMPOSITION (CARDS) 2017
styrene cards and glue
39 ¼ x 39 ¼ x 4" | 99.7 x 99.7 x 10.2 cm
Private collection

94 COMPOSITION (CARDS) 2017
styrene cards and glue
39 ¼ x 39 ¼ x 4" | 99.7 x 99.7 x 10.2 cm

97 COMPOSITION (CARDS) 2017
styrene cards and glue
22 ¼ x 22 ¼ x 4" | 56.5 x 56.5 x 10.2 cm

98 COMPOSITION (CARDS) 2017
styrene cards and glue
22 ¼ x 22 ¼ x 4" | 56.5 x 56.5 x 10.2 cm
Collection of Jack and Joy

99 COMPOSITION (CARDS) 2017
styrene cards and glue
22 ¼ x 22 ¼ x 4" | 56.5 x 56.5 x 10.2 cm
Private collection

100 COMPOSITION (CARDS) 2017
styrene cards and glue
39 ¼ x 39 ¼ x 4" | 99.7 x 99.7 x 10.2 cm

102 COMPOSITION (CARDS) 2017
styrene cards and glue
39 ¼ x 39 ¼ x 4" | 99.7 x 99.7 x 10.2 cm

105 COMPOSITION (CARDS) 2017
styrene cards and glue
36 ¼ x 36 ¼ x 4" | 92.1 x 92.1 x 10.2 cm
Collection of Dr. Jeffrey and Mrs. Mary Ellen Jay

106 COMPOSITION (CARDS) 2017
styrene cards and glue
39 ¼ x 39 ¼ x 4" | 99.7 x 99.7 x 10.2 cm
Private collection

108 COMPOSITION (CARDS) 2017
styrene cards and glue
39 ¼ x 39 ¼ x 4" | 99.7 x 99.7 x 10.2 cm
Collection of Ann and Paul Chen

110 COMPOSITION (CARDS) 2017
styrene cards and glue
39 ¼ x 39 ¼ x 4" | 99.7 x 99.7 x 10.2 cm

113 COMPOSITION (CARDS) 2017
styrene cards and glue
22 ¼ x 22 ¼ x 4" | 56.5 x 56.5 x 10.2 cm

114 COMPOSITION (CARDS) 2017
styrene cards and glue
22 ¼ x 22 ¼ x 4" | 56.5 x 56.5 x 10.2 cm
Collection of Nicole D. Liarakos

115 COMPOSITION (CARDS) 2017
styrene cards and glue
22 ¼ x 22 ¼ x 4" | 56.5 x 56.5 x 10.2 cm

116 COMPOSITION (CARDS) 2017
styrene cards and glue
39 ¼ x 39 ¼ x 4" | 99.7 x 99.7 x 10.2 cm

118 COMPOSITION (CARDS) 2017
styrene cards and glue
39 ¼ x 39 ¼ x 4" | 99.7 x 99.7 x 10.2 cm

122 COMPOSITION (CARDS) 2017
styrene cards and glue
36 ¼ x 36 ¼ x 4" | 92.1 x 92.1 x 10.2 cm
Private collection

124 COMPOSITION (CARDS) 2017
styrene cards and glue
39 ¼ x 39 ¼ x 4" | 99.7 x 99.7 x 10.2 cm

126 COMPOSITION (CARDS) 2017
styrene cards and glue
39 ¼ x 39 ¼ x 4" | 99.7 x 99.7 x 10.2 cm
Collection of Thomas and Aline Shapiro

130 COMPOSITION (CARDS) 2017
styrene cards and glue
39 ¼ x 39 ¼ x 4" | 99.7 x 99.7 x 10.2 cm

132 COMPOSITION (CARDS) 2017
styrene cards and glue
39 ¼ x 39 ¼ x 4" | 99.7 x 99.7 x 10.2 cm

134 COMPOSITION (CARDS) 2017
styrene cards and glue
22 ¼ x 22 ¼ x 4" | 56.5 x 56.5 x 10.2 cm

135 COMPOSITION (CARDS) 2017
styrene cards and glue
22 ¼ x 22 ¼ x 4" | 56.5 x 56.5 x 10.2 cm
Collection of Randi Weiss

136 COMPOSITION (CARDS) 2017
styrene cards and glue
39 ¼ x 39 ¼ x 4" | 99.7 x 99.7 x 10.2 cm
Collection of Ann and Paul Chen

138 COMPOSITION (CARDS) 2017
styrene cards and glue
39 ¼ x 39 ¼ x 4" | 99.7 x 99.7 x 10.2 cm

140 COMPOSITION (CARDS) 2017
styrene cards and glue
39 ¼ x 39 ¼ x 4" | 99.7 x 99.7 x 10.2 cm

143 COMPOSITION (CARDS) 2017
styrene cards and glue
22 ¼ x 22 ¼ x 4" | 56.5 x 56.5 x 10.2 cm
Private collection, courtesy of Pettit Art Partners

144 COMPOSITION (CARDS) 2017
styrene cards and glue
22 ¼ x 22 ¼ x 4" | 56.5 x 56.5 x 10.2 cm

145 COMPOSITION (CARDS) 2017
styrene cards and glue
22 ¼ x 22 ¼ x 4" | 56.5 x 56.5 x 10.2 cm
Collection of Dana and Richard Kirschenbaum

146 COMPOSITION (CARDS) 2017
styrene cards and glue
39 ¼ x 39 ¼ x 4" | 99.7 x 99.7 x 10.2 cm

148 COMPOSITION (CARDS) 2017
styrene cards and glue
39 ¼ x 39 ¼ x 4" | 99.7 x 99.7 x 10.2 cm

150 COMPOSITION (CARDS) 2017
styrene cards and glue
39 ¼ x 39 ¼ x 4" | 99.7 x 99.7 x 10.2 cm
Private collection

152 COMPOSITION (CARDS) 2017
styrene cards and glue
22 ¼ x 22 ¼ x 4" | 56.5 x 56.5 x 10.2 cm

153 COMPOSITION (CARDS) 2017
styrene cards and glue
22 ¼ x 22 ¼ x 4" | 56.5 x 56.5 x 10.2 cm

154 COMPOSITION (CARDS) 2017
styrene cards and glue
39 ¼ x 39 ¼ x 4" | 99.7 x 99.7 x 10.2 cm

156 COMPOSITION (CARDS) 2017
styrene cards and glue
36 ¼ x 36 ¼ x 4" | 92.1 x 92.1 x 10.2 cm
Private collection

158 COMPOSITION (CARDS) 2017
styrene cards and glue
39 ¼ x 39 ¼ x 4" | 99.7 x 99.7 x 10.2 cm

160 COMPOSITION (CARDS) 2017
styrene cards and glue
39 ¼ x 39 ¼ x 4" | 99.7 x 99.7 x 10.2 cm

162 COMPOSITION (CARDS) 2017
styrene cards and glue
22 ¼ x 22 ¼ x 4" | 56.5 x 56.5 x 10.2 cm

163 COMPOSITION (CARDS) 2017
styrene cards and glue
22 ¼ x 22 ¼ x 4" | 56.5 x 56.5 x 10.2 cm

174 COMPOSITION (CARDS) 2017
styrene cards and glue
39 ¼ x 39 ¼ x 4" | 99.7 x 99.7 x 10.2 cm
Collection of GoldenTree Asset Management

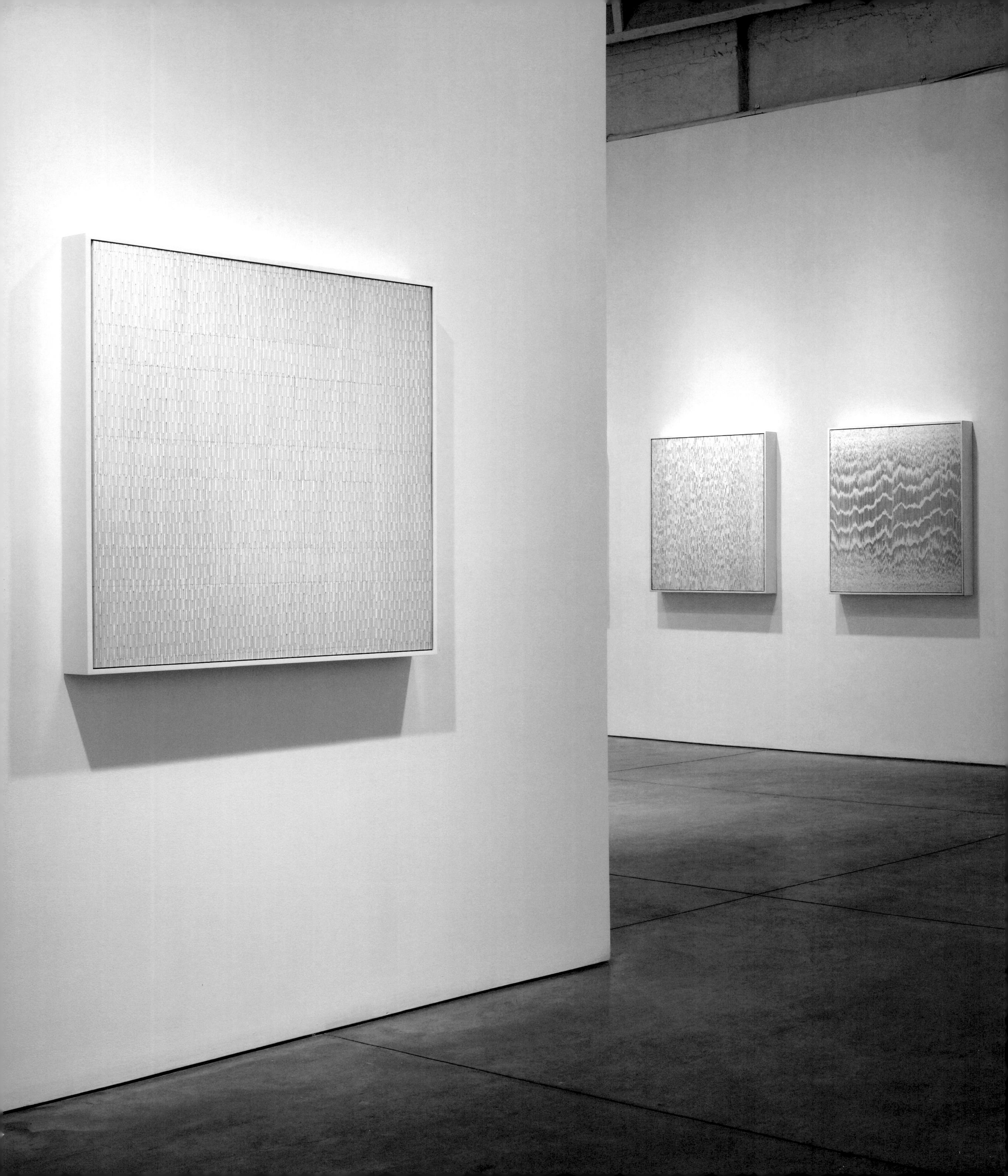

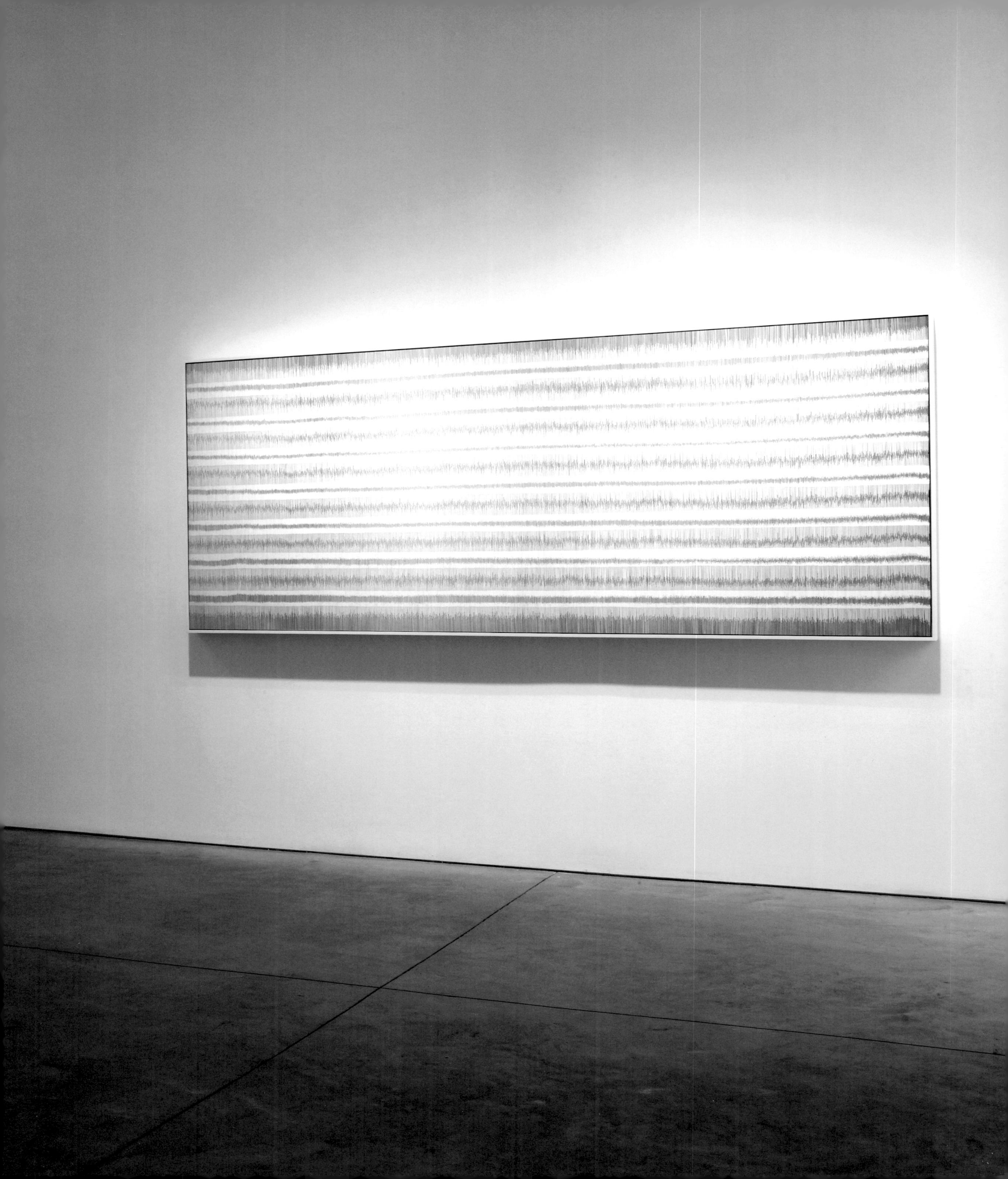

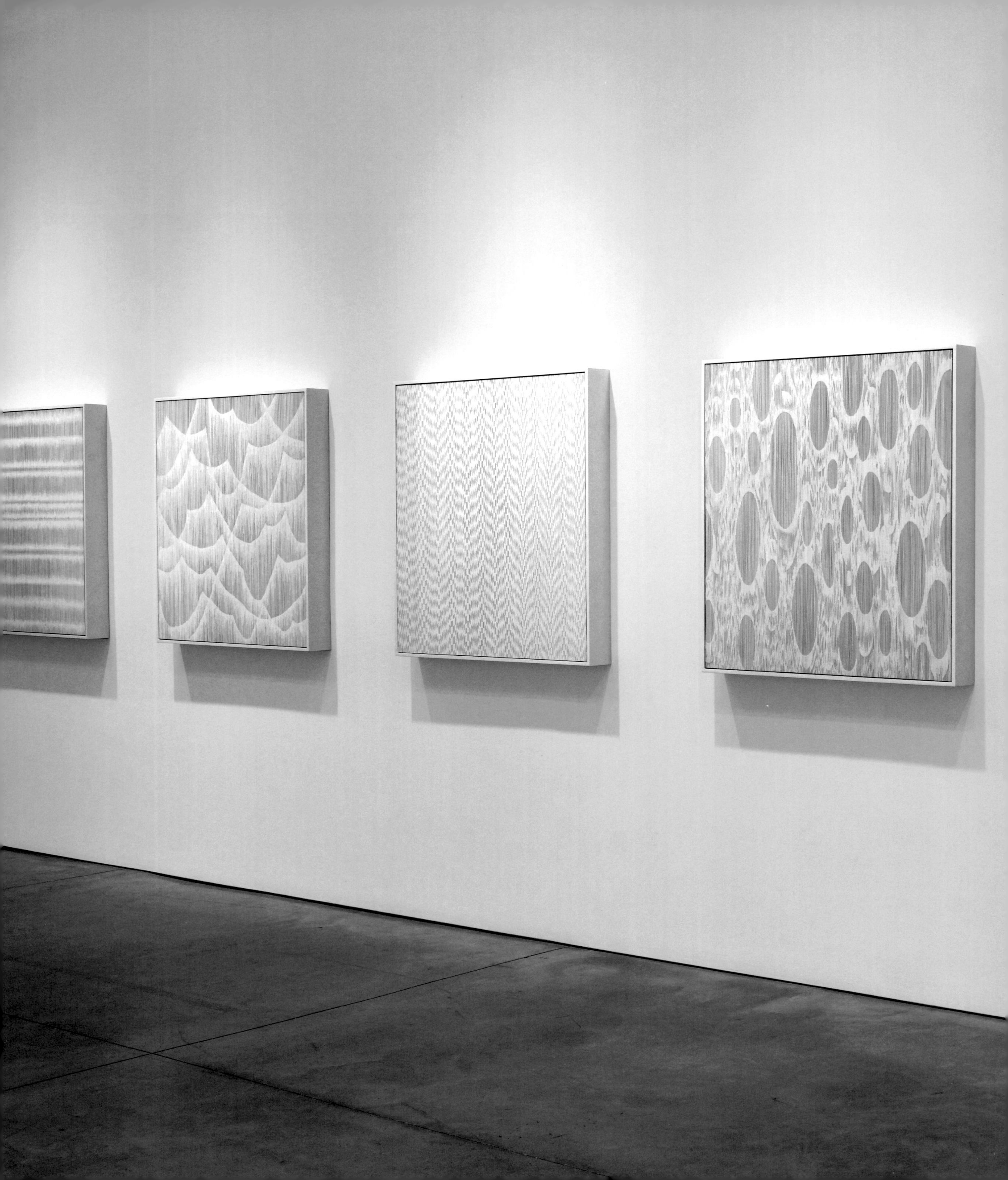

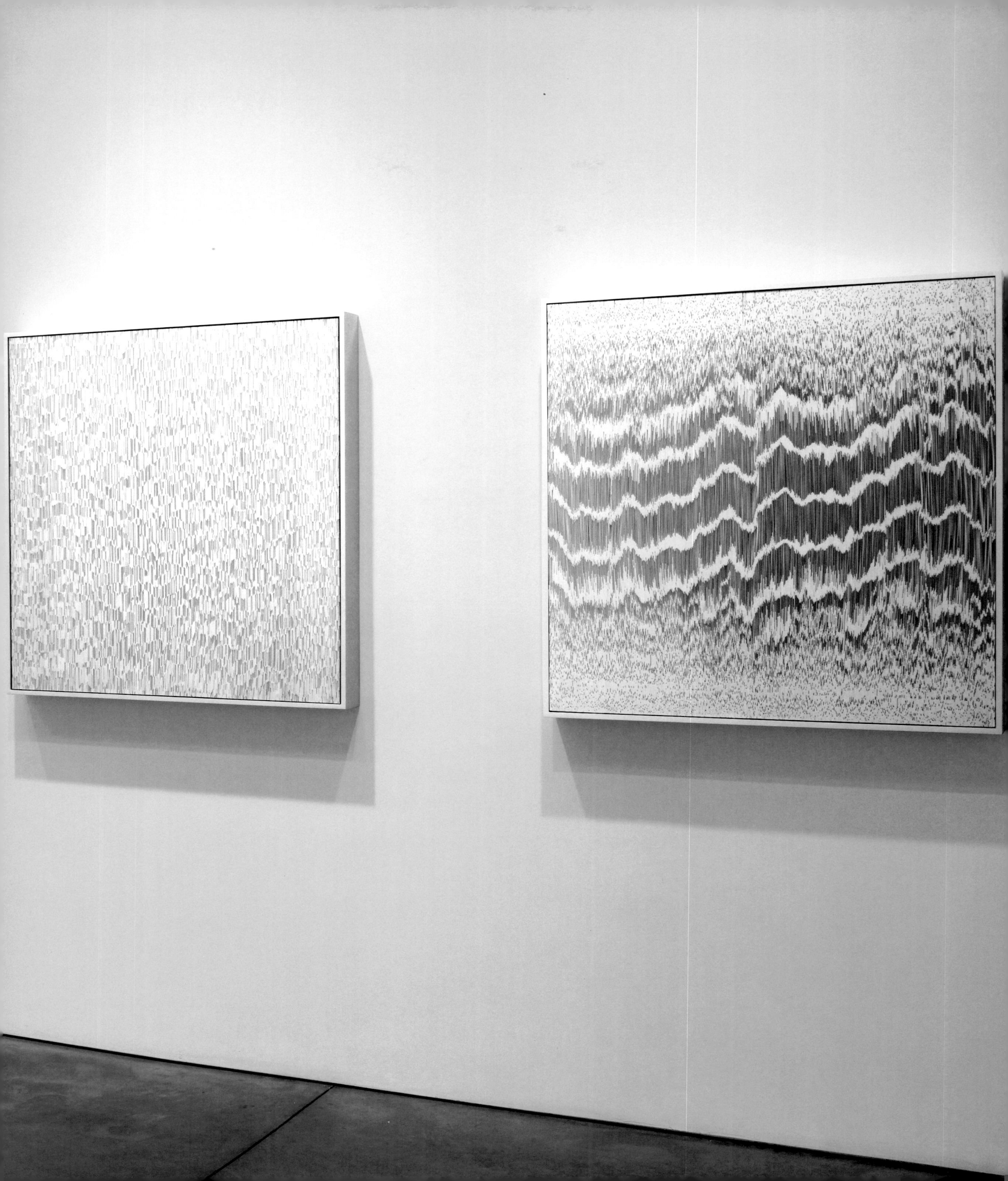

COMPOSITION (CARDS) 2017 39 ¼ x 39 ¼ x 4" | 99.7 x 99.7 x 10.2 cm

Cover: *Composition (Cards)*, 2017 (detail from page 175)

Photography:

Tom Barratt; pp. 27, 36, 39, 43–45, 47, 60, 61 (detail), 65, 67, 117, 149, 153, 162, 164–165 (detail)

Tom Barratt and Mark Waldhauser; pp. 14–15, 17, 24–26, 35, 39, 41, 43, 44–45 (detail), 50, 55, 59, 65, 69, 70–71 (detail), 73, 76–77, 78 (detail), 79, 81, 95, 96 (detail), 97, 101, 103, 112 (detail), 113, 115, 119, 120–121 (detail), 125, 131, 133, 141, 144, 147, 152, 155, 161, 163

Kerry Ryan McFate; pp. 6 (detail), 19, 21, 23, 29, 30–31 (detail), 33–34, 37, 41, 49, 51, 53, 57–58, 63, 75, 83–85, 87, 89, 91, 92–93 (detail), 98–99, 104 (detail), 105, 107, 109, 111, 114, 123, 127, 128–129 (detail), 134–135, 137, 139, 142 (detail), 143, 145, 151, 157, 159, 170–173, 175

Youngha Cho; pp. 4–5

Design: Tomo Makiura and Mine Suda

Production: Pace Gallery

Color correction: Motohiko Tokuta

Printing: Meridian Printing, East Greenwich, Rhode Island

Library of Congress Control Number: 2017962570
ISBN: 978-1-935410-98-0